The Collaborative Psychotherapist

Psychologists in Independent Practice

Leon VandeCreek, Series Editor

Michael J. Murphy, Series Editor

The Collaborative Psychotherapist

Creating Reciprocal Relationships
With Medical Professionals

Nancy Breen Ruddy, PhD
Dorothy A. Borresen, PhD, APN
William B. Gunn Jr., PhD

American Psychological Association
Washington, DC

Published by
American Psychological Association
750 First Street, NE
Washington, DC 20002
www.apa.org

To order
APA Order Department
P.O. Box 92984
Washington, DC 20090-2984
Tel: (800) 374-2721; Direct: (202) 336-5510
Fax: (202) 336-5502; TDD/TTY: (202) 336-6123
Online: www.apa.org/books/
E-mail: order@apa.org

In the U.K., Europe, Africa, and the Middle East, copies may be ordered from
American Psychological Association
3 Henrietta Street
Covent Garden, London
WC2E 8LU England

Typeset in Palatino by Stephen McDougal, Mechanicsville, MD

Printer: Sheridan Books, Ann Arbor, MI
Cover Designer: Watermark Design Office, Alexandria, VA
Technical/Production Editor: Tiffany L. Klaff

The opinions and statements published are the responsibility of the authors, and such opinions and statements do not necessarily represent the policies of the American Psychological Association.

Library of Congress Cataloging-in-Publication Data

Ruddy, Nancy Breen.
 The collaborative psychotherapist : creating reciprocal relationships with medical professionals / Nancy Breen Ruddy, Dorothy A. Borresen, William B. Gunn Jr. — 1st ed.
  p. ; cm. — (Psychologists in independent practice)
 Includes bibliographical references and index.
 ISBN-13: 978-1-4338-0338-3
 ISBN-10: 1-4338-0338-0
 1. Psychotherapists—Professional relationships. 2. Psychiatric referral. 3. Medical referral. 4. Psychiatric consultation. 5. Psychotherapy—Practice. I. Borresen, Dorothy A. II. Gunn, William B. III. Title. IV. Series.
 [DNLM: 1. Referral and Consultation. 2. Mental Disorders—therapy. 3. Psychotherapy. WM 64 R914c 2008]
 RC480.5.R825 2008
 616.89'14—dc22   2007038439

British Library Cataloguing-in-Publication Data
A CIP record is available from the British Library.

Printed in the United States of America
First Edition

To my husband, Tom, and children Natalie and Sean for their support and patience during this process.

—*Nancy Breen Ruddy*

To my husband Bill for his unwavering support.

—*Dorothy A. Borresen*

To my parents, Mary Hunter and Bill; my partner, Johane; my sons, Josh, Sean, and Will; as well as the faculty and staff of the New Hampshire/Dartmouth Family Residency Program. All taught me the joys and rewards of collaboration.

—*William B. Gunn Jr.*

Contents

Acknowledgments

This book reflects the efforts of many people. We would like to acknowledge the assistance we received from others, professionally and personally. We had a great deal of assistance in reviewing and editing the book. Marianne Hall provided much needed editorial input and helped us create the underlying structure of the book. Her hard work greatly expedited the publication process. We extend special thanks to the staff of the Books Department of the American Psychological Association, especially Margaret Sullivan, for her support and suggestions.

A number of people, including psychologists and family physicians, reviewed chapters of the book and provided valuable feedback and critiques. For this work we are grateful. They include, in alphabetical order, William Alexander, Linda Bush, Carol Goodheart, Susan McDaniel, Dael Waxman, David Seaburn, and Barry Jacobs.

This book would not have been possible without the support of the program directors, faculty, and staff of the Family Practice Residency Programs at Hunterdon Medical Center, New Hampshire/Dartmouth Family Residency Program, and the University of Medicine and Dentistry of New Jersey at Capital Health System. We specifically thank Kathy Dey for her secretarial support.

Finally, we greatly appreciate the time and effort expended by the practitioners who were interviewed: Shari Altum, Albert Bassetti, Dave Driscoll, Michael Hoyt, and Deborah Wright.

The Collaborative Psychotherapist

Introduction

Becoming a Collaborative Psychotherapist

Many psychotherapists in private practice rarely collaborate with medical professionals. Psychotherapists who do not know how to initiate and maintain collaborative relationships or do not recognize the advantages of collaboration may not make the effort to begin. Others who have tried to begin collaborating may have had negative first experiences. Many psychotherapists may perceive the barriers to collaboration to be insurmountable. We believe this is unfortunate because psychotherapists who have made the shift to collaborative care generally find it well worth the effort, clinically, collegially, and economically. We hope to help psychotherapists adopt collaboration practices that are consistent with their preferences and style, their patients' needs, and other factors.

In this introduction, we outline the case for becoming a collaborative psychotherapist. We believe that psychotherapists who take the time and effort to create collaborative relationships with medical professionals will improve their patient care, enhance their referral networks, and increase their professional satisfaction (Doherty, 2007). This introduction sets the stage for psychotherapists to contemplate a shift toward greater collaboration.

We begin by discussing various types of health care professionals and how these professionals' role and culture differences affect collaboration. We define *collaborative psychotherapist*, and differentiate the mind-set and practices of a collaborative psychotherapist from the current standard of care. We provide case examples that illustrate the potential pitfalls of separate care and illustrate how collaboration can avoid these potential pitfalls. Finally, we review numerous cultural and health care trends that support the need for psychotherapists to become more collaborative with medical professionals.

Medical Professionals 101

First, it is helpful to define some of the professionals we refer to in this introduction and throughout the book.

Medical professionals is an umbrella term that includes both primary care medical professionals (e.g., family physicians) and specialists (e.g., cardiologists).

Primary care medical professional refers to those medical professionals who practice in primary care, including family doctors, internists, pediatricians, obstetricians/gynecologists, nurse practitioners, and physician assistants within these disciplines. Family physicians treat people and families across the life span, and many provide women's health and obstetrical services. Internists treat adults, typically focusing on individuals of both genders. They do not provide women's health or obstetrical services. Pediatricians treat children and adolescents, sometimes including young adults through the college years. Obstetricians/gynecologists focus on gynecologic and obstetrical services to women of all ages but often provide advice and counsel regarding other issues and may serve as a woman's only medical professional. Nurse practitioners and physician's assistants work alongside physicians and are called *midlevel providers.*

It is important to distinguish between *medical professionals* and *primary care medical professionals.* Primary care medical professionals serve as the "medical home" for most patients. Primary care professionals often know their patients well from providing care over a long time period, often for multiple family members. They have developed relationships and understand the patient in the context of his or her family and community. Ideally, primary care is comprehensive and preventive personal medical care in which the primary care professional helps patients navigate the health care system and coordinates care among specialists and other health care providers. Patients with complicated health issues that require care from multiple specialists often look to their primary care medical professional to help them choose the right specialists and obtain referrals. Postreferral, patients seek the counsel of their trusted primary care professional to help them make difficult decisions regarding treatment options.

Specialized *medical professionals* (e.g., cardiologists, radiologists, allergists, endocrinologists) typically do not function as the care coordinator, may not have continuity of care, and tend to focus on a particular organ system or disease rather than whole-person care. However, some medical specialists do provide ongoing care for patients who have a chronic illness that falls within their area of expertise (e.g., endocrinologists for patients with diabetes).

Psychotherapists include licensed clinical and counseling psychologists, clinical social workers, marriage and family therapists, professional counselors, pastoral psychotherapists, and, at times, psychiatrists.

Psychotherapists who have little experience working with medical professionals may be struck by our choice to use the word *patient* rather than *client* throughout the text. This difference is but one example of cultural and linguistic differences between medicine and mental health. Although it is not absolutely necessary to change one's nomenclature to *patient* when collaborating with medical professionals, we use the term here because it is the more accepted term in the medical arena.

Who Is a Collaborative Psychotherapist?
Collaborative Psychotherapist Defined

Becoming a collaborative psychotherapist entails more than simply making the occasional phone call to a patient's medical professional; it entails a change of mind-set. Collaborative health care professionals expand their purview to the patient's whole health picture by asking patients about their health, encouraging them to see a medical professional to rule out physical causes for their symptoms, and becoming knowledgeable about how medical issues affect mental health. They see communication with the patient's other health care professionals as the norm, rather than the exception, and as an important part of providing comprehensive care.

Of course, there is a continuum of collaboration, from psychotherapists who seldom contact their patient's medical professionals to those who work on-site with their medical colleagues. Most psychotherapists in private practice fall between these points and vary the level of collaboration from case to case, depending on the patient's needs, the level of preexisting relationship with the medical professional, logistical issues, and other variables.

Collaboration in Action

The following two case examples illustrate psychotherapy with and without successful collaboration. Both are typical case presentations and highlight how a collaborative mind-set can alter the course of psychotherapy.

Learning the Hard Way

Mary, a 56-year-old woman, began weekly psychotherapy because she was unhappy in her marriage. After several sessions, the therapist, Dr. Brown, asked Mary's husband, John, to join them. After one session, the couple agreed to begin couples therapy. Several sessions revealed that Mary and John had been drifting apart over the last 5 years. John expressed sadness and confusion about their limited communication. He was worried and concerned about his wife's depressed mood and lack of energy. When asked for more specifics by Dr. Brown, John expressed frustration with his wife's lack of interest in sex. Mary reported that she felt guilty and pressured by her husband in this regard. They both felt sad and resigned to the situation.

Dr. Brown worked with the couple on communication skills for several months and helped them to become more emotionally intimate and physically affectionate. After 6 months, the couple told the therapist that they felt that their relationship had improved significantly, although they continued to report that Mary had almost no sexual desire. However, Mary and John felt that they had made enough improvements in their relationship to terminate couples therapy.

Dr. Brown believed that the therapy had been somewhat successful but was also frustrated and concerned that the couple's sexual relationship had not been rekindled as their communication and general marital relationship improved over the course of the treatment. He strongly encouraged the couple to remain in therapy to work on their sexual relationship.

John and Mary said that they would return to therapy if they found that their sexual relationship had not improved over time. They were hopeful that the strides they had made in communication and nonsexual intimacy would eventually lead them to an improved sexual relationship. Dr. Brown reluctantly agreed to this compromise.

A year later, Mary scheduled an individual appointment with Dr. Brown. In the session Mary tearfully related how their sexual relationship had not improved and that John had been unwilling to return to therapy, as he had earlier promised he would. Mary later had learned that he would not return to therapy because he had met someone else with whom he had developed a "wonderful" sexual and romantic relationship. John had asked her for a divorce and was unwilling to try to work things out. He had suddenly moved to a hotel the week Mary called Dr. Brown. Mary was devastated.

The therapist felt sad for the couple and was disheartened that he had been unable to help them with their sexual relationship. With Mary's permission, the therapist reached out to John by telephone. John was adamant that his relationship with Mary was over and that he was unwilling to come in and meet with Dr. Brown, even for a single session. He was determined to file for divorce.

Mary continued individual therapy to cope with the impending divorce. Six months later, after John had moved in with his girlfriend, in passing Mary mentioned that the stress had exacerbated her blood pressure problem. Previously unaware of this medical issue, the therapist asked Mary about her medical history, which was unremarkable except for the hypertension. Further probing by Dr. Brown revealed the following:

Mary's family physician had diagnosed her hypertension 5 years earlier. At his urging, she had since been taking several medications to control her blood pressure including a beta-blocker (atenolol), candesartan, and a diuretic (hydrochlorothiazide). Although the family physician carefully monitored Mary's hypertension and reviewed her improvement with the medications, he had been unaware that Mary was experiencing marital problems, fatigue, and lack of sexual desire. Mary had never told him that she and John were in couples therapy.

Dr. Brown was dismayed that he had been unaware of Mary's medical history or drug regimen, which most likely affected Mary's sexual desire and responsiveness, as well as her general energy levels. He belatedly realized that he should have been more inquisitive about Mary and John's medical history and should have consulted with her family physician. Although the therapist again reached out to John by telephone, discussing how Mary's medications had likely been a culprit in their failed sexual relationship, John was still adamant that his relationship with Mary was hopeless. He was glad to know the hypertension medication may have been at fault but said firmly that it was now too late. He was happy in his new relationship and was committed to seeking a divorce.

This case illustrates missed opportunities for the therapist, the medical professional, and, most important, the patients. If Dr. Brown had had a more collaborative mind-set, he would have asked about Mary's health conditions and related medications and perhaps made the link between the medications and her decreased libido. Dr. Brown would have contacted the family physician to discuss Mary's decreased libido and its possible relationship to her medication regimen. The physician, in turn, could have adjusted her medications to help alleviate these side effects. In short, if Mary's decreased sexual desire and fatigue were secondary to her hypertension medications, medication changes could have dramatically affected the couple's relationship and the marital therapy. Moreover, if the therapist had inquired early on about the patients' medical history and then followed up by contacting Mary's family doctor, in addition to the excellent work he did with communication and nonsexual intimacy between the spouses, the couple may not have divorced. Although this case is a dramatic illustration of the potential pitfalls of not collaborating, it is not a rare presentation.

In contrast, the following case illustrates how implementing collaboration can positively alter the course of psychotherapy. Again, it is a common clinical presentation.

Health Care Professionals Use Teamwork to Manage Somatic Anxiety

Pat, a 40-year-old mother of two children, sought psychotherapy with Dr. White, a psychologist. She had endured a lengthy course of medical testing for multiple physical symptoms including dizziness, palpitations, tingling down her left arm, and generally "not feeling well." She was frustrated that the testing had not resulted in a definitive diagnosis.

Dr. White completed a detailed history of Pat's presenting problem. When Dr. White questioned Pat about her medical health, Pat described a year-long course of multiple diagnostic tests that she took to rule out cardiac problems including echocardiograms, electroencephalograms, stress tests, and extensive laboratory tests. She had worked with two internists, two cardiologists, a neurologist, and a gynecologist. When the last round of tests failed to yield a diagnosis, Pat made an appointment with a third cardiologist, because she believed that "something must be wrong." None of her physicians had recommended that she see a psychotherapist, but her husband made the suggestion. Pat was reluctant to start psychotherapy because she feared that her doctors would attribute everything to anxiety and advise her to stop seeking a physical cause of her symptoms.

When Dr. White reviewed Pat's history, Pat disclosed that she had epilepsy as a child. She described feeling ashamed and frightened because her family never spoke about the epilepsy neither during her childhood nor later in her life. Eventually, she had grown out of the epilepsy and had not taken seizure medication since adolescence. She acknowledged that her current physical symptoms reminded her of the epilepsy and her shame about having another problem that was "in [my] head." She recognized that this history made it difficult for her to consider that her symptoms could be secondary to anxiety.

Pat expressed a great deal of frustration with her medical experiences. Dr. White saw Pat several times before she suggested that Pat see a different internist, Dr. Hale, whom she collaborated with frequently. Dr. White focused on Pat's physical symptoms of nausea and reflux which had not been addressed during the past year, and she suggested that a physician who considers the whole person during diagnosis may be helpful to Pat and may integrate the findings of multiple specialists that Pat had visited.

Pat was able to see Dr. Hale quickly after Dr. White called her office to expedite an appointment. On the basis of their history of working together, Dr. White felt she could request and receive special service for her patient from Dr. Hale, just as Dr. Hale trusted that Dr. White would make a special effort to help a needy patient of hers in return. After obtaining a release of information, Dr. White requested that Dr. Hale see Pat as soon as possible because her frequent episodes of panic and dizziness were increasingly affecting her functioning. These symptoms left Pat exhausted, and she was beginning to feel depressed. Dr. Hale requested that Pat schedule a full physical to allow adequate time to review the various issues. Dr. White faxed a one-page treatment summary and diagnostic impressions to Dr. Hale for her to review before the first appointment.

At their first appointment Dr. Hale spent almost an hour with Pat reviewing Dr. White's impressions, which helped Dr. Hale understand Pat's symptoms in the broader context of Pat's history. She believed, as Dr. White believed, that Pat was experiencing severe anxiety and panic and was beginning to feel depressed. Dr. Hale also addressed those physical symptoms she could treat symptomatically. She recommended that Pat begin a reflux medication, and a very low dose of sertraline, an SSRI, to address her symptoms of anxiety, panic, and depression. Pat was receptive to these recommendations because of Dr. Hale's relationship with Dr. White as well as Pat's sense that Dr. Hale understood her complex situation.

At her next psychotherapy appointment Pat reported that her symptoms were only minimally better. However, she felt a sense of relief that Dr. White and Dr. Hale were working together to help her with her symptoms. Pat was beginning to consider that these symptoms might be related to anxiety.

In this case, Dr. White's careful medical history enabled Dr. Hale to better understand Pat's difficulty with accepting a diagnosis of anxiety. Dr. White's sensitive referral to a physician that she trusted, and her recommendation to not continue the expensive and unhelpful, even damaging, cycle of repeated diagnostic testing, helped Pat begin to consider that her problems were not based in a cardiac or neurological problem. The collaboration helped Pat trust that her team was taking her difficulties seriously and examining all of the possible contributing factors. Pat's fear that she had a life-threatening medical condition was somewhat reduced, especially as she recognized that her history of epilepsy, and the way her family had managed her epilepsy, affected her experience of her current symptoms. The therapy likely would have progressed very differently if Pat's therapist had not completed a thorough medical history or had not been able to offer her a collaborative approach.

Why Should Psychotherapists Collaborate?

Many psychotherapists are surprised to learn that less than one third of patients with diagnosable mental health conditions ever meet with a psychotherapist. Even the majority of those with significant symptoms of depression and anxiety seek treatment solely from their primary care medical professional (Miranda, Hohnmann, & Attikisson, 1994). Similarly, research indicates that approximately 30% of primary care visits are for psychosocial issues (Kessler et al., 2005; Robins & Regier, 1991).

Research on mental health issues in primary care reflects the centrality of these issues in patients' lives and how unlikely it is that patients who need mental health services ever access them. Consider the following facts:

- ☐ Between 25% and 30% of visits to primary care physicians have depression, anxiety, alcohol abuse, and somatoform disorders as part of the presenting issue (Ansseau et al., 2004; L. S. Kahn et al., 2004; Ormel et al., 1994).
- ☐ Primary care medical professionals prescribe 60% to 70% of the psychotropic medications prescribed in the United States (Lewis, Marcus, Olfson, Druss, & Pincus, 2004; Miranda et al., 1994).
- ☐ The incidence of depression rises as patients seek more intensive medical care: from 5% in the general population to 10% in medical outpatient settings, to 15% in medical inpatient settings (Katon, 2003).

- □ Although only 20% of people who commit suicide had contact with a psychotherapist in their last month, 45% had contact with a primary care medical professional (Luoma, Martin, & Pearson, 2002).
- □ Whereas 68% of patients with a diagnosable mental health condition will seek care from a primary care medical professional, only 28% of such patients will see a psychotherapist (Miranda et al., 1994).
- □ Whereas 32% of undiagnosed, asymptomatic adults say they would first turn to their primary care medical professional for assistance with a mental health issue, only 4% state that they would approach a psychotherapist (National Mental Health Association, 2000).
- □ One quarter of patients who present in an emergency department for chest pain has depression or panic disorder (Fleet et al., 1996).

In our collective 30-plus years of experience in primary care settings, one of the most striking discoveries has been that few people whose lives are negatively affected by psychological symptoms ever obtain psychotherapy or meet with a psychotherapist in any capacity. Even when patients do ultimately connect with a psychotherapist, the frequent lack of collaboration between the psychotherapist and the patients' medical professionals reduces the effectiveness of both the medical and the psychotherapeutic treatments.

Primary care professionals often do not have the time or skills to deal adequately with these psychological problems, and thus they often welcome and genuinely require assistance from psychotherapists. Unfortunately, they rarely have established relationships with psychotherapists and therefore do not know to *whom* they should refer a patient. Primary care medical professionals spend a good part of their day making referrals, yet they are stymied by mental health referrals, resulting in frustration for them and missed opportunities for their patients.

The research just cited reflects the reality that the mental health care system simply does not reach the vast number of patients who need its services. Some factors such as social stigma and payment issues that inhibit optimal care and access to mental health care are beyond medical professionals' and psychotherapists' control. However, psychotherapists can choose to engage in proactive collaboration with medical professionals to improve access to care, caseload management, and professional satisfaction (Gilbody, Bower, Fletcher, Richards, & Sutton, 2006). One way that collaboration may reduce health care costs and improve care is by reducing care fragmentation. Poor collaboration increases care fragmentation because the lack of communication from the psychotherapist impedes the primary care professional's efforts to oversee and manage the patient's overall health care. Research supports the contention that service fragmentation is particularly likely and problematic for patients with mental health issues (Kathol, Saravay, Lobo, & Ormel, 2006).

In addition, collaboration may improve the standing of psychotherapists in the medical arena. Currently, medical professionals often do not know whether patients follow through on psychotherapy referrals or, if they do seek such assistance, whether the psychotherapy was helpful. If psychotherapists communicate more regularly, medical professionals will become more aware of the positive effect psychotherapy can have. In addition, increased dialogue between medical professionals and psychotherapists will highlight how psychotherapists' skill sets could be of great assistance to medical professionals as they help patients successfully manage many illnesses. Unfortunately, in the current system medical professionals have little or no access to our expertise and therefore may not recognize when psychotherapeutic intervention could be helpful.

Trends That Support Collaboration Between Mental Health and Medical Professionals

In this section, we describe seven trends that bode well for collaboration between mental health and medical professionals. These trends reflect changes in society, media, commerce, politics, and demography, as well as changes in medical professionals' and patients' expectations regarding the medical system. As with most change, these trends present both opportunities and challenges.

1. *As a large segment of the population lives longer, more people will live with chronic illnesses and struggle to manage the related "lifestyle" and psychological issues.* The demographics are clear: the population is aging. As baby boomers approach their "golden years," they are likely to experience unprecedented longevity—and the chronic illnesses that accompany it. This is relevant to the interface of mental health and medicine because chronic illness management requires lifestyle changes, yet medical professionals do not have the time or the skills of psychotherapists to intervene optimally. Mental health professionals can help medical professionals use psychoeducational programs to help patients manage their chronic conditions optimally (Cummings, 2000). Also, as patients struggle with the impact of their illness on their relationships and day-to-day living, they are twice as likely to develop mood disorders (Kessler, Ormel, Demler, & Stang, 2003; Polsky et al., 2005; Russell & Hui, 2005).

   Beyond simply stressing the current health care system, the aging baby boomers may redefine old age and end of life much the way they changed childbirth and child-rearing practices from previous generations. They may push our health care system to become more patient-centered and provide treatment that takes into account the mind, body, and spirit.

2. *Patients increasingly see themselves as "consumers" of medical services.* In the past, patients approached their physicians as if they were omnipotent, godlike figures and rarely asked them questions. Medical care and patient–medical professional relationships have changed dramatically over the past few decades. Many patients now view health care as a commodity to which they have a right, expecting the latest and greatest technology, regardless of the cost. They come to their medical professional armed with information and expectations, sometimes creating a challenging dance and negotiation between their agenda and the medical professional's capabilities. This change in the power differential can be helpful, because patients can use information to advocate for themselves and take ownership of their health management. However, this change becomes problematic when patients have unreasonable expectations. Psychotherapists who have established collabora-

tive, consultative relationships with medical professionals can help when conflict arises out of this dynamic. The
psychotherapist's agenda setting and negotiation skills
have the potential to be helpful to medical professionals
in the current health care environment.

3. *Mind–body integration is becoming a societal norm, in part because the media has focused on integration of the two entities.*
The popularity of yoga classes as well as highly attended
information sessions and multiple best-selling books focusing on the mind–body connection, provide evidence
of the widespread acceptance of the integration of mind
and body. Psychotherapists, medical professionals, and the
general public increasingly believe that integrated "whole-
person" care is better than care that focuses on only one
organ system. Insight regarding the connection between
one's emotional life and physical well-being varies, but
most people acknowledge that stress has a direct effect on
one's health.

This cultural shift has created opportunities for psychotherapists to motivate patients toward healthy lifestyle
habits, help patients explore wellness strategies, and help
patients and their families cope with the changes associated with illness. However, these opportunities material-
ize only if psychotherapists reach patients who are experiencing health difficulties. Because these patients
primarily obtain services in the medical arena, psychotherapists who have established relationships with medical professionals are more likely to receive these referrals. Such working relationships will also help medical
professionals better understand what psychotherapists
have to offer these patients, increasing referrals to psychotherapists who have a track record of successful patient outcomes.

4. *Medical professionals increasingly realize that psychosocial
health is important to heal physical illness and promote physical
wellness.* Many medical professionals, particularly those
in primary care, recognize the importance of mental health
in the maintenance of physical health. Some primary care
disciplines are actively working to establish the concept
of a "medical home," encouraging patients to manage their
various health care needs with a single primary care medical professional as much as possible. This professional

oversees their health care, increasing the likelihood that they will obtain appropriate preventive care and care co-ordination because of this continuity. The medical home concept also may facilitate detection and treatment of mental health issues that tend to get short shrift when there is not an established medical professional–patient relation-ship (Future of Family Medicine Project Leadership Com-mittee, 2004).

Although primary care medical professionals are trained to appreciate the importance of psychosocial issues, there is a gap between these beliefs and the active integration of psychosocial issues into medical care. Although many medical professionals try to screen for mental health diffi-culties, they have little time, training, or inclination to ad-dress the issues they uncover, creating opportunities for psychotherapists. As more medical professionals assess for mental health symptoms, they will ultimately need a cadre of psychotherapists they trust to help manage these issues optimally.

In the current disjointed system, primary care medical professionals are often frustrated with the barriers to get-ting their distressed patients into psychotherapy. The frus-tration continues after patients obtain psychotherapy because of the lack of communication from the psychother-apist (Chantal, Brazeau, Rovi, Yick, & Johnson, 2005). This frustration and the breach between medical and mental health treatment systems negatively affect patient care and set the stage for change in practice delivery patterns. Those psychotherapists who adapt their practice to meet these needs through greater collaboration and communication will thrive.

Many psychotherapists may not agree that medicine has become more psychosocially focused because this is counter to the stereotype of the technology- and prescription-obsessed medical professional. Skeptical psychotherapists might be surprised to learn that all family physicians have at least one psychotherapist on faculty during residency and that psychosocial issues are integrated into the cur-riculum. Pediatricians likewise are trained to recognize when family or other stressors are related to a child's medi-cal presentation or a parent's level of concern about a child. As a result, they are trained to ask about stress and psychological distress. The Accreditation Council for Graduate Medical Education (2005), a regulatory board for medical residencies, highlights "interpersonal and communication skills" as one of six core competencies in which residencies must teach and evaluate all residents. In short, medical professionals have greater exposure to psychosocial aspects of medical care than most psychotherapists have to the medical aspects of mental health care.

5. *Psychotherapists increasingly recognize the importance of physical health in healing mental illness and promoting mental health.* Psychotherapists increasingly focus on the link between sound body and sound mind, recognizing that a person's brain, neurons, and the various associated chemicals affect one's mood, behavior, and relationships. Psychotherapists also are becoming increasingly knowledgeable about psychotropic medicines and regularly refer patients for medication consultation. In addition, many psychotherapists now ask patients about their physical health, recognizing that people with physical illnesses often need psychosocial support and that physical illness can lead to emotional problems. Those psychotherapists who understand this interplay and have relationships with medical professionals have the opportunity to provide better patient care and create flourishing professional referral networks.

6. *As community mental health center funding dwindles, more mental health care is occurring in the primary care setting.* Community mental health centers are struggling to meet the needs of their patients, and their waiting lists are growing. Patients who finally recognize that their suffering has a psychological etiology and decide to seek help often find that help is weeks or sometimes months away. Even patients who can choose private therapy often cannot obtain services quickly. While these patients wait for mental health intervention, they often receive support and medical intervention from their medical professional. Collaborative psychotherapists can provide consultation during these waiting periods and can ensure that patients with urgent needs are seen, at least for screening. Collaborative psychotherapists will get "repeat business" from medical professionals who have found them to be helpful in difficult situations or who have created space for a truly needy patient.

7. *New psychotropic medications and pharmaceutical marketing campaigns have increased patient awareness of mental health problems and heightened their expectations.* Pharmaceutical marketing campaigns have been incredibly successful in creating a demand for specific medications and facilitating medical professional–patient dialogues about sensitive issues (Elliot & Chambers, 2004). Many of the advertisements specifically advise patients to, "Talk to your doctor about . . . ," and patients actively follow this advice, looking for a "quick fix." Most psychotherapists who do not prescribe medications would be amazed at how effective these marketing campaigns have been in creating and broadening the market for specific and usually costly medications. The selective serotonin reuptake inhibitors have been most aggressively and profitably marketed. These marketing campaigns have encouraged depressed or anxious patients to talk to their medical professional about their emotional problems, partially because there is a greater recognition that depression and anxiety are now treatable conditions. Also, there is less of a stigma for a "medical condition" as opposed to a "psychological weakness."

In a parallel fashion, medical professionals have been more likely to ask patients about their emotional well-being because they now have pharmacological interventions to treat the symptoms of depression or anxiety that they uncover. This increased dialogue about emotional concerns results in a greater recognition of depression and anxiety disorders in the medical setting. Many medical professionals strongly encourage patients for whom they prescribe psychotropic medication to also pursue psychotherapy, emphasizing that the two treatments work best together (Croghan, Schoenbaum, Sherbourne, & Koegel, 2006).

Purpose and Organization of This Book

In this introduction, we have sought to help psychotherapists contemplate changing their attitudes and behaviors toward establishing collaborative relationships with medical professionals. We have defined our use of terms to describe various medical professionals and what we mean by the term *collaborative psycho-*

therapist. We have outlined reasons that psychotherapists must begin to reach out to medical professionals, particularly primary care medical professionals, to improve patient care in the current system and to adapt to ongoing and anticipated system changes.

Despite cultural shifts toward a more integrated view of health and wellness, medical professionals and psychotherapists still operate in parallel, largely separate universes, creating a treatment system with a mind–body split inconsistent with "whole-person" care. How can the mental health community respond to popular and medical culture slowly redefining *health* as general wellness of both the mind and body?

The purpose of this book is to guide psychotherapists through practice pattern changes designed to create collaborative relationships. Collaboration occurs along a continuum related to professional preferences and practice patterns, practice setting, and patient needs (Doherty, McDaniel, & Baird, 1996). Currently, many psychotherapists practice *minimal collaboration* in which they practice separately from medical professionals and rarely communicate. The first part of the book, "Routine Collaboration," discusses ways to move from minimal collaboration to *basic collaboration at a distance.* In basic collaboration, the psychotherapist and medical professionals practice separately, but there is ongoing, basic communication driven by patient needs. The psychotherapists and medical professionals view each other as resources in providing optimal patient care. Many patients who obtain mental health services do not need greater collaboration, typically when their difficulties are situational or do not have major implications for long-term health and wellness.

Psychotherapists who integrate basic collaboration into their daily practice need to have an understanding of the cultural difference that can create difficulties in collaboration and how to manage these differences to minimize their negative effect. The "Routine Collaboration" portion of the book reviews the barriers to, and advantages and disadvantages of, such collaboration. We share what we have learned from our collective decades of experience in medical settings that all psychotherapists, regardless of setting, need to know to practice collaboratively. Finally, we describe the skills and practices psychotherapists need to develop, implement, and maintain to become more collaborative.

The second part of the book focuses on *intensive collaboration*. It discusses challenging patients who need more intensive collaboration and reviews psychotherapeutic and collaborative strategies that optimize their care. We discuss cutting-edge models of collaborative mental health provided in the medical setting and how many health care systems are beginning to create environments of mental health–medical collaboration.

In Part III, we apply these concepts using clinical material and interviews with collaborative psychotherapists. The cases and interviews therein illustrate how collaborative care works and how collaboration can alter the treatment process, outcomes, and patient and professional satisfaction.

In chapter 1, we discuss some of the barriers to collaboration. These include both very real barriers as well as myths and stereotypes that hinder collaborative relationships. Psychotherapists who seek to improve their collaborative relationships benefit from understanding these potential issues as they begin to journey toward greater collaboration.

I

Routine Collaboration

To a collaborative psychotherapist, every new patient is an opportunity to create a new collaborative relationship with a medical professional or strengthen an old relationship. Collaborative psychotherapists develop ongoing relationships with medical professionals by sharing care of patients and helping each other provide optimal treatment. Although not all medical professionals will work closely with a psychotherapist, most welcome the assistance and camaraderie. Practicing collaboratively expands your support system, facilitates referrals, and improves patient care.

Of course, it isn't that easy. In this part of the book, we help you make a plan for increasing your level of collaboration in a pragmatic and realistic way. We chose the word *routine* carefully, because in this context it has numerous meanings. First, and foremost, we emphasize routine collaboration because the key to becoming a collaborative psychotherapist is to make collaboration *routine*—part of your everyday, usual care of patients. Second, we want to ensure that psychotherapists realize there are various intensities and methods of collaboration, from *routine*, or what can be expected within the range of normal, to *intensive*, that which goes beyond the norm. The reader who is only contemplating collaboration or currently engages in minimal collaboration is recommended to start with routine collaboration.

We realize that some readers may already have implemented many of our suggestions for routine collaboration and thus will expand their collaborative practices from the concepts presented in the second part of the book, which focuses on intensive collaboration. It is our hope that psychotherapists who are not yet collaborative will eventually evolve their practice style to implement some of the intensive collaborative techniques we discuss later.

For now, we focus first on issues that contribute to the current status quo of noncollaborative care. Then, we describe the world of primary care, the important role that mental health issues play in it, and how these issues tend to present and be managed in the primary care medical arena. Finally, we describe a step-by-step process for psychotherapists to increase their collaboration and make it a part of their daily routines.

1

The Hidden Benefits
of Collaboration

In this chapter, we address some of the specific challenges psy-chotherapists face in building collaborative relationships with medical professionals. First, we address some of the myths that psychotherapists who are reticent about collaboration may believe. In addition, we describe some of the real barriers that psychotherapists and medical professionals must creatively overcome on the road to productive collaborative care.

Before reviewing barriers to collaboration, we suggest that you take a minute to evaluate your current status on the collaboration continuum. This assessment will help you to identify where you are now and where you want to be in the future. The tool is an informal scale and not validated by research, but psychotherapists have found it a useful instrument in setting the stage to become more collaborative.

Self-Assessment Tool:
Evaluate Your Current Level of Collaboration

1. I ask my patients about their medical health history.
    Never   Sometimes   Always

The discussion of myths that inhibit collaboration is based on work outlining cultural differences between medicine and mental health (e.g., Bray & Rogers, 1997; McDaniel & Campbell, 1986). Please see Appendix D for additional references on this topic.

2. I ask my patients about all of their medications, not just psychotropic medication.
   Never   Sometimes   Always
3. I obtain a release of information to contact my patient's medical professional at the beginning of treatment.
   Never   Sometimes   Always
4. I believe that collaboration with medical professionals is important.
   Not at all   Somewhat   Very important
   important   important
5. I contact my patient's medical professionals.
   Never   Sometimes   Always
6. I believe that collaboration should be the standard of care.
   Never   Sometimes   Always
7. I believe that medical professionals value my input about a patient.
   Never   Sometimes   Always
8. I believe that medical professionals are willing to collaborate.
   Never   Sometimes   Always

Each question evaluates your beliefs regarding various potential barriers to collaboration and your motivation to overcome these perceived barriers. Although there are very real barriers to collaboration, some barriers assessed in this instrument are based on myths and stereotypes. In the following sections, we discuss the basis of these issues, and contrast these myths with realities that may surprise the reader and encourage a reconsideration of the collaborative process. Throughout this discussion, we illustrate points with comments from an Internet survey we conducted through the American Psychological Association (APA) Practice Directorate in 2006.

The Myths and Realities About Collaborative Relationships With Medical Professionals

Myth: Strict patient confidentiality is critical to the therapeutic relationship. Confidentiality precludes interprofessional communications.

Mental health training and practice, particularly traditional psychoanalytic psychotherapy, historically emphasized that strict confidentiality is necessary to successful treatment. The inadvertent result has been minimal interprofessional communication although with proper consent disclosure is permissible and desirable. For example, in the APA "Ethical Principles of Psychology and Code of Conduct" (2002) the following tenets advise: (a) Principle B and Standard 3.09 (Cooperation With Other Professionals) state that "when it is indicated and professionally appropriate, psychologists cooperate with other professionals in order to serve their clients/patients effectively and appropriately" and (b) Standard 4.05 states that "psychologists may disclose confidential information with the appropriate consent of the organization client, the individual client/patient, or another legally authorized person on behalf of the client/patient unless prohibited by law." These ethical guidelines are consistent with other mental health professional associations (American Association for Marriage and Family Therapy, 2001; National Association of Social Workers, 1999).

Many psychotherapists believe that their patients will be offended by a request to talk to their medical professionals, or that sharing information will adversely affect the psychotherapeutic process. Some psychotherapists have concerns about how medical professionals will manage sensitive, confidential information. They may need to see a clear benefit to collaboration before they will be willing to make such a large change in their way of thinking and practicing. Psychotherapists' lack of information and experience with collaboration may reduce their motivation to talk to patients about collaboration. They may believe that they cannot justify collaboration to a reluctant patient, fearing that they will not have a good answer if a patient asks them, "Why do you need to talk to my doctor?"

Reality: Psychotherapists who ask their patients for a release to speak to the other health care professionals rarely encounter resistance.

Generally, patients are not at all reluctant to give a release of information to their medical professional. In fact, they are often pleased and reassured that there will be communication between the members of their health care team. Many patients assume that professionals involved in their care do talk and are surprised to learn that this is not the case.

When patients are unwilling to give permission for communication and collaboration with their medical professionals, it may signal that there are more complex issues to discuss. Patients appreciate and often require an explanation of how sharing information can positively affect their health care. In addition, psychotherapists can reduce patient concerns about information disclosure by clarifying and negotiating what information will and will not be shared with the medical professional. Patients should be reassured that particularly sensitive information that does not have a specific link to their medical care does not need to be shared. In fact, medical professionals do not always need or want specifics of the psychotherapy, generally preferring a "broad-brush" picture. Throughout this dialogue, however, patients need to understand that they can rescind their permission at any time.

Psychotherapists themselves must come to terms with sharing sensitive information about their patients and challenge their patients' fears that medical professionals will not maintain patient confidentiality. When psychotherapists have an established relationship with specific medical professionals, they can openly discuss how to maintain the safety of patient information. The Health Insurance Portability and Accountability Act regulations have increased pressure on medical professionals to maintain privacy, and they now have privacy practices more in line with mental health standards than in the past.

Myth: Collaborative care is extremely time-consuming.

Psychotherapists may assume that they must write a formal report or provide a significant amount of detail about their treatment. They may dread the amount of time they believe written collaboration will take but feel that more direct communication is impossible because they believe that reaching a medical professional directly will be difficult and time-consuming.

Reality: Written collaborative communication can be brief and not time-consuming, and direct contact can be streamlined.

The type of written communication medical professionals want about their patients is not time-consuming to compile or communicate. Psychotherapists "plumb the depths" whereas the medical professionals "skim the surface" of mental health issues.

Whereas psychotherapists gather details and slowly construct a narrative about the patient, typical medical professionals want only pertinent information such as diagnosis, symptom profile, and treatment plans. They appreciate regular updates about the patient's progress, especially if they are prescribing psychotropic medications or if the patient's medical problems and emotional status are intertwined. They often want suggestions from the psychotherapist about treatment strategies that will help them provide better care to the patient. Most medical professionals desire written communication that is brief and to the point.

The psychotherapist may anticipate that direct contact with a medical professional will be a frustrating game of "phone tag." Most medical professionals are used to being interrupted by beepers, pages, and phone calls. Although telephone contact may not always be the most efficient form of communication, facsimiles, voicemail, and electronic mail provide multiple means for the busy psychotherapist or medical professional to leave and retrieve pertinent data quickly. When actual conferencing is needed, cell phones are useful in the prearranged collaborative relationship. These technologies can promote regular, brief, and effective communication. In addition, an established, collaborative relationship facilitates direct communication because the professionals agree in advance about the best ways to share information.

Myth: Medical professionals are not interested in nor do they value the input of the psychotherapist.

Negative stereotypes are another barrier to collaboration. The stereotype of a brusque, "arrogant doctor" at the top of the hierarchical health care world may intimidate some psychotherapists. The medical professional, too, may have negative stereotypes of "touchy-feely shrinks" who do "talk therapy" that takes forever and who never provide feedback. One bad experience for either the psychotherapist or medical professional can be generalized and may deter further efforts to collaborate. A survey respondent illustrates this point well:

> Physicians I have run across do not seem to understand or trust psychological treatment and talking therapy. I have a few physicians who are patients. They explain that they are

taught to be very cynical about psychological intervention. My physician patients were very surprised how much therapy helped them. (APA Survey, 2006)

Many psychotherapists assume that they will be questioned or challenged about their assessment and treatment of the patient and the value of their communication. They may be uncertain about what to discuss and disclose about their patient. They may worry that the medical professional will view them as interfering or as a nuisance. The notion that medical professionals are "too busy" to be interrupted is ingrained.

All of these issues fuel isolation and deter psychotherapists from initiating collaboration. Like the stereotypes, these "myths" have a grain of truth. Medical professionals seem busy and rushed because they are busy. Also, medical professional receptivity and willingness to collaborate varies. Some medical professionals are difficult and do not appear to value communication from psychotherapists. The fear of rejection is a powerful deterrent to collaboration.

Reality: Most medical professionals are receptive to and interested in receiving feedback about their patients. They routinely get this feedback from other medical specialists.

Although medical professionals are time pressured, they do welcome specialists' input. Depending on the patient's situation, medical professionals may or may not be aware of the patient's emotional or psychiatric issues. If they are aware, they want to know how to provide better care for the patient and how the patient's mental health treatment is progressing. If medical professionals refer the patient to psychotherapy, they expect some sort of feedback on the treatment. In the medical world, it is normative to "close the loop" with the medical professional who referred the patient. Usually, this is done with a brief letter from the consultant or specialist. The lack of feedback to the referring medical professional from psychotherapists is seen as problematic and almost rude.

If medical professionals are unaware of a patient's emotional struggles, they need this information to provide optimal care. When they learn that their patient has sought mental health services, many medical professionals will invite the patient to come in and discuss their overall wellness and ensure that stressful life situations are not negatively affecting their health. When psychotherapists fail to communicate in this situation, both the medical professional and the psychotherapist have lost an opportunity to provide more optimal supportive care. More important, the patient has lost a potential ally in an effort to improve his or her life.

Myth: One-way communication is a brush-off or rejection of the psychotherapist's communication.

Psychotherapists frequently complain about the limited communication they receive from medical professionals. "They generally do not return phone calls. I'm never contacted by them for information about the psychotherapy. It's one-way communication. They rarely respond back or initiate contact. Communication is primarily one-sided" (APA Survey, 2006).

Reality: It is true that many medical professionals will not acknowledge receipt of information or respond in kind. This should not be interpreted as a "brush-off."

When medical specialists send a report or a letter regarding their consultation to other medical professionals, it is to inform them of their impressions and recommendations. They do not expect a reply because it is not the norm unless the receiving medical professional has questions or disagrees with the recommendations. Medical professionals treat information from psychotherapists in the same way. They are interested in the psychotherapist's impressions, recommendations, and updates and use them to provide overall health and wellness care to their patient. This correspondence, whatever form it takes, becomes part of the patient's medical record. However, they are unlikely to respond to the correspondence unless they have a question or concern.

Myth: The psychotherapist's purview is patients' emotional and psychological health, not their physical health.

Some psychotherapists may feel uncomfortable asking about their patient's physical symptoms despite their knowledge of behavioral medicine and psychopharmacology. Psychotherapists tend to be cognizant of scope of practice laws and may fear questions about health will be misinterpreted as an attempt to make medical diagnoses.

Reality: Integrated, collaborative health care depends on the psychotherapist and the medical professionals considering the "whole" person.

The biopsychosocial model, first described by George Engel in 1977, was a challenge to medical orthodoxy that was reductionistic and focused on disease to the exclusion of the person. He believed that a biomedical perspective limited understanding of illness, and he based his model on the assumption that the person's body, mind, relationships, and social context interact and influence each other continuously, shaping the person's overall health (Engel, 1977, 1980). Historically, the *bio, psyche,* and *social* aspects of care were attended to by different disciplines that ignored the parts of the patient for which they were not directly responsible. Primary care specialties and nursing embraced the biopsychosocial model in their training, whereas other specialties have continued to be disease oriented. The more recent mind–body paradigm shift described by Herbert Benson in the early 1970s and popularized in his book *The Relaxation Response* (1975) described the negative impact of stress on health and challenged the belief that the mind and body were separate entities.

Both of these paradigm shifts provide a framework for increasing collaboration between medical professionals and psychotherapists. Just as many medical professionals have expanded their purview beyond physical disease processes, psychotherapists must recognize the relevance of the patient's mind and body. They must be knowledgeable and actively assess the possibility of medical causes of psychiatric symptoms. They need to recognize the impact of chronic diseases such as obesity, hypertension, diabetes, and heart disease, as well as the role of stress in disease progression.

It is important to ask questions about patients' physical health and hypothesize how it may affect their emotional functioning—and vice versa. Thinking through patients' symptoms may result in the psychotherapist recommending that patients consult with their medical professional.

Myth: Medical professionals do not know their patients well and rarely have meaningful, emotional relationships with them.

Psychotherapists do not always appreciate the depth, importance, and permanence of the relationship that can develop between patients and their medical professionals. They may believe that medical professionals spend so little time with each patient, there is little opportunity for relationship development. They may believe that medical professionals see so many patients in a day that they cannot possibly feel a personal connection with so many people.

Reality: Many patients have a close bond to their medical professional. Many medical professionals know their patients well.

Psychotherapists may be surprised how often patients value their relationship to their medical professional and want that person to be apprised of status of their mental health care. This is particularly true of the patient with a chronic or life-threatening condition or one who has been with a primary care medical professional for many years. Patients have contact with their medical professional in times of health and illness; they share births, deaths, diagnoses of new illness, and declining health. This continuity of care creates a shared history that can result in a relationship important to both the patient and the medical professional.

In summary, there are many reasons collaborative care is not the norm. Medical professionals and psychotherapists are not trained to work together, so myths and stereotypes remain unchallenged. Separate cultures and physical distance are self-perpetuating. Often, the only link between professionals is the actual patient whose needs straddle both the "medical" and the "mental health" treatment worlds, particularly for patients with concomitant mental health and chronic physical problems. Yet psychotherapists usually do not consider themselves part of their patient's overall health care team and do not consult other involved professionals.

Of course, not all barriers to collaboration are myths. There are many real barriers to collaboration that relate to large system issues. Although large system issues are difficult to change, it is important to acknowledge how they both cause and reflect the separation of mental and physical health in our health care system. The following section outlines these barriers.

Real Barriers to Collaboration: The Large System Issues

Public Health Structure. Physical and mental health care and research operate under separate government funding streams and regulations. In 2007, the National Institute of Mental Health (NIMH) budget was $1.4 billion, in contrast to the National Institutes of Health (NIH) total budget of $28.4 billion (NIH, 2006; NIMH, 2006). Publicly funded medical and mental health care typically occurs in separate locations, so medical professionals and psychotherapists practice in separate worlds, reducing or eliminating opportunities to integrate health care research. The disparities are a reflection of the stigma attached to mental illness and promote the "mind–body split."

Separate Training and Practice Settings. Many of the cultural differences between medicine and mental health stem from the fact that psychotherapists and medical professionals usually train and practice separately. Psychotherapists train in universities and colleges that have little or no educational overlap with medical or nursing schools. The only contact with the medical world most psychotherapists have during their education and training is with psychiatrists. Similarly, medical professionals trained in many specialties may have limited exposure to psychotherapists.

Insurance Reimbursement Structure. Like the government, insurance companies often have completely separate systems and funding pools for physical and mental health treatment. "Carved out" mental health may be provided by a smaller company that manages only mental health and substance abuse issues. Some insurance companies have higher patient copayments for mental health treatment, negatively affecting access to mental health treatment. In addition, a referral process that requires patients to choose a psychotherapist on the basis of input from the behavioral health arm of the company can prevent the medical professional from managing the referral process directly by helping the patient select a psychotherapist.

Insurance reimbursement systems also impede collaboration by creating intense time pressure. The current reimbursement structure emphasizes volume and medical procedures over taking time to talk to patients. Medical professionals see a large volume of patients in any given day and are frequently rushed and behind in their schedule. No matter how psychosocially oriented, they genuinely may not have time for lengthy discussions about patients' emotional lives and stressors. The perception and reality that medical professionals are busy may increase the psychotherapist's discomfort initiating contact. One psychologist surveyed said, "Most physicians seem very impatient when they are contacted by phone, even though I keep the contact short, organized, and try to speak their language" (APA Survey, 2006).

Most medical professionals and psychotherapists are pressured by insurance companies to see more patients in less time for less reimbursement. High patient volume and cost control measures such as precertification generate more documentation. These factors leave many professionals feeling that they have no time for collaboration. The lack of insurance reimbursement for phone calls or e-mail communication regarding patient care serves is a further disincentive to collaboration. Although patients value collaboration between their health care professionals, they are usually unwilling to pay for nonreimbursed services.

Fortunately many of these large system issues are slowly beginning to change. Integrative, mind–body approaches to treatment of acute and chronic illnesses such as heart disease and pain use a team approach that often includes psychotherapists. Health psychology has become an important area of study and specialty (Chesney & Antoni, 2002). Parity legislation, which would require insurers to reimburse mental health and substance abuse treatment at the same rate as physical health, has been introduced in many states and at the federal level. In some states, serious mental illness, which may include schizophrenia, bipolar disorder, and depression, is already reimbursed at the same rate as medical problems. These examples suggest a paradigm shift toward a more integrative approach to treatment of the whole person. However, as we review in the next section, larger system issues are not the only barriers to collaboration.

Systemic and Cultural Differences Between Medicine and Mental Health

Differing Treatment Philosophies. In the biomedical model, the medical professional directs treatment decisions and bears responsibility for motivating the patient toward positive outcomes. Treatment and cure traditionally have been understood to be the medical professional's responsibility, even when patients are not cooperative in treatment. Although medical professionals may get frustrated and angry with noncompliant patients, they rarely terminate treatment. The medical professional–patient relationship is evolving toward more of a partnership, but most medical professionals still feel a sense of overarching responsibility for care outcome.

In contrast, in the mental health world, the patient and psychotherapist share responsibility for change, but the onus is on the patient to create change. When patients do not progress in psychotherapy because of lack of motivation or chronically missed appointments, these issues become the treatment focus. Sometimes psychotherapists will terminate their therapeutic relationship using APA ethical guidelines for termination and referral when the patient is unwilling or unable to participate actively in treatment.

Although both the mental health and medical culture consider the patient's readiness to change, the medical culture is to provide care to all, even those patients who are not ready to change their health behaviors. Outside of treatment for the chronically and persistently mentally ill, psychotherapists more readily terminate treatment for unmotivated patients. But then what happens? Patients who terminate mental health treatment may then return to their medical professional in search of symptom relief. Thus, the most challenging, often most needy, patients ultimately obtain whatever care they get from the medical system, which is poorly situated to meet their needs. This cultural difference can affect collaboration negatively because medical professionals view the mental health systems' discharge of such patients as highly problematic.

Action Versus Process Orientation. Medicine is action-oriented. Medical training emphasizes action over discussion and dialogue.

Patients hold the expectation that their medical professional will "do something" and may feel that their appointment was not helpful unless they leave with a prescription for medication, diagnostic tests, or a referral to a specialist. Medical professionals focus on outcome and ideally strive to practice "evidence-based medicine" in which they use current research evidence to guide their treatment decisions.

Psychotherapy tends to be more process oriented. Psychotherapy patients expect only that the psychotherapist will listen to them and offer insights and ideas about how to solve their difficulties. Psychotherapists are trained to assess and understand behavior and contextual factors to help people effect change. Often, the focus is on patterns of behavior and process as much as the final outcome.

These differences in focus need to be understood and respected because they can interfere with collaboration. Medical providers are unlikely to find collaborative communication focusing on the psychotherapeutic process and patterns helpful and prefer a focus on symptom description, treatment plan, and outcome indices.

Different Professional Languages. An obvious difference between these cultures is that medical professionals and psychotherapists use different languages (Seaburn, Lorenz, Gunn, Gawinski, & Mauksch, 1996). For example, medical professionals use the term *myocardial infarction* or *MI* for *heart attack,* and psychotherapists might refer to *undifferentiated ego mass,* or an *enmeshed family* in describing an abnormally close family system. Psychotherapists who experience difficulty understanding "med-speak" may be unaware that their own jargon is equally noncommunicative. Ideally, both psychotherapists and medical professionals avoid jargon in their communication. However, psychotherapists may need to learn some "med-speak" to enhance collaboration.

Roles and Logistics. Most psychotherapists are not familiar with the various layers of professionals in the medical system or the differences in training and philosophy between them. Nor are they familiar with the logistics of the medical office. Only a few graduate programs in psychology have expanded their curricula to include behavioral health and specific training in the workings of the larger medical system. Thus, many psychotherapists may be unfamiliar with the medical hierarchy, training, and philosophy of different specialties and with the role of midlevel providers such as advanced practice nurses and physician assistants. As a result, psychotherapists may be less able to adjust their collaboration to the different styles of family physicians and internists, for example, if they do not understand how these disciplines differ in training and culture.

Similarly, most medical professionals are confused by the vast array of disciplines, training, skills, and specialties in mental health. Psychotherapists with different theoretical orientations further confuse the medical professional. Although medical professionals understand why, when, and how to refer to medical subspecialists such as a cardiologist and endocrinologist, they may be uncertain about specifics of a psychotherapy referral. Ultimately, they may have difficulty matching the patient's needs to the most appropriate psychotherapist.

Confidentiality. The medical culture is organized around referrals and consultation with others. In contrast, the mental health culture values strict confidentiality. Medical professionals often engage in "curbside consults" in which they discuss their patients passing in the halls of hospitals or at professional meetings. Informal phone consultation regarding a patient is not uncommon. In this culture of openly sharing patient information, medical professionals may be confused and skeptical about psychotherapists who do not routinely communicate and seem secretive about their patients. Medical professionals often complain, "I never hear anything from psychologists or psychiatrists" after they make the referral. Although some programs have tried to encourage psychotherapists to communicate in writing to the patient's primary care medical professional, regular communication never became common practice (see also chap. 3, this volume).

Conclusion

In summary, there are very real barriers to collaboration, particularly separate cultures, time pressure, and reimbursement policies. Personal stereotypes, myths, and negative experiences can decrease the likelihood that psychotherapists and medical professionals are willing to make the effort necessary to collaborate. To collaborate effectively and overcome these barriers, psychotherapists must be willing to take a leap of faith to alter their practice patterns and trust that collaboration will ultimately be worth the time and effort. They must become educated about the medical world and make a personal paradigm shift.

In chapter 2 we help collaborative psychotherapists begin to understand the world of primary care medicine. More specifically, we review how mental health issues tend to be presented by patients in primary care and how primary care professionals attempt to help those patients. We discuss the challenges primary care medical professionals face as they attempt to help patients with emotional issues and how collaborative relationships with psychotherapists can alleviate some of these issues.

2

Primary Care:
Where the Patients Are

Many psychotherapists are not familiar with the world of primary medical care, aside from their own experiences as a patient or those of their family and friends. They might find the high volume of mental health issues in the primary care setting surprising. Consider the following commentary about a typical day from an average primary care physician.

Medical professionals see patients in half-day sessions. A family doctor might describe a typical session something like this:

□ *8 a.m.:* I arrive at my office to find my mailbox filled with charts to be reviewed, phone messages for prescription refills, patient questions, reams of papers for managed care referrals, and lab results to be reviewed with patient follow-up if the result is abnormal.

□ *8:30:* I am scheduled for a 15-minute appointment with a 48-year-old woman whom I diagnosed with adult-onset diabetes 18 months ago. At that time, I counseled her about diet and exercise to control her diabetes. In this visit, we focus on the patient's difficulty managing her diet, which resulted in poorly controlled blood sugar. After I review my recommendations, I refer her to a dietician but doubt she will follow through with the referral.

□ *8:45:* I am scheduled for a 15-minute appointment with a 34-year-old woman who thinks she has a sinus infection, even though she's only been sick for 2 days. I obtain a history of her symptoms and examine her. When I tell her that her symptoms are consistent with the common cold so antibiotic treatment is not warranted, she becomes angry. She pleads her case, and I try to forge a compromise by giving her a prescription to fill in a few days if she does not feel better. She may wait, but I think it is more likely that she will go directly to the pharmacy after her appointment.

☐ *8:50:* Just as I start the physical examination with my 8:45 patient, my pager goes off, and I step out of the room to answer the page. This definitely does not help my negotiation regarding antibiotics with the patient, but I am able to have a conversation with the cardiologist about shared patients.

☐ *9:00:* Next, I have a 30-minute well-child check on a 3-month-old. The parents are tired but happy, and the baby looks great. I answer questions about feeding, growth, and sleeping. I offer reassurance to the parents that they are doing a great job.

☐ *9:30:* I am scheduled for a 15-minute appointment with a 42-year-old woman with chest pain. She has been to the emergency department on numerous occasions, and all of her chest pain episodes have been attributed to panic attacks. She is certain that she is going to die of a heart attack and that no one believes her. I spend almost 45 minutes discussing her symptoms and concerns. She acknowledges that the fear of a heart attack makes her anxious and concedes that anxiety is at least part of the problem. She agrees to consider starting medication and will return in 1 week.

☐ *10:15:* I begin to see my 9:45 patient who is scheduled for a 15-minute appointment. Fortunately, this is an elderly woman who is patient and understanding about the delay. Unfortunately, she has multiple complicated medical problems and is not a great reporter of her conditions. I make a mental note to contact her daughter and ask the patient to come back in 2 weeks for follow-up because she got short shrift today.

☐ *10:30:* I am now seeing my patient who was scheduled for a 10:00 appointment. Unfortunately, he is a busy, impatient executive who is clearly annoyed by the delay. Fortunately, he has a simple upper respiratory infection that

takes only 5 minutes to diagnose and prescribe. He men-
tions at the end of the appointment that he needs a physical. It has been 5 years since his last one, and he is a 53-
year-old smoker. I would like to talk to him about his
smoking, lifestyle modification, and the need for a routine
colonoscopy, but I'm running behind. I have to hope just
mentioning it will motivate him.

☐   *10:40:* The 10:15 appointment is allotted 45 minutes for a
physical. It feels luxurious to have so much time to treat
one person! The patient has had a significant problem with
depression in the past but has done well on antidepressants. She has never followed up on my referrals for counseling. She is under a great deal of stress and feeling more
depressed but is still not willing to see a psychotherapist.
I increase her antidepressant dose and encourage her to
talk to family and friends about how she is feeling. I end
up spending almost an hour with her because she really
needs to talk to someone.

☐   *11:40:* I am just starting to see the 11:00 appointment as
lunch, phone calls, and charting should start. Late again!
11:00 is a 15-minute appointment with an asthmatic who
smokes. I review the treatment plan and note that her
emergency room visits have decreased. The inevitable
smoking discussion ensues, and surprisingly the patient
agrees to try a medication to help her quit smoking. Perhaps all that lecturing does pay off!

☐   *12:05:* My last patient of the morning. The 11:15 appointment is allotted 15 minutes for a toddler who fell down
the stairs 2 days ago. Her arm may be broken. Do her parents supervise appropriately? Why was treatment so delayed? I do not know this family well, and the mother's
story does make sense. I make a mental note to see them
back and try to get to know more about the family situation. I hope that this is not child abuse.

☐   *12:30:* Lunch—15 phone calls and 10 charts to be completed. All in 30 minutes before the next whirlwind session starts!

At the end of this chapter, we revisit this schedule to see how a
collaborative psychotherapist's perspective might help the physician provide optimal patient care.

The Primary Care Worldview

Most primary care medical professionals view emotional distress and mental health disorders as central to care because so many patients they treat have psychosocial issues. Of course, there are some primary care medical professionals who try to ignore these issues and focus solely on biomedical presentations. However, in general, most attempt to detect and diagnose mental health problems and provide first-line treatment. When a patient's difficulty exceeds the medical professionals' expertise or time constraints, the patient is referred to a psychotherapist, as the patient with complex heart problems would be referred to a cardiologist. Psychotherapists only see those patients who were not helped in primary care, which may give them a negatively skewed view of the skill level and success ratio of primary care medical professionals.

How Primary Care Medical Professionals Help Patients in Psychological Distress

Primary care medical professionals do not provide in-depth mental health services, but they often help patients with situational stressors and mild to moderate depression and anxiety. The following example illustrates how this care can occur in a primary care setting with a perceptive and skilled physician:

> During an evening patient care session, Dr. Franklin entered the room of a patient he knew only from a few appointments when she was acutely ill. Her presenting concern was insomnia, but as he walked in the room, he instantly knew it was more. The patient, Janet, was in tears and started crying harder when Dr. Franklin asked how he could help. She told Dr. Franklin that she had not slept in 2 days because her brother had tried to commit suicide. She felt responsible, because this attempt followed an argument in which she had told him he could no longer live with her unless he sought treatment for his addictions. Her brother had a serious drug problem, and Janet felt she was enabling him.
>   Dr. Franklin was concerned about Janet. He only had 15 minutes allotted for her visit and realized her needs were too

great for him to address fully. He worked to put aside his frustration and emotionally regroup to be able to help Janet. First, he acknowledged to Janet how difficult her situation must be. Second, he realized that Janet was exhausted and needed sleep, so he decided to give her a sleep aid. Third, he recognized that Janet needed more help than he could provide, so he asked Janet if she was willing to talk to a counselor. Janet also felt she needed counseling and was willing to call her company's employee assistance program in the morning. Finally, Dr. Franklin felt that Janet needed reassurance that her brother's suicide attempt was not her fault and that she did the right thing by setting a firm limit with him. Furthermore, it was imperative that she not allow her brother back in her home. He coached Janet to call her brother's case manager in the psychiatric unit to clarify that she was not willing to receive him at discharge. Dr. Franklin asked Janet to come back within a week to ensure the sleep aid worked and to allow him to check in with her and offer more support. Also, Dr. Franklin stressed that Janet could call the office at any time and talk to him or another medical professional on call. Dr. Franklin spent approximately 20 minutes with Janet.

This example illustrates how primary care medical professionals help patients cope. They use their relationships and continuity of care to reassure patients that they have an ally. They counsel patients with simple reassurance and empathy, and some have skills in using anxiety-reduction and problem-solving strategies, as well as simple cognitive–behavioral techniques. They often write prescriptions for symptom relief. Finally, they refer patients to psychotherapy. Each major concept is described in the following sections.

The Role of the Relationship

When primary care medical professionals have established relationships with patients in emotional distress, they are in a unique position to help. Although psychotherapists only know patients in the context of significant emotional distress, primary care medical professionals see patients under more typical circumstances. Their knowledge of the patient's baseline can serve as a helpful comparison point to determine the patient's distress level and treatment progress. Also, medical professionals may know the patient's family and social context, allowing them to enlist the patient's personal support system when appropriate. Patients who trust their primary care medical professional may be more likely to adhere to the prescribed treatment plan or to follow through on a referral to a psychotherapist or other specialist. The continuity of care that medical professionals have with patients facilitates healing.

Additionally, medical professionals sometimes find themselves in an advocacy role for their patients. Patients who need disability benefits or even brief work respites secondary to stress get this permission from their medical professional. The medical professional's advocacy role can facilitate a sense of partnership.

Counseling Patients

Patients often look to medical professionals for reassurance and guidance regarding their health. Providing the same kind of reassurance and guidance regarding life stresses is a natural extension of these skills. The combination of reassurance and empathy often soothes patients and helps them regroup and manage the stresses in their lives. Medical professionals also may be more comfortable than psychotherapists with offering advice to patients given that psychotherapists have been specifically trained *not* to offer advice. Many patients appreciate this type of input.

Appropriate Use of Medications

Primary care medical professionals often turn to medications for several reasons. Medical professionals look at most problems through a biomedical lens and recognize ways in which medications may be helpful. They tend to be pragmatic, and many patients do improve on medication alone. Prescribing medication can save time, because many patients expect to receive a medication and the "quick fix" that they believe it will bring, and writing a prescription takes less time than talking to patients. Also, most primary care medical professionals feel more comfortable prescribing medication than providing counseling for their patients. The poor insurance reimbursement that medical professionals receive for counseling is another disincentive to talking versus doing.

An Artful Referral

When medical professionals feel that a patient's difficulties exceed their time or expertise, they can use their relationship with the patient to facilitate a referral to a psychotherapist. Medical professionals who regularly collaborate with several psychotherapists can discuss the history of successful shared patient care with their patients. This engenders trust "by association" and reassures the reluctant patient that the psychotherapist is competent and likely to be of assistance. This trust and the likelihood that the patient's positive expectations for psychotherapy facilitates referrals and may even help patients engage more fully in the therapeutic process are yet more advantages of established collaborative relationships.

Many patients look to and receive a great deal of psychological help from primary care medical professionals. A sincere desire to help, genuine empathy, reassurance, and assistance in problem solving can be extremely helpful to patients struggling to cope with situational stressors such as death, divorce, job loss, motor vehicle accidents, and illness. These interventions can be sufficient, especially with patients who have a good personal support system to help them cope. However, medical professionals also know that their skills and treatments cannot address the full range of mental health problems that present routinely. Patients dealing with chronic and multiple stressors, lack of social support, abuse histories, personality disorders, and major mental health disorders need a team approach to address their issues. In the next section of this chapter, we describe these and other issues that need consideration to understand the role of primary care medical professionals in treating patients in emotional distress.

The Challenges of Mental Health Treatment in Primary Care

Primary care medical professionals face many challenges as they attempt to help their patients with emotional issues. The following sections review a number of factors and specific situations that complicate this task in the primary care setting.

The Patient's Presentation and Definition of the Problem

In primary care, patients often present mental health issues indirectly, rarely listing "depression" or "anxiety" as the reason for their visit. Patients experiencing physical symptoms associated with their emotional distress seek medical care to learn the cause and treatment for their somatic symptoms. Primary care medical professionals will miss underlying emotional or mental health issues unless they actively attempt to assess emotional functioning. They must then adroitly shift the dialogue from the patient's physical concerns to their emotional well-being and communicate the connection between these issues to create a shared definition of the problem. It can be difficult to transition adeptly from the patient's presenting somatic concern to a discussion of his or her stress level. Throughout this process, the medical professional must take care to rule out fully any possible physical causes of patients' symptoms and ensure that patients do not feel dismissed because their symptoms are "in their head."

Ideally, medical professionals manage this balancing act between investigating biomedical and nonbiomedical causes of physical symptoms carefully to avoid alienating the patient. In reality, this conversation takes time and skill that many medical professionals simply do not have. They are less likely to detect mental health issues when the patient communicates indirectly, is unaware of the link with their physical concern, or has multiple concerns at a given visit (Rost et al., 2000).

Mental Health Access Issues

Helping the patient make a link between stress and physical symptoms is key to the detection and treatment of underlying emotional distress. Most primary care medical professionals use the concept of "stress" to ask patients about the emotional context of symptoms in a nonpejorative, normative way that most people will understand and acknowledge to be relevant to the presenting concern. However, some patients often define the source of their distress as solely biomedical and are not open to the idea that at least some aspects of their physical health problem may stem from psychological distress.

Helping patients make this link is only half the battle. Even patients who recognize they are struggling with emotional issues are unwilling to seek treatment from a psychotherapist. Brody, Khaliq, and Thompson (1997) found that although 89% of depressed primary care patients desired counseling by their primary care medical professional, only 11% wanted a referral to a psychotherapist. There are many reasons that so few wanted a mental health referral, including cost, stigma, privacy concerns, and the belief that "just talking" with a psychotherapist will not help.

Even when a patient agrees to seek mental health care, the barriers to entering the mental health treatment system often derail the medical professional's referral (Chantal, Brazeau, Rovi, Yick, & Johnson, 2005). Patients complain that psychotherapists do not return phone calls, cannot begin treatment for an extended period of time, or do not take their insurance. Prior negative experiences with psychotherapy can further complicate the referral process for both the patient and the medical professional. Primary care medical professionals find it extremely frustrating to work so hard to get patients to try to seek psychotherapy, only to be derailed by systemic barriers to care.

Chronically Distressed Patients

Many patients experience depression or anxiety for years but do not realize that their baseline emotional functioning is different from the norm. The average latency between onset of illness and treatment for depressive disorders is 6 to 8 years, and the average treatment latency for anxiety is 9 to 23 years (Wang, Bergland, & Olfson, 2005). Prior to their diagnosis and treatment, these patients often make frequent medical appointments, presenting with vague, unclear complaints related to their overall low level of wellness, yet they may not have made the link between their emotional struggles and their symptoms.

Patients with moderate to severe chronic depression and anxiety commonly need both psychotherapy and medication. They may require numerous trials before they find the right medication at the right dose. Likewise, patients who need pain or anti-anxiety medications are often difficult for primary care medical professionals to manage. The patient's primary agenda of obtaining medication can preclude the development of a therapeutic relationship. In the best of circumstances, the medical professional makes the medication contingent on establishing a relationship with a psychotherapist with whom they have a collaborative relationship. Unfortunately, this is rarely the case.

Patients Newly Diagnosed With a Serious Chronic or Life-Threatening Illness

Patients with a new diagnosis of a serious chronic or life-threatening condition can be challenging for medical professionals. The diagnostic process itself can be a major life stressor, particularly when the patient's symptoms affect quality of life or when the diagnostic process is protracted and inconclusive. The stress of illness, the potential brush with mortality, role and function loss, and anticipatory grieving associated with illness relate to the high rate of depression among the chronically medically ill. These patients often need therapy from a psychotherapist who understands the psychological and relational issues inherent in chronic illness.

Sometimes, the medical diagnostic process does not yield answers. Between 25% and 50% of all primary care visits yield no organic cause for the presenting symptom (A. A. Khan, Khan, Harezlak, Tu, & Kroenke, 2002), with rates of 80% to 90% in specific symptom presentations (Bleijenberg & Fennis, 1989; Kroenke & Mangelsdorff, 1989). Some 20% to 40% of the patients seen by medical specialists do not receive a clear diagnosis (Barsky & Borus, 1995; Bass, 1990). Patients who experience symptoms and undergo a diagnostic process without a clear biomedical cause are in limbo; they may fear their medical professional has missed a disease process or views the illness as being "all in their head." They have no prognostic or treatment information to help them cope. Often, these patients fall into a dysfunctional illness role that ultimately can become their primary identity. The larger cultural bias is that illness stems from *either* the head or the body. When the patient's difficulties stem from both the soma and the psyche, our health system does not support an integrated view of the cause or the treatment and forces the patient to choose one or the other as the cause of distress.

Patients Who Somaticize

A subset of patients has a number of unexplained physical symptoms in multiple organ systems, fitting the criteria for somatization disorder. Many medical professionals find somatically fixated patients extremely frustrating. The patients often "doctor shop" searching for a cure, believing the source of their misery and their salvation rests in finding the correct diagnosis and treatment of their perceived biomedical illness. They tend to avoid any discussion of emotional issues because they believe their problems are strictly biomedical. They request many diagnostic tests, believing the right test will reveal the source of their discomfort and unhappiness. Medical professionals find it difficult to deny the patient's requests for testing and referrals to specialists out of fear that the patient does have some strange underlying illness that they might miss, resulting in a poor outcome or a liability claim. Yet the ongoing testing and referrals to specialists only fuel the patient's fears, exacerbating and perpetuating the problem (Escobar, Waitzkin, Silver, Gara, & Holman, 1998; Katon et al., 1990; Katon & Walker, 1998; Smith, Monson, & Ray, 1986).

Continuity of care and collaboration can help somatizing patients make slow but steady improvement. Primary care medical professionals sometimes can convince these patients to see a psychotherapist to help them cope with the stress of their elusive illness. In fact, most of these patients are depressed or anxious (or both), and a significant percentage of them have trauma histories (Haugg, Mykletun, & Dahl, 2004; Simon, Gater, Kisely, & Piccinelli, 1996; Simon, VonKorff, Piccinelli, Fullerton, & Ormel, 1999). Specific collaborative and psychotherapeutic strategies to optimize care for patients with somatic fixation are reviewed in chapters 4 and 5.

Patients Who Have Personality Disorders or Who Abuse Substances

Medical professionals often struggle with patients with personality disorder and substance abuse issues, particularly if patients tend to be extremely demanding or become frustrated when they feel misunderstood or believe that their needs are not being met. Psychotherapists who work primarily with patients who have substance abuse or personality disorders are accustomed to helping patients avoid these dysfunctional patterns through limit setting and relationship building. Medical professionals may not have the sophistication to recognize personality disorders or substance abuse problems, ultimately feeling manipulated after spending time and energy on patients with a poor outcome. Medical professionals may respond to these patients with anger, frustration, and blame. Issues in treating such challenging patients are discussed further in chapters 4 and 5.

Medical Professional's Differing Skill and Interest Level Regarding Psychological Issues

Medical professionals fall along different points on a broad continuum of skill and intuition regarding mental health issues, resulting in variable care quality. Some medical professionals do not have the skills, time, or interest to delve into patient's lives and better understand the role of stress and mental health issues in the patient's presentation. These professionals are unlikely to realize when patients are struggling with emotional issues. Even when the mental health issue is the stated presenting problem, they tend to refer to a psychotherapist with little preparation for this transition.

Some primary care medical professionals are more skilled at identifying psychosocial problems but do not have the time or the training to address them. Medical training does not include psychotherapy skills. Most medical professionals recognize the critical differences between primary care counseling and psychotherapy provided by a psychotherapist, and they understand that many patients need psychotherapy to improve.

The medical professional's ability to differentiate patients who need situational support from those who need psychotherapy is critical. Medical professionals may not realize when the patient's needs exceed their expertise until after the patient feels committed to the therapeutic process with them. In these situations, the medical professional must carefully discuss a referral to a psychotherapist. Patients sometimes feel rejected, betrayed, or "dumped" by the medical professional or assume that the referral means that their mental health problems are more serious. A poorly managed referral can set the stage for trust issues between the patient and the psychotherapist. This is particularly problematic for patients with underlying personality pathology.

A patient's psychotropic medication needs may exceed the primary care medical professional's expertise; often primary care professionals are comfortable prescribing only a few antidepressants and anxiolytics. Most tend to shy away from complicated combinations of medications or antipsychotic medications. Even when the patient's medication regimen is not complicated, there is evidence that primary care medical professionals do not follow patients as closely as psychiatrists and do not counsel patients regarding medication side effects as effectively (Schulberg, Block, & Madonia, 1997; Simon & VonKorff, 1995; Wells, Katon, Rogers, & Camp, 1994). Patients with intractable symptoms are referred to a psychiatrist or psychiatric nurse practitioner. Again, patients in such situations may feel that the psychiatric referral means they are "sicker than they thought," or they may feel rejected or betrayed by the medical professional. Taken together, these factors may result in suboptimal care (Katzelnick, Kobak, Greist, Jefferson, & Henk, 1997; Simon, VonKorff, Wagner, & Barlow, 1993).

The Opportunities for Psychotherapists

Primary care medical professionals "see it all" and have a unique vantage point for viewing the human condition. They see patients at every level of health and wellness, illness and suffering. It is impossible to provide good medical care and ignore mental health issues. However, it is also impossible to address the needs of all patients with emotional distress without some type of mental health system support. Primary care medical professionals need to work with a cadre of competent psychotherapists who can provide services to those patients whose needs exceed their capabilities.

In the following section, we revisit the typical schedule of the primary care medical professional from the beginning of the chapter, focusing on those patients who could be referred to a mental health professional. The clinical questions regarding the patient's presentations illustrate cases in which collaborative psychotherapists might begin their work to benefit the patient, the primary care physician, and the mental health professional.

1. The 48-year-old woman with adult-onset diabetes diagnosed 18 months earlier who was experiencing difficulty making the necessary lifestyle changes:

    Is it simply difficulty with changing habits, or has she not really accepted that she has diabetes and must make these changes? Is she scared and depressed about the diagnosis? What are her health beliefs about diabetes, given her prior experiences? Does she view herself as able to have an impact on the course of her illness, or does she see herself as a hapless victim? Does this pattern play itself out in other aspects of her life? A psychotherapist would address these questions and concerns as part of a therapeutic intervention to help the patient cope with her new illness. A collaborative psychotherapist could then help the medical professional create a treatment plan that addresses her specific barriers to optimal care.

2. The 42-year-old woman with chest pain who fears she has cardiac problems and is frustrated by the medical system:

    Can she begin to consider whether stress plays a role in the onset of her chest pain? Can this patient learn anxiety management techniques to help her tolerate and wait out her panic attacks, rather than overusing and misusing the health care system? Again, the psychotherapist and medical professionals need to work together to appropriately reassure her, while ensuring that any biomedically treatable issues are dealt with appropriately.

3. The depressed woman who made an appointment for a physical has chronic depression but will not see a psychotherapist:

    Thus far, the patient has gained some relief through occasional conversations with a medical professional.

However, the medical professional does not have the time and skills to treat her optimally. If the medical professional could personally recommend a psychotherapist, or if a psychotherapist would be willing to meet briefly with the patient in the primary care setting before the referral, the likelihood that the patient would follow through is much higher. Meeting the proposed psychotherapist in the medical setting can be a powerful antidote to the anxiety and dread that some patients have about beginning psychotherapy. This patient requires a team approach.

4. The family with the child with a broken arm:
    This family may be in crisis. The medical professional may find that there is domestic violence, substance abuse, or extreme life stressors related to the child's injury. The family members will require immediate assistance if they agree to referral, although they if the physician suspects abuse, the resulting report to the authorities may force them to seek services. An appointment in 4 to 6 weeks would not be useful. In medicine, it is normative to "make room" for emergent situations. Just as a cardiologist might clear an appointment for a patient who may be critically ill, psychotherapists may need to accept new patients who are not in "psychiatric crisis" but will be soon if they do not obtain appropriate intervention.

Conclusion

Psychotherapists have an opportunity to create professional relationships with medical professionals to facilitate referrals and enhance care. The current state of affairs creates enormous opportunities for savvy psychotherapists to establish relationships with medical professionals who work on the front lines—"where the patients are." In chapter 3, we take you, the reader, to a hands-on approach to collaboration in your own practice. You will learn how to create a network of collaborative medical professionals, make contact with medical professionals both within and outside your current referral network, and weave collaborative practices into your daily routine to facilitate collaboration.

3

The Nuts and Bolts of Routine Collaboration

Building collaborative relationships into the routine of your practice need not be an anxiety-provoking process. In this chapter, we break this process into seven specific steps and describe how to implement each step. Some of the steps relate to the psychotherapist's mind-set, whereas others focus on practice-management techniques that facilitate collaboration. Different readers, depending on their particular backgrounds, will spend a different amount of time working on each step. For example, readers who already have a collaborative mind-set may find Steps 1 and 2 easy to complete but require more time to adopt Steps 3 through 7. This is because, despite their collaborative mind-set, they have not been exposed to the practicalities of making collaborative relationships part of their routine. Others may need to think through the collaborative mind-set itself to determine how they want to integrate these concepts into their current practice.

Although this chapter focuses on routine collaboration, the steps that we propose here also are highly relevant to less routine and more intensive collaboration discussed in Part II of this book.

Step 1: Making a Commitment to Collaborate

As with most changes in behavior, it takes motivation to step outside one's comfort zone and practice differently. The first step is to assess one's own level of motivation as reviewed in the self-assessment tool at the beginning of chapter 1. Collaborative psychotherapists must be willing to adapt their practice to aspects of the medical system culture that are different from the mental health culture. Some psychotherapists feel this puts mental health in a "one down" position to the medical system. However, an alternative perspective is to see oneself as a systems consultant. Much as psychotherapists adapt to each patient and family, they can and must adapt to work more effectively with medical professionals.

Step 2: Establishing a Collaborative Mind-Set

Once psychotherapists have committed themselves to becoming more collaborative, they must make a critical shift in their assessment, conceptualization, and treatment planning process. Psychotherapists must expand their thinking and processes to assess actively patient's collaborative needs. What role can collaboration play in this particular clinical presentation? How do the patient's medical and mental health care currently synergize each other, and what can be done to improve their combined power?

Psychotherapists who actively assess for the patient's collaboration needs will find that the appropriate level of collaboration varies across cases, from a minimum of a form letter at the beginning and end of treatment to contact after each session. Ongoing communication tends to be more important when the medical professional is prescribing psychotropic medication or when the patient has a chronic or life-threatening illness, presents with somatic symptoms, has chronic pain or substance abuse issues, or a combination of these. These types of cases are discussed further in Part II of this book. It is essential that psychotherapists evaluate these issues during the assessment process.

A psychotherapist with a collaborative mind-set recognizes the interplay of physical illness, medications, and mental health. For example, is the patient fatigued and having difficulty concentrating secondary to depression or hypothyroidism? Any patient who has not had a general physical for 2 or more years or who presents with somatic concerns, substance abuse, an eating disorder, or significant vegetative symptoms should be referred for medical examination. Many medical conditions can present as symptoms frequently associated with mental health conditions. Psychotherapists must familiarize themselves with medical conditions that have symptoms similar to depression and anxiety. Appendix A outlines some of the "medical suspects" that should be ruled out by a medical professional. This is by no means an exhaustive list but reviews some of the most common issues. Appendix B similarly reviews some medications that can cause psychiatric symptoms. Psychotherapists who have established collaborative relationships with medical professionals can easily refer patients who do not already have a primary care medical professional when appropriate. Referring a patient to a medical professional for evaluation or treatment also creates an opportunity to make contact.

A collaborative mind-set may alter how, and to what degree, psychotherapists facilitate better medical professional–patient relationships. It is not uncommon for patients to complain about their medical care in psychotherapy. Psychotherapists who do not collaborate only hear the patient's perspective on these issues and may unwittingly play into relationship issues between the medical professional and patient or into manipulation by the patient. In contrast, a collaborative psychotherapist recognizes the importance of hearing both sides of the story. Patients who tend to "split" their health care professionals may benefit from a collaborative approach that prevents them from fragmenting their own treatment team. A patient who actively complains about previous or current professionals or who has a history of "doctor shopping" may fall into this category. Alternatively, collaborative contacts can indicate that the patient has good reason for his or her dissatisfaction. The medical professional may be frustrated as a result of providing care to this patient, or there simply may be a mismatch between the patient's needs and the professional's style. In these situations, the psychotherapist may be able to help mend the medical professional–patient relationship. When this is not possible, the psychotherapist can empower the patient to seek more appropriate care.

Psychotherapists with a collaborative mind-set recognize that the time and energy spent on collaboration can ultimately save time and energy spent on patient care. This can help to maintain motivation to prioritize collaboration even when it is challenging.

Step 3: Creating a Collaborative Practice Toolbox

To maintain collaborative relationships, collaborative practices must be integrated into daily practice patterns. Becoming collaborative is a process. Each psychotherapist must experiment with various practice management techniques to determine which fit best with his or her practice style and within the community. As with any behavioral change, attempting a collaboration "practice overhaul" is probably not realistic. Rather, it is recommended that psychotherapists start with those techniques that seem least time-consuming or difficult and allow their collaboration practices and style to evolve with time and experience.

It is helpful to create a "toolbox" of communication aids. To reduce time spent collaborating, streamline communication by creating form letters for common points of communication. Such form letters allow the psychotherapist simply to add relevant information to a preexisting letter, distilling written communication into its easiest form. They are most useful at the beginning and end of treatment.

Postreferral and Intake Letter

It is recommended that psychotherapists have a standard "thank you for the referral" letter (Appendix C, "Sample Postreferral Letter") to be sent after the first appointment. Even a letter that discloses only that the patient followed through on the mental health referral helps the medical professional, because in the current system, they often have no way of knowing if or when the patient connected with a psychotherapist. A form letter with a space for diagnosis and a few words about treatment plan can be even more helpful and takes little extra time and energy.

Clarification of Communication Expectations and Means

Additional elements to the postreferral letter can facilitate future collaboration. Include your contact information, and request the same in return from the medical professional. You can include a business card with the correspondence that contains information on all forms of contact, including e-mail address. Psychotherapists and medical professionals are notoriously difficult to contact directly. Determining how the medical professional prefers to be contacted under emergent and nonemergent situations can reduce time-consuming and frustrating attempts to connect. In the medical culture, it is normative to interrupt medical professionals during patient care or to use a paging system to facilitate communication. In contrast, these methods are typically used only under emergent conditions in the mental health culture. Because many psychotherapists are reluctant to use these methods without the expressed permission of the medical professional, simply ask directly. Include a form that indicates preferred modes of communication with the postintake letter, and ask the medical professional to return it (Appendix C, "Medical Professional Communication Preference Form"). Psychotherapists can request information from the medical professional about desired means and frequency of contact and specific referral concerns in a checklist format. Include a self-addressed stamped envelope and a fax number. Although some medical professionals will not take the time to complete this form, others will as a matter of course or when they have particular concerns about the shared patient.

Termination Letter

The communication toolbox should also include a letter to be used to alert the medical professional when treatment has been terminated (Appendix C, "Sample Termination Notification Letter"). The letter can simply state that treatment has stopped, or it can go into more detail about the treatment and future options. This letter should describe the patient's progress and symptoms or warning signs the patient and medical professional should monitor for early detection of relapse. If the termination is mutually agreed on between the patient and the psychotherapist, they can cocreate the termination letter. Writing this letter is a therapeutic exercise in and of itself because it reviews material that the patient and psychotherapist would generally discuss as part of the termination process. Cocreation of letters to the patient's medical professional is one way to reduce the out-of-session time involved in collaboration.

Psychotherapists who create a structure for easy communication with medical professionals will find ongoing clinical collaboration much easier to maintain. In addition, basic collaboration techniques tend to evolve into a routine as professionals establish a relationship over time and multiple shared patients.

Step 4: Finding Partners for Collaborative Care

The fourth step is to find medical professionals who are receptive to collaboration. This may entail some rejection from those professionals who do not focus on psychosocial concerns and mental health issues in their practice. However, they are in the minority. A survey of family physicians indicated that 13.5% already have mental health professionals providing services in their office, and an additional 60.2% indicated they value collaborative care to the point they would consider having an in house psychotherapist (Chantal, Brazeau, Rovi, Yick, & Johnson, 2005).

The process of finding collaboration partners is similar to the networking psychotherapists use to expand their referral network. Ask colleagues, friends, and even one's own medical professionals who is known to be psychosocially focused or particularly skillful in working with distressed patients. As Doherty, McDaniel, and Baird (1996) reviewed in their model, medical professionals fall along a continuum of styles regarding the integration of psychosocial issues in medical practices. Those medical professionals who are already psychosocially focused are more likely to be receptive and helpful in further networking.

Another way to find collaboration partners is to investigate the medical professionals who practice near you. Psychotherapists can begin by researching all the primary care medical professionals who practice within a 2- to 5-mile radius of one's office, or greater distances in rural areas. Geographic proximity facilitates collaboration, particularly when practices are in the same office building or office park, where there is face-to-face interaction among the professionals. Additionally, a convenient and familiar office location is often a consideration to patients when they first are seeking mental health services.

Some psychotherapists facilitate networking by giving professional presentations on a topic that medical professionals would
find of interest. Topics could include depression in primary care,
managing chronically ill patients, or increasing patient compliance to medical regimens. Many medical and nursing professional
associations have ongoing lecture series and would welcome this
assistance. Also, it is likely that the medical professionals who
would choose to attend a conference on psychosocial issues are
more interested in detecting and treating these issues in their
practices.

Step 5: Making Contact Within
Your Current Referral Network

The best source of potential collaborators is the medical professionals who currently refer patients to you. Many psychotherapists who do not regularly collaborate may not know the names
and contact information of their current patients' medical professionals. To begin, ensure that all patients routinely disclose the
name, phone number, and address of their primary care medical
professional during the intake process, and routinely request a
release of information to each patient's primary care medical professional. Although patients rarely have concerns when this request is presented in a routine manner with a rationale regarding
the importance of collaboration, their wishes must be respected if
they express reluctance. If this becomes a treatment issue (e.g.,
the medical professional is prescribing psychotropic medication,
the patient has medical issues that affect his or her mental health
care, etc.), then the topic can be addressed as a therapeutic issue.

After obtaining the necessary information and permissions,
contact the medical professionals of current and recent patients.
Many collaborative psychotherapists first send a letter, followed
up by a phone call in which they discuss shared patients and then
focus on opportunities for future networking. There is one important caveat to relying on letters for communication. Psychotherapists who use letters as a primary mode of communication
should be aware that the medical professional may not always
have the opportunity to read the letter when it is received in the
office. Patient correspondence generally is reviewed by a medi-

cal professional prior to filing, but it may not be reviewed by the one who works most closely with the patient. When this occurs, the primary medical professional does not have the opportunity to read the letter until the next patient visit and may not read the letter then, if he or she is unaware of it. Some psychotherapists attempt to avoid this problem by adding a note at the top of the letter requesting that the medical professional who works most closely with the patient review it prior to filing. However, if later conversation reveals the medical professional is unaware of the letter, do not interpret this as disinterest in collaboration.

Phone calls to medical professionals who previously have made referrals are often well received, even to discuss a patient from the past. The psychotherapist can then express an interest in further collaboration and assess the needs of the medical professional. If primary care medical professionals have made numerous referrals in the past, it is likely they will continue to be interested in collaboration. This may present the opportunity for the psychotherapist to meet in person, or at least to forward information about his or her practice to that medical professional. When contacting the medical professional of a former patient, you can focus the conversation on the patient's functioning posttermination and the medical professional's impressions of the patient's response to the psychotherapy. If there was no collaboration during the psychotherapy, it may be helpful to explain that the current contact is an attempt to change your practice style to become more collaborative and that you hope for the opportunity to provide collaborative care to the medical professionals' patient in the future.

In a later section, we review ways of ensuring appropriate follow-up to maintain collaboration. In general, referrals beget referrals, and collaboration begets collaboration, in both directions.

Step 6: Making Contact
Outside Your Current Referral Network

If there is no pattern of referrals or current shared patients with a medical professional, a letter of introduction can serve as a first contact (Appendix C, "Sample Letter of Introduction"). This letter should provide educational background, types of patients seen in the practice, office hours and location, and accepted insurance plans. Emphasize a desire to collaborate and communicate about shared patients. Suggest a face-to-face meeting and offer a means of arranging it. Be aware that sending letters alone tends to be a low-yield exercise because it puts the onus on the medical professional to make first contact and is likely to get little attention in the volumes of paperwork most medical professionals receive in a day.

If the medical professional does not respond to the letter within a week or two, complete a follow-up phone call. If it seems impossible to talk to the medical professional directly, try to talk to the office manager or a midlevel provider as an entry point. Explain that you are developing a psychotherapy practice that includes collaboration with medical professionals, and you are interesting in learning more about the needs of the medical professionals the office. Offer to come to the office to talk with providers about your services. A face-to-face meeting is a powerful tool in establishing a collaborative relationship. Unfortunately, arranging a meeting can be extremely difficult because of the time pressures in both practices. These barriers are real and do not necessarily reflect a lack of interest on the medical professional's part. Most medical professionals do not manage their own schedules. Because the office manager has the gestalt of the office routine, he or she may be able to suggest a time to capture the most medical professionals in one meeting. It may be necessary to make individual contacts with the more interested medical professionals. It is common for one medical professional in a practice to be the "go-to" person for psychosocial issues. This person, who is often a midlevel professional, is an excellent first contact, who may then encourage other professionals to make time to meet.

During the initial phone call or meeting, try to determine what the medical professionals perceive their needs to be. How often do they refer for mental health services? Do they have a cadre of psychotherapists that they use? Are they happy with the level of communication and the outcomes they obtain with these psychotherapists? Do they have patients with mental health needs who are reluctant to see a psychotherapist? After a brief needs assessment, psychotherapists can then present how they would assist with the problem areas. Medical professionals will welcome information on how the psychotherapist will communicate regarding shared patients because this is something most of them desire from any consultant to whom they refer.

The conversation should focus on pragmatic issues. Psychotherapists can market their services by emphasizing how they can make the primary care medical professionals' jobs easier and enhance patient care. A solution-oriented approach to the first meeting will reassure the medical professionals that the psychotherapist will use a similar, pragmatic approach with his or her patients. Patients often complain that psychotherapists "just listen" and do not offer any suggestions or pragmatic help. If the primary care medical professional perceives the psychotherapist as grounded and helpful, he or she will refer the psychotherapist with confidence.

Finally, most psychotherapists underestimate how much a personal conversation facilitates relationship development. Medical professionals often need to convince and cajole patients to follow through on a mental health referral. It is much easier for them to do so when they can personally vouch for the psychotherapist. Making a psychotherapy referral has been likened to arranging a blind date. Patients are often ambivalent about the referral and anxious about talking to a new person. When medical professionals can reassure patients that they have spoken with the psychotherapist and have found him or her to be personable or can say they have received positive feedback from other patients, it can lessen the patient's ambivalence and anxiety, facilitating the referral.

It is appropriate and helpful to give business cards to medical professionals as well as office managers and front-desk staff. In addition, many practices employ a managed-care referral specialist, who processes all referrals and helps patients navigate the managed-care system. Make contact with referral specialists to familiarize them with details about your practice such as location, hours, and which insurances you accept. Referral specialists may also be helpful when there are insurance issues with a patient, in that they often have established relationships with insurance system workers and thus can facilitate referrals and decisions that are delayed by bureaucracy.

When the needs assessment reveals that a practice has an established relationship with a psychotherapist, be mindful of respecting that relationship to avoid upsetting a colleague. In fact, if this colleague practices collaboratively, he or she may be a valuable resource to you. Gathering the names of psychotherapists who receive many primary care referrals may help you discern which local psychotherapists practice collaboratively. You may choose to contact these individuals to join or form a supervision group or negotiate other means of working together to learn from and support each other in providing collaborative care.

Step 7: Collaboration Follow-Through: The Moment of Truth

Although the initial conversation with medical professionals is critical to laying the groundwork for collaboration, it is the follow-up that will create and maintain a mutually beneficial working relationship. This section reviews critical junctures for collaboration.

When the initial conversation focused on a consultation regarding a shared patient, send a follow-up note reviewing details of the patient's clinical presentation and treatment plan and review the collaboration agreement, both for the specific patient and in general. This type of follow-up letter helps in the following ways:

- □ It communicates to medical professionals that their concerns and requests were heard and internalized.
- □ It helps the psychotherapist keep track of agreements made with different medical professionals and offices.
- □ It reminds the medical professionals that they have a potential ally in caring for their patients.

Create a collaboration tracking system to ensure that the follow-up collaboration is consistent with the collaboration agreement. Some psychotherapists track collaborative contacts separately from progress notes, listing the contact information for medical professionals, copies of letters sent, and notes regarding any verbal communication in a segregated section. Some psychotherapists create space on their normal progress notes to track communication with medical professionals such as a separate prompt or check box. One advantage of integrating the collaboration tracking system into routine paperwork is that the prompt can also serve as a reminder to the psychotherapist to make contact. Appendix C illustrates samples of both separate tracking and integrated tracking methods ("Sample Integrated Collaboration Tracking System" and "Sample Separate Collaboration Tracking System").

Psychotherapists must be mindful of customizing the collaboration to the patient's needs as they learn more about the patient, and the interplay of their emotional and physical health. As noted earlier, sometimes the minimal collaboration of a form letters at the beginning and end of treatment is not sufficient. When ongoing collaboration is necessary, sending routine letters that briefly update information and review of salient issues is the least time-consuming. Such letters give medical professionals an overview of the patient's mental health care, allowing them to use medical care contacts to support the issues being discussed. In addition, it informs the medical professional of ongoing stresses that may be relevant to the patient's medical care. These letters often need such a high level of specificity that form letters are less helpful than they are at the beginning and end of treatment.

Although letters are the least time-consuming form of collaboration, even multiple letters can be insufficient when the clinical presentation calls for reciprocal conversation. Common situations include patients with medical conditions affecting their mental health, patient or family questions about the patients' medical condition, or patients who have expressed dissatisfaction with their medical or mental health care. In these clinical presentations, occasional phone conversations help the professionals solve problems and share perspectives more effectively. Alternatively, some professionals have started to use e-mail as a means of reciprocal conversation; however, care must be taken to ensure confidentiality. In this manner, the psychotherapist receives information about the patient's health status, medical professional's impressions of coping and treatment progress, and other information the professional may have gleaned during medical visits. Often, when a patient has regular medical visits, his or her medical professional knows them (and their larger system) extremely well. Input from the medical professional can enhance care by giving history or context, ongoing assessment, and an alternate perspective. The following questions can frame the conversation with the medical professional:

☐ What is the medical professional's primary concern for this patient?
☐ What would constitute therapy "success" for this patient?
☐ How well does the medical professional know this patient and his or her social situation?
☐ Does the medical professional have any advice about developing a working relationship with this patient?
☐ Are there any medical problems, now or in the past, that might be relevant to the patient's psychological distress?
☐ How well does the patient follow medical advice? If this is a problem, how can the psychotherapist help the medical professional with this issue?
☐ Does the patient require psychotropic medication?
☐ How would the medical professional like to proceed with communication and collaboration regarding this patient?

Not all of these questions must be addressed with every patient. However, they provide a template of the types of issues that can be helpful to discuss, particularly with more complex situations.

Finally, it is essential to advise medical professionals when their patient terminates mental health treatment prematurely because it may be the only notification that the patient is no longer receiving services. Medical professionals can play an important role in facilitating ongoing care for patients who have difficulty engaging in psychotherapy. When the patient terminates psychotherapy prematurely, the medical professional can address the patient's decision in subsequent medical appointments and may be able to refer to another psychotherapist or encourage a return to treatment, if advisable. Because many patients use mental health treatment episodically, medical professionals are in a unique position to help patients realize when it would be helpful to return and to keep this possibility open at all times. The more medical professionals know about a patient's experiences with mental health and level of satisfaction with previous psychotherapists, the better prepared they are to intervene productively. Collaborative communication during mental health services facilitates rereferral if necessary in the future.

A Note on Compensation for Collaboration

No matter how much you streamline your collaborative practices, the bottom line is that collaboration does take time. In some cases, the time invested in collaboration pays off in reducing frustration, in crisis intervention, and in improving professional satisfaction. However, there is no monetary compensation because the current reimbursement structure does not pay psychotherapists to collaborate.

As psychotherapists become more collaborative, they can expect to serve more patients with psychological and social issues that have a negative impact on their medical conditions. When treating patients in this category, it is helpful to be aware of the new Health and Behavior Current Procedural Terminology (CPT) codes, which may open the door to reimbursement for psychotherapy and psychoeducation for patients with medical diagnoses. Basically, the new CPT codes allow psychologists, nurses, licensed social workers, and, in some states, licensed counselors to bill for services that address social and behavioral aspects of physical health problems as diagnosed by a medical professional. The interested reader is referred to *Behavioral Consultation in Primary Care* (Robinson & Reiter, 2007) for detailed, state-of-the-art instructions on the use of these codes, including how to choose the appropriate codes and necessary documentation. It should be noted that some private insurers may not reimburse these codes, but Medicare currently reimburses for five of the six CPT codes (Robinson & Reiter, 2007). It is our hope that psychotherapists will experiment with using these codes because the more frequently they are used, the more likely more insurers will adopt them, creating expanded opportunities for psychotherapists to be part of health care provision.

Conclusion

Psychotherapists who routinely collaborate find that the time spent making and maintaining these contacts often saves time, energy, and frustration in the end. The routine collaboration outlined in this chapter should be part of everyday practice for all patients. For more information on this general topic, see *Primary Care Psychology* by Frank, McDaniel, Bray, and Heldring (2004). The following chapters describe complicated patient presentations and situations that require more intensive collaboration and specialized psychotherapeutic techniques. Most psychotherapists have a range of patient presentations in their practice, and sometimes it is difficult or impossible to know the patient's needs from the outset of treatment. If a psychotherapist has set the foundation for ongoing collaboration from the first appointment, it is much easier to seek assistance and input from the medical professional if the treatment becomes complicated as it progresses. An established collaborative relationship with the patient's medical professional also facilitates a shift to more intensive collaboration when necessary. Practicing routine collaboration sets the stage for more intensive collaboration for patients who need it.

II

Intensive Collaboration

In this section, we describe situations in which more intensive collaboration is advantageous. We illustrate how to use collaborative strategies to treat optimally patients with challenging and complex presentations. As we have noted, it would be difficult to jump from nonexistent or minimal collaboration to intensive collaboration, both as a practitioner and within the constraints of our clinical care system. Psychotherapists who routinely collaborate are able to shift into more intensive collaboration when the patient's complex problems benefit from a team approach. Often they have established collaborative relationships with specific medical professionals, so that when a shared patient needs more intensive collaboration, the foundation of trust is already in place. The process of shifting to more intensive collaboration is parallel to the process medical professionals must make with patients as they shift from a purely somatic focus to a more integrated understanding of the patient's difficulties. If the medical professional does not include questions about emotional well-being from the beginning and only asks these questions once all biomedical causes have been explored and dismissed, patients may not accept the idea that their emotions are relevant. Similarly, if the psychotherapist does not include the medical professional from the beginning of care and then later decides that professional could be of assistance, the patient, and perhaps the medical professional, may balk.

Some of the patient presentations in this section are challenging to manage, for both medical professionals and psychotherapists. Both struggle with many of the same presentations working with "overserviced and underserved" patients who take a great deal of time and energy. However, these patients frequently are poorly served as evidenced by their struggle through daily life regardless of medical professionals' and psychotherapists' interventions. The patient's sense of hopelessness and helplessness reflects this reality. We believe collaboration optimizes care with these patients, both because the providers have each other's support and because of the synergy collaboration can create. Nothing is a panacea, but we find it telling that many collaborative psychotherapists say they would never go back to practicing in a vacuum. In our decades of experience, collaboration has all too often been the saving grace in challenging patient situations in which nothing else seemed to help.

So, what is intensive collaboration? When and how should you practice it? In which clinical presentations that challenge medical professionals are collaborative psychotherapists most able to assist and facilitate optimal care? In addition to answering these questions, Part II reviews intensive collaborative methods useful with patients who will and will not engage in psychotherapy. We describe primary care counseling techniques that medical professionals can be coached how and when to use. Finally, we review psychotherapy strategies that are useful with patients who have somatic concerns, as well as those facing medical illness.

4

Challenging Patients, Challenging Interactions

In this chapter, we introduce collaboration that goes beyond the routine. Intensive collaboration is generally most useful with complex cases that frustrate, infuriate, confuse, and dishearten even the most seasoned medical and mental health professional. To begin, we draw from a highly competent and experienced medical professional's report of her internal monologue when faced with such a case. Second, we describe factors that influence medical professionals' management of such cases. These two sections are intended to help psychotherapists "walk in the shoes" of medical professionals to increase their understanding of how disruptive and challenging they find these situations. Third, we describe the kind of cases that typically need intensive collaboration and provide examples of difficult interactions that commonly occur in these challenging situations. Finally, we present typical scenarios in primary care and specialty settings and describe how collaboration with a psychotherapist could greatly benefit the medical professional, and more important, the patient. In chapter 5, we expand on this last topic by detailing intensive collaborative strategies useful in these situations.

Facing That Patient Again:
Confessions of a Compassionate Doctor

Danielle Ofri captures the dilemma faced by many medical professionals in the following essay from her book, *Incidental Findings* (2005). Dr. Ofri provides an insightful view into how even the most compassionate physician can be personally affected by complex individual and family dynamics presenting in the expert-oriented medical setting.

I groan when I catch sight of her name on the patient roster. Nazma Uddin. Not again! She is in my clinic office almost every month. I dread her visits, and today is no exception. A small, plump woman, Mrs. Uddin is cloaked in robe, head-scarf, and veil, all opaque blue polyester. Only her eyes peer out from the sea of dark blue. She is trailed, as usual, by her 11-year-old daughter Azina, who wears a light-green gown with a flowered headscarf, pinned under her chin but no veil covering her solemn, bespectacled face.

Mrs. Uddin flops into the chair next to my desk, with a postural sprawl that is almost teenagerly. Azina perches on the exam table, her white Nikes peeking out from under the full-length gown. Mrs. Uddin unsnaps her veil—something she does only with her female doctor—revealing her weathered cheeks, and the litany begins. "Oh, doctor," she says, pinching the sides of her head with skin-paling force, "the pain is no good." After this brief foray into English, she slides into Bengali, aiming her barrage of complaints at Azina, who translates them to me in spurts while fiddling with her wire-rim glasses. There is abdominal pain and headache, diarrhea and insomnia, back pain and aching feet, a rash and gas pains, itchy ears and a cough, no appetite. And more headache.

The feeling begins: a dull cringing in my stomach that gradually creeps outward, until my entire body is sapped by foreboding and dread. I feel myself slipping into her morass, and the smothering sensation overcomes me. If she doesn't stop, I will drown in her complaints.

I fight it, but it seems impossible. I know that I should be focused on Mrs. Uddin's words, but I fear for my sanity and my ability to get through this visit and move on to the next 10 patients.

And so I begin to filter. I begin to ignore a certain percentage of what is being said, nodding vaguely, murmuring offhandedly—shortcuts to suggest that I am engaged but that are merely smokescreens to keep her at bay. I scan the computer while she moans about her shins and her coccyx, and I see that she has been to the Neurology Clinic, Rehab Clinic, Pain Management Clinic, Gynecology Clinic, Podiatry Clinic, GI Clinic . . . all in the five weeks since I last saw her.

I desperately want to get Mrs. Uddin out of my office. I dread my visits with her, and it is increasingly difficult to mask my annoyance. Like all the other doctors who see Mrs. Uddin, I'm anxious to write a few more referrals or a few more prescriptions just to get her out of my hair.

The truth is I can't do anything for Mrs. Uddin. I've talked to her endlessly about stress and depression, which I am sure underlie many of her pains, but she never follows through with the psychiatry referrals or antidepressant prescriptions. Her resistance to my efforts sometimes makes me feel as though she is in a personal battle against me.

I start to resent her, to hate her, to hate everything about her. I hate to see her name on the roster. I hate to see her in the waiting room. I hate the whine in her voice that is detectable even when she is speaking Bengali. I hate that she keeps her daughter out of school to facilitate her wild overuse of the medical system.

And I hate how she makes me feel so utterly useless.

Whenever I've tried to treat one complaint, another bursts to the surface like a mocking hydra: an antacid temporarily relieves her stomach pains, but then she will have palpitations. A migraine medication partially assuages her headache, but then she will have intractable hiccups and swollen knees.

"I can't breathe," she says. "I don't eat. I don't sleep."

Well, if that's truly the case, I want to retort, how is it that you are still alive?

I stop listening to what she says. I stop believing what she tells me about her symptoms. Stop it, I want to yell at her. Just stop complaining. Go away. Stop bothering me. You know and I know that this is hopeless.

I shudder as I realize that I am slipping too far. The annoyance and resentment are getting the better of me. I wish she would just disappear—out of my office, out of my hospital, out of this city, off this planet. How is it that she emigrated thousands of miles from her obscure village in Bangladesh to end up precisely in the catchment area of our clinic, and then in my office when there are 150 other medical attendings and residents she could have been randomly assigned to?

Why, I plead with myself, can't I unearth some grain of humanity? Why can't I put my feelings aside to help a patient in need, no matter how annoying?

Back at our first visit—if I can even remember that far—I was probably compassionate. I'm sure I asked open-ended questions and responded with concern to each of her problems.

Now I am the model of the curt, hyperefficient doctor. I ask as few questions as possible for fear of eliciting new, unsolvable complaints. I avoid eye contact. I focus on the computer, tuning out her words, as I copy from my previous note: "multiple somatic complaints, noncompliant with recommendations for psychiatric therapy."

I have tried to prioritize her complaints. I have tried setting modest, attainable goals. I have tried to reassure her of her basic good health. I have tried to set limits by refusing to order the tests she requests. I have tried to placate her by ordering every test she requests. I have tried to help her see the connection between stress and symptoms. Nothing helps.

And now I am angry. (p. 71)

Dr. Ofri ultimately manages her reaction to Mrs. Uddin by focusing on the context of her illness, particularly its effect on her daughter.

In medicine we always seek objective data to confirm a diagnosis, something that is often tricky with "difficult" patients. But Azina is the objective data, the stark evidence of the magnitude of my patient's pain. Though I'd like to write Mrs. Uddin off as just another complainer, as one who can't hiccup without demanding an MRI, she is truly suffering. Her daughter is truly suffering.

I am not suffering.

I am actually the complainer. I'm the one who can't face this patient without immediately rolling my eyes and turning off my compassion. The reality is that I am profoundly discomfited by my inability to treat Mrs. Uddin, and she is simply the thorn that continually reminds me how limited my skills can be.

Though physicians inquire about patients' social history as part of the full medical interview, it is usually given only lip service. We tend to view our patients as just that: patients. They exist only in our office, on our wards, in our clinics. We forget that 99% of their lives are lived—or suffered—without us. We often react as though their illness is a personal battle between doctor and patient, when, in fact, we are bit players. The real battle is between the patient and his or her world: spouse, children, work, community, daily activities. It is within this grander tapestry that the threads and snags of bodily dysfunction introduce rents in the fabric, even wholesale unraveling. It is often only when we are allowed to glimpse the greater weave of our patients' existence that we can truly understand what illness is.

I take the hands of both Azina and her mother, for they are both my patients now. "Depression is a painful illness," I say. "Broken souls hurt as much as broken bones, and the pain spreads to everyone around them." I explain about antidepressant medications and the importance of psychotherapy, and we negotiate a contract for treatment. This time, I include a stipulation that Mrs. Uddin come alone or with her husband, that Azina must stay in school.

Azina wipes her tears. Mrs. Uddin gathers her papers and snaps the veil back over her face. She promises to take the medications and to see the psychiatrist.

Of course, we have been down this road many times before, and I won't be surprised if she's back next month with a new physical ailment, not taking her antidepressants, having missed the appointment with the psychiatrist. And I won't be surprised if I, again, dread the visit.

But I think, or at least I hope, that I will no longer view Mrs. Uddin as a personal torment. Azina has cured me of that. (Ofri, 2005, pp. 68–74)

In this example, Dr. Ofri captures the common experience of many medical professionals. Although setting and medical professional variables contribute to challenging encounters, the medical literature focuses primarily on patient factors. Numerous articles categorize challenging patients and describe effective practice methods. These articles tend to have titles such as "Dealing With the Angry, Seductive, Weeping, Silent Patient" (Kuritzky, 1996; Murtagh, 1991; Nyman, 1991). To psychotherapists, this kind of labeling and stereotyping of patients may seem pejorative and blaming, thus reinforcing existing stereotypes of medical professionals as unsympathetic and controlling. However, these articles have set the stage for productive dialogues about the "challenging patient" in the medical community.

Medical Professional Factors in Difficult Interactions

Bright, motivated people choose medical careers because they are drawn to the science and to helping people solve health problems. Although medical school does focus on the importance of whole-person care, more emphasis is placed on science and problem solving. Medical students are trained to gather information from a patient by asking a series of closed-ended questions in a particular order to generate a differential diagnosis. This pattern, designed to converge quickly into a diagnosis and treatment plan, is further reinforced in the practice environment of short, symptom-focused visits. These pressures prevent medical professionals from gathering contextual information that will help them understand and have compassion for their challenging patients.

Medical professionals are taught: "Don't just stand there, do something." In other words, give the patient a specific diagnosis, describe the course of the illness and the prognosis, and then generate a treatment plan. They give patients advice under the assumption that the rational patient will follow it faithfully. In addition, many medical professionals and patients equate the "do something" mantra with "write a prescription for medication." Ideally, the patient follows the treatment plan and the problematic symptoms dissipate.

This model works well with cooperative, stable patients who have simple, acute issues with clear symptoms that fit neatly into a diagnosis, medication prescription, or treatment plan. However, the majority of primary care patient presentations do not meet these conditions. Most medical professionals are painfully aware that one third of patients, both pediatric and adult, do not follow advice. (DiMatteo, 2004; Winnick, Lucas, & Hartman, 2005) Yet few medical professionals are trained in how to work with nonadherent patients.

Challenging encounters call for a more curious, exploratory, respectful approach that can feel like the opposite of "doing something." David Keith, a psychiatrist in Syracuse, New York, advises the medical residents he teaches to "Don't just do something, stand there," to emphasize that engaging the patient is often more important than quick advice and medications (D. Keith, personal communication, March 1998). Careful listening and psychotherapeutic techniques contradict the "do something" model, so they are difficult skills for many medical professionals.

Medical professionals' reactions to patients' behavior are understandable and natural. They feel angry when patients do not put effort into getting well or try to manipulate the medical professional or the staff. They are irritated by entitled patients who make unjustified disability claims or demand inappropriate tests or treatment. They are concerned when the diagnosis and cure eludes them. Yet medical professionals do not have support in coping with these internal reactions. Most medical schools and residencies do not address these emotional reactions to complex patient presentations. Case discussions rarely focus on medical professionals' reactions to patients or how the professional's approach and response contributes to the difficulties. Medical professionals attempt to apply the same objective science uniformly to each patient's presentation. When this does not work, they may focus on the patient's reaction. In this vacuum, medical professionals are prone to a fight-or-flight reaction, either avoiding the patient or blaming the patient, overtly or covertly.

With experience, many medical professionals make the link between their personal history and the types of patient care situations they find difficult. In an exploratory, qualitative study, Gunn and Stulp (1989) asked experienced primary care medical professionals about their most difficult patients and encounters. The majority of these professionals attributed the difficulties to their personal history. For example, one medical professional found patients with a large number of undiagnosable physical complaints particularly challenging. He linked his reactions to his mother often canceling family activities because of her own physical problems. Another medical professional always felt his brother was favored. This medical professional found patients who sought a specific prescription difficult, stating, "I could be a cardboard cutout, and it wouldn't make any difference" (n.p.)

As with routine collaboration, psychotherapists who become involved in intensive collaboration benefit from making note of the type of patients with whom a particular medical professional struggles. The therapist may become aware of some of the medical professional's "issues" in this process (we all have "issues"). However, instead of confronting or questioning medical professionals about these issues, the competent collaborative psychotherapist focuses on devising and communicating specific management strategies that they might use to deal with such patients. In ensuing dialogues, medical professionals, depending on their degree of personal insight, may become more aware of their own issues in dealing with these patients. However, if this occurs, it is a secondary benefit of collaboration. As always, the patient's well-being defines the primary purpose of collaboration.

Patient and Family Factors to Consider in Intensive Collaboration

Challenging is the general term used to describe the following four types of patients. *Complicated* patients have multiple factors influencing their health in ways that are not linear and not easy to understand. *Chronic* patients have long-standing conditions for which there is no cure. Chronicity becomes problematic when the patient continues to expect a cure rather than accepting their new reality and exploring ways to cope and adapt. *Conflictual* patients may have conflict within their family or support system, with their medical professionals, or both. *Chaotic* patients are disorganized in their approach to care. They have little family support, do not come to scheduled appointments, and are nonadherent with treatment plans. Zubialde, Shannon, and Devenger (2005) used a single label of *complex* to describe the small number of patients who use the greatest amount of services. Lucas and Peek (1997) have described this group as "overserviced and underserved high utilizers" (p. 374), which reflects these patients' overuse of the medical system in the context of poor overall health and wellness, and the inability of the health care system to meet their needs. Population-based studies indicate that about 15% of patients use 70% of services (Hahn et al., 1996). Many of these patients first turn to the medical system as primary treatment for all distress, physical or psychological. Hahn's results also indicated that only about 20% of the *overserviced–underserved* obtain mental health services. The next four sections give examples of these kinds of interactions as they present in a medical outpatient office.

Interactions With Complicated Patients

A woman with a diagnosed heart problem and a history of cardiac surgery also has an anxiety disorder that focuses on her cardiac conditions. She searches the Internet for information about potential causes of her problems. She calls her primary care medical professional frequently and demands tests to rule out possible disorders. Her fears have resulted in multiple hospitalizations. Despite all of these interventions, both the patient and medical professional are frustrated, and the patient reports an overall low sense of health and wellness.

Although patients in primary care often report medically unexplained symptoms and often disagree with their medical professional about the etiology of the symptoms (Greer & Halgin, 2006), they always have a *chief complaint*. Patients with many chief complaints are likely to be described as "difficult" or "challenging" by the medical professional. Furthermore, multiple issues within a given appointment make it more difficult for medical professionals to set an agenda, complete an evaluation, and determine and implement an appropriate treatment plan. (Marvel, Epstein, Flowers, & Beckman, 1999)

Beyond the challenges within a given appointment, patients who have multiple health problems are often referred to multiple specialists. The primary care medical professional must then manage the complicated and often confusing information associated with various specialists' assessments and treatment plans. In the best circumstances, the primary care medical professional is able to integrate the various findings into a cohesive treatment plan. Unfortunately, specialists commonly disagree about the "correct" diagnosis or treatment plan (or both), resulting in confusion or increasing the likelihood of conflict. Primary care medical professionals may be left interpreting the specialist's opinions and attempting to negotiate a reasonable treatment plan that cares for the whole patient and his or her family.

Medical professionals struggling with complex or vague medical problems often fear they are "missing something." They know that a missed diagnosis can have serious consequences, some even resulting in death. Although psychotherapists face this in extreme cases, it is more common for medical professionals to worry about an error. These fears lead to more medical tests and more hospital admissions. The specialists' focus on a particular symptom or organ system often prevents them from seeing the issues in the context of the whole person. This is particularly true when mental health issues may be exacerbating physical symptoms, yet no psychotherapist is involved. For some patients, the escalating medical intervention feeds into their mental health issues, creating a vicious cycle. Is the chest pain a deadly cardiac problem or anxiety (in which case, multiple emergency department visits to rule out cardiac disease exacerbate the anxiety)? Are headaches and dizziness a result of a brain tumor or secondary to stress (in which case, the fear of a brain tumor escalates the stress)? It is difficult, and anxiety provoking, to differentiate various diagnostic possibilities. One family medicine resident described this cycle well:

> I precept these patients over and over again, often with different attendings. The more input from experienced minds, the better. New ideas are thrown around. New blood tests are mentioned, new medications cited. I feel encouraged. Maybe I can help these patients. I create a new treatment plan. They walk out the door with the new prescription, more blood work, another radiologic study and more referrals. Temporarily, their

mood brightens and they forgot about their pain. Temporarily, I believe I've actually found the secret recipe to heal them. Then, soon after, the messages begin to reappear on my desk again. Three "while you were out" messages taped together—"med made patient vomit," "doctor you referred patient to does not accept insurance," or "cannot afford new medication you prescribed." Shortly thereafter, the blood work and X-ray results return—all normal. Back to the drawing board. Again. (Rice, 2006, p. 40).

Interactions With Chronically Ill Patients

A professional woman is diagnosed with fibromyalgia and does not feel she can continue in her career as a lawyer. She adopts a life view that she is not able to control her symptoms, needs to retreat from work and relationships, and avoids any potentially stressful situations. When she comes to the doctor, she describes her symptoms but is not willing to try any new treatments or engage in a conversation about the underlying depression she feels.

Chronic medical conditions such as hypertension, arthritis, diabetes, pulmonary disease, and obesity are increasingly prevalent (Institute of Medicine, 2001). Medical professionals are also treating more patients with chronic pain syndromes and other syndromes diagnosed primarily by symptom profile, such as fibromyalgia, chronic fatigue syndrome, and irritable bowel disease (Gallagher, Thomas, Hamilton, & White, 2004). These conditions have been shown to have a high prevalence of psychiatric comorbidities (Kato, Sullivan, Evengard, & Pedersen, 2006). All of these chronic medical conditions are similar to chronic mental health conditions such as bipolar illness, schizophrenia, or substance dependence in that treatment focuses on symptom management and maximizing quality of life, rather than a "cure."

It is difficult to achieve optimal chronic illness management and virtually impossible without a motivated, active patient. Medical professionals are taught a collaborative model of chronic care delivery in which patients and medical professionals work together to achieve the best possible outcomes. Patients' role is to take charge of their illness by educating themselves and making necessary lifestyle changes. The medical professional's role is to provide information to facilitate decision making. In theory, the collaborative model reduces the patient's reliance on the medical professional to "fix" the problem and gives power to the patients to optimize their own health and wellness (Funnell, 2000).

Unfortunately, many chronically ill patients experience depression and anxiety related to being "sick all the time." This makes it difficult for them to take a proactive role in their own care. Furthermore, the hopelessness, fatigue, poor concentration, and vegetative symptoms associated with depression often mimic or exacerbate the symptoms of the chronic illness itself. It becomes a vicious cycle, particularly if the illness is but one of many life stressors with which the patient is struggling. Despite these connections, many patients with chronic illnesses will not seek mental health services because they fear their medical professionals will shift the diagnostic focus to mental health issues.

Chronically ill patients who have a preillness disposition of external locus of control can pose challenges. They view themselves as victims of uncontrollable circumstances. Without a sense of personal power to "take charge" of their health, they tend to respond to problems with passivity and blame. They often have rigid, dysfunctional interactional patterns with medical professionals, resisting or rejecting possible health improvement strategies, and may angrily blame the medical professional for their ill health and demand that their problems be "fixed." Given that morbidity and mortality in chronic illness is heavily attributed to the inability to make lifestyle changes, a "helpless victim" mentality is a poor prognostic sign (Cross, March, Lapsley, Byrne, & Brooks, 2006; Dec, 2006; Hamilton, Karoly, & Zuatra, 2005; Van de Putte et al., 2005).

Psychotherapists are well trained to help chronically ill patients mitigate the effects of ambivalence and denial on self-care. Patients need help making behavioral changes in eating habits, stress reduction, and smoking cessation. Medical professionals do not have the time or expertise to help even motivated patients in this way. Psychotherapy also can help patients cope with the stress of chronic illness and its impact on their personal relationships.

Conflictual Interactions

A middle-aged man fell from a ladder and developed a chronic back problem that required narcotic medication to control the pain. He appears depressed and reports that the pain is worse. His wife also comes to the appointments, demanding that more be done to help him. She calls angrily between appointments to request more medication. Some staff feel sorry for the patient, but others are angry at behavior they see as manipulative. The medical professional feels caught in the middle of a high degree of emotional conflict.

Health problems can create or exacerbate conflict within a family or support system. A wife can feel her husband is using the sick role to abdicate his responsibilities. A daughter can get frustrated when her mother ignores significant symptoms and refuses to seek medical care. Children can disagree about how to approach an aging parent who wants to continue driving but may not be safe. Old family conflicts may arise anew when family members must make difficult decisions about an ill family member or when a child needs medical attention. All of these situations call for compassionate, skilled mediation. These are the situations that are well suited to mental health intervention.

Conflict among family members is not the only challenge. Tension and conflicts can arise between the medical professional and the patient when they do not agree on the appropriate diagnosis or treatment plan. Conflicts also occur when symptoms do not improve, causing fear of misdiagnosis or inappropriate treatment. Some medical professionals become angry when a patient does not follow recommendations or questions their medical advice. Patient care can become fragmented if a patient seeks multiple medical opinions or does not have an organized approach to understanding his or her condition. Some patients do not follow any advice. When staff and medical professionals become the least bit defensive, conflict can escalate to the point that neither side listens to the other.

Challenging interactions also occur when the patient and medical professional have different agendas. Unfortunately, overt agenda setting rarely occurs at the beginning of the medical encounter (Marvel et al., 1999). Mismatched agendas are most common when patients have complicated chronic issues, particularly chronic pain syndromes and anxiety disorders. Patients want symptom relief, but medical professionals must take care to avoid addiction to narcotic pain or anxiolytic medications, and many fear legal sanctions stemming from overprescription of these medications. Although only a small minority of patients with chronic pain abuse or sell narcotic medications, any patient on opioid medication has the potential for abuse and is suspect until proven otherwise. Medical professionals routinely establish *medication contracts* to monitor the patient's use of opioid or anxiolytic medications. These contracts outline how the patients are to take the medications and the consequences for requesting early refills, overuse of the medication, or selling it on the street. Sometimes, medical professionals prescribe involvement of a psychotherapist as part of the medication contract. These issues can result in an adversarial relationship between medical professionals and patients.

Emotionality and conflict in the medical professional–patient relationship often replicates itself in a parallel process in the medical professional's office. If a patient argues directly with the medical professional, makes disparaging comments about the care given or about the care facility, or abuses staff members, tensions rise rapidly. Intrastaff conflict may arise over the best way to assist in these situations. Some medical professionals and staff members may be engaged by the patient's problems and advocate an understanding, compassionate approach, whereas others feel the patient must be held responsible for his or her behavior and focus the treatment plan on limit setting and consequences.

Psychotherapists, particularly relationship-oriented therapists, have many skills to help medical professionals best manage conflictual situations. As psychotherapists consult about difficult situations, they can explore how conflict affects care and help medical professionals recognize and manage these issues more effectively.

Interactions With "Chaotic" Patients

A young woman who is a single parent with three children and an angry ex-husband misses half of the appointments she makes for herself or her children. She continually reports feeling overwhelmed and has been referred for counseling on multiple occasions. She sometimes attends these sessions but does not fully engage in therapy. The sessions consist of reporting the crisis of the week. She is always apologetic and promises to be more attentive but finds it difficult to manage her chaotic life and care for herself and her children.

Chaotic patients and families have difficulty organizing their lives. They tend to respond to frequent crises with denial, disorganization, and confusion. These patients often are overwhelmed with the complexity of their life and have difficulty prioritizing health care issues among the many stressors. This pattern can be catastrophic in the context of chronic or severe acute illness. Patients with chaotic lives may underrespond or ignore symptoms until they are a crisis, which can result in irreversible medical damage. For example, a person with diabetes who does not proactively make lifestyle changes will have high blood sugars, ultimately resulting in damage to various organs. The patient is then largely unable to cope with the resulting ill health and disability.

Chaotic patients are often given the label of *noncompliant* or *help rejecting* for their lack of cooperation and treatment plan adherence. These patients miss appointments and reject treatment options. Although medical professionals and staff intellectually understand that the patients' denial and dismay at their own illness underlies the emotional reactivity and self-destructive behaviors, they struggle to manage their own emotional reactions and to maintain a productive treatment relationship.

An interesting isomorphic process sometimes results between these families and their health care practices. A chaotic, unfocused treatment team becomes the ineffective counterpoint to a chaotic, unfocused family. Psychotherapists who have worked in a live team supervision model may have experienced the team dissolving into chaos when working with particularly chaotic families. Each team member is struck by different aspects of the situation and proposes a different theory about the problem and potential solutions, resulting in unhelpful disorganization. This parallel process also occurs in a medical office. Staff becomes frustrated and angry with patients who call frequently with small problems because they don't have time to continually solve the "issue of the day." Medical professionals bite their tongues when patients call emergency lines for nonemergent issues (e.g., the 2:00 a.m., "I can't sleep" call). Understandably, medical professionals sometimes respond with anger and frustration. They feel they are working much harder than their patients as they struggle to contend with extensive documentation, appointment no-shows, unmet treatment plans, and multiple unreasonable requests. Medical professionals ultimately feel they are being used, abused, and manipulated.

Many patients who need mental health services are functioning in a chaotic, dysfunctional way. Psychotherapists can help these patients focus and organize themselves to facilitate problem solving and behavior change. They recognize the relevant contextual issues, fostering compassion that facilitates joining with and caring for these patients. When psychotherapists share care of patients with chaotic lives, they can help the medical professional understand this context and set appropriate expectations and plans. Psychotherapists also understand how important it is not to work harder than a patient and how to motivate patients. In addition, sharing care of these patients helps both medical professionals and psychotherapists manage reactivity, frustration, and burn out to remain optimally effective.

Facing "Those" Patients: How a Collaborative Psychotherapist Might Help

The following are actual encounters with patients in a typical week in a typical family practice setting. During one morning session, four medical professionals faced cases that reflect the challenging issues that are common and that can be, without collaboration, extremely disruptive to the provision of optimal medical care.

Mary: A Patient Who Somaticizes

Mary is a 55-year-old woman who has had significant symptoms of "racing heart" and pain in her arm. She is concerned that she will die of heart disease the way both her mother and her aunt did at an early age. She requests appointments about two times a month, reporting vague pains and concern about her heart. Mary does not drive and spends her day helping her daughter take care of her children. Although she likes the connection with her grandchildren, she feels used. She does not feel she has anything in her own life. She feels she cannot talk to her daughters about these feelings and hides her internal distress. A complete cardiac assessment revealed no abnormalities. She changed medical professionals three times on referral to a psychotherapist and has been unwilling to see a psychotherapist for fear this would confirm that her symptoms are "not real." She lives in constant fear of dying of a sudden heart attack. Her current medical professional is frustrated that his attempts to reassure Mary fall on deaf ears; he has become very curt in his language and cuts short his appointments with her.

This case falls into the chronic, complicated categories. Mary somaticizes her distress, frustrating medical professionals. The more they have tried to reassure her that there is nothing wrong with her heart, the more she worries about it. The less they schedule appointments with her, the more she calls.

Psychotherapists providing consultation could recognize stressors that affect Mary's emotions and behavioral reactions. They could help the medical professional listen to the symptoms as an expression of isolation and perceived incompetence in addition to the physical sensations. In addition, they could help the medical professional realize that withdrawing from Mary only fuels her pursuit of medical care. In addition to addressing Mary's physical symptoms, she needs to have conversations about her life, challenges, and frustrations. Mary needs regular appointments, regardless of her symptoms. She might be more open to a psychotherapy referral if the focus was to help her understand the stresses of her illness rather than eradicating the cause and if her medical professional could personally recommend a specific psychotherapist.

Bill: A Patient Dealing With Medical, Legal, and Psychological Problems

Bill is a 45-year-old brick mason who works for a large construction company. He had a back injury 3 months ago and is now awaiting workers' compensation settlement. He has always worked outside. Although he realizes his body cannot tolerate physical labor, he does not see retraining as an option, and fears he will not be able to provide for his family financially. He is very depressed and has stated that life is not worth living. He has refused to seek any mental health services out of fear it would negatively influence the settlement of his workers' compensation case. Although he does not have a plan to kill himself, the medical professional worries about the wisdom and liability issues of treating him without mental health assistance. Although the medical professional feels Bill's back pain should be resolving somewhat posttherapy, Bill does not report any improvement. The medical professional wonders whether Bill does not report improvement because waning symptoms might negatively affect his settlement.

This case is complicated because it involves both the medical and legal systems. This man has suffered a life-altering event for both himself and his family, and he feels that his life is in chaos. At this point, he may be malingering or somaticizing the symptoms for financial gain. Although the medical professional understands his motivation, she is frustrated by the conflict of interests and her inability to address the clear underlying psychological distress he is experiencing.

A psychotherapist could provide a consultation to both the patient and the medical professional regarding pharmacological and nonpharmacological treatment for depression. The issue of disability could be discussed openly for both its practical and emotional implications. The medical professional could be advised to talk directly with Bill about the implications of disability and help him set realistic goals in the context of the depression and the outstanding disability and workers' compensation claim. Without this type of goal readjustment, the medical professional is likely either to feel the treatment is failing or to become angry with the patient.

Anita: A Patient Facing Chronic Illness and Grief

Anita is a 45-year-old woman who was first diagnosed with Type 1 diabetes at age 5. Born to an upper-middle-class family, she had excellent care throughout childhood and adolescence. In early adulthood, she began to develop diabetic retinopathy and lost her eyesight. She also developed a heart condition, requiring additional medications. She has not been able to drive since age 25. She has been married twice; she believes both marriages ended because of the medical care and attention she required. She acknowledges lifelong depression and now has developed increasingly debilitating panic attacks. Thoughts of suicide are increasingly prevalent. She has continually received mental health treatment and is currently engaged with a medical professional whom she likes. However, their sessions focus on social and emotional issues and not on her medical problems. Recently, she lost her insurance, forcing her to leave the care of her trusted medical professional. She reports a great deal of conflict with other medical professionals in the past, feeling they minimized her physical pain and emotional distress and wanted to "punt" her to a psychiatrist. She is now enrolled as a patient in a community health center. She likes her new medical professional, a woman about her age; however, because she now feels understood and cared for, she calls frequently to vent to the staff and to request antianxiety medication.

This case reflects the mind–body perception split that pervades our culture. Anita was willing to seek treatment for her depression and panic attacks, but this treatment does not address the impact of her chronic medical problems. She also does not discuss the impact of her medical conditions on her life with the medical professional. The medical office staff is frustrated and has been complaining about the amount of time she takes on the phone.

The psychotherapist could provide a consultation and assessment using the health and behavior service codes. These codes were designed to reflect care that evaluates the effects of stress on chronic illness and vice versa. Anita's stress could be normalized and discussed in a developmental framework. The grief and loss associated with her chronic illness could be discussed, and she could be encouraged to use her natural support system. These efforts could be framed as an intelligent use of resources rather than a weakness to encourage her to follow her treatment care plan.

Bob: A Medically Disabled Patient Unconsciously Creating Chaos

> Bob is a 55-year-old former communications officer for a local company who lives with his wife and grown son. He is unemployed currently because of his health issues, which include diabetes and obesity. His son had significant behavioral problems in school and has been incarcerated several times. Bob attends most of his appointments but admits he does not always take his medication and that he overeats when stressed. He feels losing weight is impossible for him, which is consistent with a general sense of helplessness in his life. He tries to set limits with his son but he and his wife are not a team, creating constant tension in the house. Bob obtained mental health services related to his son but did not feel it was helpful. Although reluctant to seek psychotherapy for himself, he recently set up an appointment. His medical professional is frustrated and feels helpless to get Bob to take care of himself. He is secretly glad when Bob does not show for appointments and is hoping the psychotherapist will be able to make a difference.

The chaos in the patient's life replicates itself in Bob's attempts to get help. He does not feel he can get better and yet continues to ask the medical professional to help him. Appointments are frustrating to both parties and result in halfhearted plans that neither of them expects to be followed.

The psychotherapist could start the initial appointment by focusing on the medical issues. He could ask for permission to talk freely with the medical professional and suggest a joint meeting. He could help the medical professional understand the importance of not working harder than the patient. The pull to "fix" by finding the right medical regimen is strong, and medical professionals need support to realize there is a limit to what they can do to be helpful. The psychotherapist could suggest a family meeting with Bob and his wife to discuss the relationship issues that contribute to his illness role, depression, and nonadherence to the treatment plan. Marital therapy could occur if both partners are willing.

Conclusion

The cases and issues described in this chapter represent those with which the medical community struggles. Psychotherapists may notice parallels in these cases to those with which they, too, struggle. Despite training in identifying and managing patient resistance through communication and rapport-building strategies, psychotherapists also experience frustration in caring for certain patients with whom they have challenging interactions (*stuck cases*). However, psychotherapists typically are trained to reflect on their personal reactions to patients to understand the factors that make such cases so challenging. Effective psychotherapists attempt to mitigate the treatment effects of their personal issues by understanding and managing countertransference and by seeking professional and informal peer supervision.

Psychotherapists' training focuses on influencing attitudinal and behavior change in patients, and this training can be invaluable to providing optimal health care for these patients. Sharing these insights, skills, and strategies through collaboration with medical professionals can help them broaden their range of interventions, manage their internal reactions, and reduce the frustration, isolation, and sense of futility they experience in caring for their most challenging patients. Psychotherapists who help medical professionals in this way will see their stock rise markedly with their medical colleagues and will find their own frustration and isolation reduced as well. Medical professionals truly appreciate and respect other professionals who help these patients improve or help the professionals manage the situation more effectively. Sharing even one particularly challenging case can often cement a collaborative relationship that secondarily will create referrals for years to come. Most important, the patients often benefit.

In short, intensive collaboration is needed in the kinds of complex situations described in this chapter. Psychotherapists have the training and skills to collaborate with medical professionals to create comprehensive treatment plans based on contextual factors and interpersonal dynamics to optimize care. This team approach can help transcend the mismatch between these patients' needs and the contemporary medical system. In the following chapter, we describe in greater detail the collaborative and psychotherapeutic strategies that can be used in these challenging situations.

5

Strategies and Techniques in Intensive Collaboration

Psychotherapists can use a range of strategies in their collaborative efforts, including prereferral consultation, specific psychotherapy techniques, and ongoing collaborative techniques. This chapter is divided into three parts. In the first part, we describe collaborative strategies that the psychotherapist can use when medical professionals call to consult on patients they are not yet ready to refer or with patients who would benefit from psychological intervention but are currently unwilling to accept such a referral. In the second part of the chapter, we describe techniques that we have found helpful in conducting psychotherapy with patients who have been referred by medical professionals. In the third and final part of the chapter, we describe intensive collaborative strategies that are useful during ongoing therapy. This therapy may follow a referral from the medical professional or may have been initiated by the patient. Note that the fields of health psychology, medical social work, addiction medicine, and the new area of medical family therapy offer techniques, models, and approaches for these patients (Gatchel & Oordt, 2003; McDaniel, Hepworth, & Doherty, 1992; Seaburn, Lorenz, Gunn, Gawinski, & Mauksch, 1996).

Although these strategies can be useful with a variety of patients, they can be critical with challenging patients and interactions. Throughout this chapter, we use the case of Julia to illustrate the concepts and strategies and their implementation. Julia was initially resistant to a referral to a psychotherapist. Once she eventually accepted the referral, her care was complex. Her story illustrates how many of the strategies and techniques described here can help the patient, the medical professional, and the psychotherapist.

Julia: An Introduction

Julia was a 24-year-old nursing student. She had suffered from vague, recurrent abdominal pain since adolescence. Ultimately her medical team diagnosed her with endometriosis. She had multiple surgeries to remove endometrial tissue. Each surgery would reduce her pain temporarily, but her symptoms would slowly return. She required high doses of narcotic pain medication. After multiple surgeries, her condition was exacerbated by surgical adhesions (internal scar tissue). Julie had been told that a hysterectomy would probably end her pain.

Julia struggled to cope with her severe pain and the effect it had on her life. Her illness frequently interfered with her schooling. Although members of her nursing program were supportive, they had standards to maintain and tried to convince Julia to leave the program. Her illness also affected her relationships because her peers viewed her as "the sick one" and were tired of hearing about her pain and illness. She felt alone and isolated as a young woman with a chronic, recurrent, painful illness.

Prereferral Collaborative Strategies for the Psychotherapist

Collaboration regarding a patient who is not concurrently under your care usually occurs when the patient is resistant to accepting a referral. Sometimes medical professionals seek help when they are not sure how to be helpful to the patient or feel frustrated with the situation. We have found the following four strategies most helpful:

□ building a trusting, supportive relationship with the medical professional;

□ recognizing and assessing relational patterns between the patient and the medical professional;

□ offering a collaborative consultation session; and

□ coaching the medical professional with regard to psychotherapy techniques.

Building a Trusting, Supportive Relationship

Psychotherapists and medical professionals who discuss challenging patients and families build trust and a sense of partnership. Some medical professionals may not immediately feel comfortable discussing difficult cases because they believe the patient's potential for change is low. They may have a sense of failure and feel embarrassment or discomfort with their own angry, frustrated reactions to the patient. Medical professionals will respond best to psychotherapists who create an atmosphere of curiosity, provide support, and give advice, *in that order*. After hearing the story, it is helpful to empathize with the medical professional's conundrum. This is a key step. Avoid responding to stories about difficult encounters with diagnostic and therapeutic possibilities or by focusing on changes the medical professional should make. Rather, ask curious questions about the history of the situation and the reactions of the patient and family members. This conversation may help the medical professional see his or her own part in the problem and better understand the patient's perspective.

Recognizing and Assessing Relational Patterns in the Medical Professional–Patient Relationship

In most situations, diagnosis is secondary to recognizing the patterns, motivations, agenda, and blind spots of both the medical professional and the patient. The following two patterns are particularly common in the treatment of complex, challenging patients.

The *distancer–pursuer pattern* is when a psychotherapist realizes that the medical professional is trying to avoid seeing a demanding patient (distancing) and that the patient is escalating symptoms and office visits to get attention (pursuing). The psychotherapist can help the medical professional alter the distancer–pursuer pattern by moving toward the patient and setting up regular visits. In their review of best practices in treating "difficult patients," Haas, Leiser, McGill, and Sanyer (2005) implored the medical professional to see challenging patients frequently and for longer appointments to ensure patient needs are being met.

Triangulation occurs when the patient involves a third party such as a family member or another medical professional to mediate a conflict. When this occurs, the consulting psychotherapist can suggest that the medical professional work to extricate himself or herself from the other conflict and help the patient deal with the conflict more directly. When another person (family member or another health care professional) is triangulated in a conflict between the medical professional and the patient, the medical professional can be coached to discuss the situation directly with the outside party. Sometimes inviting the third party to a medical visit can mitigate the situation.

These dynamics and strategies are common in chronic pain and anxiety syndromes. Psychotherapists can also help medical professionals decide how and when to discuss the medical professional–patient dynamic with the patient.

Consultation Session

If the patient is unwilling to seek mental health care, the psychotherapist can offer to see the patient either conjointly or alone in consultation. Patients unwilling to consider therapy will often agree to a consultation visit. These visits can be billed using either psychotherapy or the new health and behavior codes (H & B) for reimbursement (B codes are described in more detail in chap. 3). Psychotherapists serving this role must recognize that these patients are not "customers" for therapy, and the goal of the consultation is to provide information to the medical professionals and staff to facilitate improved health outcomes. Although the consultation is an opportunity to create a connection with the patient and may facilitate a future referral, this must not be its ultimate goal.

During the consultation, psychotherapists can explore patients' hopes and fears about their illness. Particular fears are often based in the patient's experiences of loved ones who have had the same or similar illness. This contextual information can help the medical professional understand how the patient's history may contribute to health or adherence issues. Psychotherapists can explain and reframe patient resistance to help implement a treatment plan mindful of the patient's "readiness to change" (Prochaska et al., 1994). A consultation session helps the psychotherapist make individualized recommendations to both the patient and the medical professional. The combination of the medical professional's knowledge of the patient over time and the focused efforts of the psychotherapist can maximize behavioral change.

Prochaska's stages of change model (Prochaska & DiClemente, 1983) is a helpful way to conceptualize a patient's progression in understanding his or her distress, but many psychotherapists may be unfamiliar with it. We use the example of helping patients work toward mitigating the effects of emotional issues on their physical distress to illustrate this five-stage model of change. The first stage is *precontemplation*. Patients who do not recognize a link between their emotional life and physical distress are in a precontemplative stage. Medical professionals must work to move patients from precontemplation, when they do not view themselves as having a mental health or substance abuse issue, to the second stage of *contemplation* in which they begin to recognize that emotional issues are negatively affecting their lives. From there, the medical professional must help the patient begin to strategize treatment options in *preparation* of making changes— Prochaska's third stage. If the patient is willing to pursue mental health treatment, obtaining it is one step in the *implementation* of true behavioral change. The final step is *maintenance* of the behavioral changes. Some medical professionals are familiar with this readiness to change model because it is a theory behind smoking cessation programs taught in medical training. However, they may have difficulty applying the concepts to more amorphous issues, such as the link between physical symptoms and emotional distress. Using this model to frame a consultation can help medical professionals set appropriate expectations and use interventions consistent with the patient's level of readiness to change.

Coaching the Medical Professional to Implement Psychotherapeutic Techniques

Psychotherapists can recommend brief psychotherapeutic techniques that the medical professional can use to reduce symptoms. For example, the psychotherapist could coach the medical professional to teach brief relaxation strategies to an anxious patient, involve important support people, customize motivational strategies, and anticipate barriers to care. Brief problem-solving strategies can increase activity levels and reduce depressive symptoms in chronically ill patients. Julia's story illustrates the use of these techniques.

> Julia saw Ms. Howard, an ob-gyn nurse practitioner, for most of her primary care. Recently, Ms. Howard became concerned because Julia had made six emergency room (ER) visits for pain in a 1-month period. Now the medical team in the ER was threatening to refuse future pain medication for Julia because they worried she was becoming addicted and was visiting the ER simply to get more drugs. Ms. Howard was not sure how to handle this escalation in Julia's symptoms and the ER team's threats.
>
> Ms. Howard had in the past collaborated with Dr. Norwalk, a psychologist, on a few challenging patients. Ms. Howard hoped Dr. Norwalk could help now in managing the crisis with Julia. She called him, and after a bout of telephone tag, the two finally connected.
>
> Dr. Norwalk listened to Ms. Howard's concerns and noted how difficult it can be to care for a patient like Julia with intense pain. He asked Ms. Howard about her interactions with Julia. Ms. Howard admitted that she dreaded seeing Julia because she felt she couldn't do anything more for her and was very uncomfortable with prescribing her narcotics. Ms. Howard stated she tried to get Julia to be more independent by encouraging her to try to push through her pain and do "normal 24-year-old things."
>
> Dr. Norwalk noted to himself that there might be a "pursuer–distancer" relational pattern between Ms. Howard and Julia. After also noting that his relationship with Ms. Howard had been supportive and that there was enough trust between them now to be more open about his hunches, he decided to

discuss the pursuer–distancer hypothesis with Ms. Howard. She was intrigued but somewhat wary because seeing Julia was not the highlight of her day. Dr. Norwalk empathized with this but encouraged Ms. Howard to experiment. Could she see Julia more frequently? Ms. Howard said she could, at least for an experimental period of time, perhaps 6 weeks. Dr. Norwalk thought this was reasonable. He further stressed that Julia should be encouraged to attend these more frequent appointments regardless of whether she was having symptoms. As far as the ER team was concerned, Ms. Howard decided that she would cease using them as a resource.

Dr. Norwalk ended the telephone consultation by offering a collaborative consultation session, if Julia was agreeable to meeting with them both together. Ms. Howard said she would consider this after she tried to alter the relational pattern, as Dr. Norwalk had suggested.

So far, Dr. Norwalk has used all four strategies without ever seeing this particular patient. He trusted that if his suggestions worked, Ms. Howard would be (and feel) more helpful to Julia in managing her pain. He also trusted that if his suggestions did not work, Ms. Howard would likely take him up on his suggestion for a collaborative session, either soon or possibly much later because they had both found such sessions helpful in the past.

Strategies in Conducting Therapy With a Patient Referred by a Medical Professional

In addition to the psychotherapist's repertoire of therapeutic skills and techniques, we have found the following strategies particularly useful in working with a patient who has been referred by a medical professional. These nine strategies are derived from health psychology, family therapy, and narrative psychology. For more in-depth information on specific behavioral health strategies for patients with specific presentations, the reader is referred to *Clinical Health Psychology and Primary Care* (Gatchel & Oordt, 2003). For specific information on relational therapy concepts and strategies for families facing medical illness, the reader is referred to *Medical Family Therapy* (McDaniel et al., 1992).

Partnering With the Patient to Distinguish Disease From Illness

One core psychotherapeutic strategy is to help the patient and the medical team distinguish between the "disease" and the "illness." The disease is the organic, physiological, and symptomatic presentation. The illness is the unique experience of the patient as he or she grapples with understanding and coping with the disease. Sometimes, work toward this goal cannot begin until after the patient expresses concerns, frustrations, and perceived lack of control over the disease or the treatment system.

Exploring the Curing Coping Continuum—Soliciting the Illness Story

Patients with chronic, complicated conditions often struggle to accept their illness without accepting "defeat." Psychotherapists can help a patient understand the curing–coping continuum and assess the appropriateness of patients' expectations for cure and improvement. Many patients struggle to transition from seeking a cure to managing an illness. They must seek a new normal that adapts to the realities of the illness but that does not result in a redefinition of self in a helpless, hopeless sick role. Acceptance of limitations must be balanced with a sense of agency or the ability to affect outcome (McDaniel et al., 1992). Patients must learn to accept that their health has changed but that they can work to optimize functioning despite their limitations. Psychotherapy can help patients explore what they can control and what they simply must accept.

Soliciting the illness story is important because patients need to experience being heard before they can move toward self-care. Multiple authors have proposed questions to elicit the illness experience of the patient and family (Kleinman, 1988; McDaniel et al., 1992; Seaburn et al., 1996). Appendix E presents a compilation of these questions. Julia's entry into psychotherapy and ongoing care illustrate these techniques.

> Julia agreed to see Dr. Norwalk when Ms. Howard explained that she felt Julia needed help coping with her illness. Initially,

Julia focused her psychotherapy sessions on discussing her pain and how her illness was ruining her life. Dr. Norwalk encouraged her to express these feelings and did not try to create insight about the interplay between her emotional functioning and her pain. He realized that Julia did not recognize any link between her emotions and her pain and was not ready to explore this. However, he did reserve some of each session for "nonillness" talk, encouraging Julia to focus on other aspects of her life, including her extraordinary effort toward becoming a nurse despite her illness. This helped Julia realize that she was more than a "patient."

As Julia completed a timeline of her illness, she recognized a cyclical pattern of surgery resulting in short-term relief, followed by escalating symptoms, leading to another surgery. Over time, she shifted her focus from assuming that a surgery could "cure" her to finding ways to delay surgical intervention to elongate this cycle. Rather than viewing surgery as her cure, she realized that surgery potentially exacerbated her problems and worked to find alternative ways of reducing her pain and improving her functioning. In a similar vein, she recognized that side effects from the narcotic pain medication also caused many problems. Although she had previously sought more medication both for relief and to convince others that her pain was "real," she agreed to work toward reducing her narcotics. This was a huge step for Julia, because she started to trust that the treatment team was not trying to take away her pain relief regimen and that she could work collaboratively with the team members to reduce her medication use.

Suggesting Symptom Diaries

One specific, useful intervention is a symptom diary. When pain or other medical symptoms dominate and create problems in the patient's life, a careful recording of these symptoms, as well as the events and feelings associated with them, can help the patient to assess patterns and make plans for change. Such a symptom diary also helps psychotherapists better understand how patients' difficulties are affecting their daily lives.

Symptom diaries also assess patients' investment in treatment and their willingness to follow recommendations. Some patients follow directions exactly as prescribed, others will modify the request, and some simply ignore directions. Medical professionals can use the results of the symptoms diary to help them engage the patient or to modify their expectations or treatment plan.

Creating Health-Focused Genograms

The genogram is a frequently used family therapy technique to obtain a quick, graphic understanding of the patient's relationships with immediate and extended family members (Jolly, Froom, & Rosen, 1980; McGoldrick, Gerson, & Shellenberger, 1999). Psychotherapists can use the genogram to take a family history and to document how family members manage health care issues. A thorough history outlines family health beliefs, loss history, and illness history, including how other family members coped with their own illnesses and their illness course. This can be particularly enlightening when a patient has a health condition that other family members experienced. These family experiences may affect patients' beliefs and expectations about the course of their illness and how much control they have. This exploration provides context for the present problem, helping the patient problem solve and reduce self-blame for failing to prevent the problem or struggling to cope with it.

> Dr. Norwalk encouraged Julia to keep a diary of her pain, ranking the pain level three times a day for 2 weeks. For the following 2 weeks, Dr. Norwalk asked Julia also to note her emotions both in general and in response to her pain level. This symptom diary was a key step in helping Julia realize that focusing on her pain and becoming upset with herself and the illness for "ruining her life" worsened the pain and sharply reduced her ability to function. She also realized that this focus preceded ER visits and set a goal for herself to "stay ahead of the pain" to reduce these emergent visits.
>
> Dr. Norwalk reviewed Julia's family medical history using a genogram. The history was not remarkable for chronic pain. However, when Dr. Norwalk asked about family health beliefs Julia stated that her mother did not believe that she had "real pain," even after multiple medical professionals had told her otherwise. She was incredibly angry at her mother for "not

believing" her and felt she had to prove that her pain was "real."

Focusing on the Basics—Exercise, Diet, Spirituality, Lifestyle Change Strategies

The area of most clinical overlap between medical and psychotherapy worlds is in encouraging positive lifestyle patterns. These include regular exercise, good nutrition, spirituality, good sleeping patterns, and not smoking or abusing alcohol. These basics can get lost when patients have complex issues that require both medical and mental health involvement (Gatchel & Oordt, 2003). Focusing on improving lifestyle patterns is an excellent opportunity for collaboration and provides a way to engage patients in positive changes. For example, in Keene, New Hampshire, the local mental health center created a wellness program with their most difficult, chronic, and severely disturbed patients. They partnered with the local YMCA to provide training and encouragement for patients to make dietary and exercise changes and have had significant, positive results in both lifestyle change and mental health improvement of these patients (Ellen, 2005).

Coordinating and Facilitating Family Meetings to Increase Support and Concordance With the Treatment Plan

Some of the most effective interventions with complex patients target the patient's family and social context (Gatchel & Oordt, 2003). Collaboration with medical professionals and family members creates what Seaburn et al. (1996) called the *therapeutic rectangle,* referring to the relationships between the psychotherapist, the patient, the medical professional, and the family. The goal is to have quality relationships around the system to create a "culture of collaboration"—a team of people who come together to optimize the patient's health. Often "stuck" patients have a saboteur in their lives, and progress will be limited as long as that person is not actively involved in their care. Sometimes the issue stems from mistrust in one of the rectangle's quadrants.

When interactional dynamics influence the patient's medical treatment, conferences involving the family and medical professional can be a powerful tool. A protocol for conducting these meetings is included in *Family-Oriented Primary Care, Second Edition* (McDaniel, Campbell, Hepworth, & Lorenz, 2005). At a family conference, the psychotherapist and medical professionals can hear the family's perspective on the illness, and family members can ask questions about the patient's illness, prognosis, and treatment. Families often experience difficulty discussing the illness because it is too painful, or they wish to protect each other from harsh realities. The fear of discussing an illness is often a barrier to mutual support and problem solving. Also, people who are ill often hide their needs out of a fear of burdening others. Family members struggle to know when to help and when to step back. These dynamics can result in dysfunctional patterns in which the patient feels unable to access needed help and may even feel abandoned. Family conferences can strip away some of these barriers and begin dialogues about moving forward and working together. Frank discussion may reveal that support people are feeling burned out or resentful, and the family needs help in more evenly distributing caregiving tasks. Understanding the impact of the illness on the family enables the professional to coach them to obtain support and ward off illness-related family crises. Finally, family conferences give the professionals insight about the family's dynamics and each individual's functioning, helping them determine who best can help the patient.

> Julia's spiritual life was important to her. She had a supportive community at her synagogue and started to talk with her rabbi about her illness. She found great comfort in this. Julia recognized that one of the ways she "fought back" against her illness's effect on her life was to ignore the reality that she couldn't tolerate the "normal" college student lifestyle of late nights, poor nutrition, and little exercise. She decided that a healthy lifestyle and listening to her body was one thing she could control. She felt empowered by starting an exercise program and trying to eat a healthier diet. At the same time, Dr. Norwalk stressed that she didn't have to have a "perfect" lifestyle.

Julia's parents were divorced, and her father was not part of her life. She was reluctant to include her mother in treatment. Julia felt she had not been supportive in the past but did ultimately sign of a release of information. Julia's mother was thrilled when Dr. Norwalk called because she was concerned about her daughter. She said she did not know how to talk to Julia about her illness and expressed concerns about the recommendation that Julia have a hysterectomy and her pain management regimen. After the conversation, Dr. Norwalk felt that Julia's mother was well intended and trying to be supportive but also could understand how Julia interpreted her mother's concerns as invalidating her illness. After a great deal of work with Julia, she agreed to a session with her mother. Although the session started with an argument, by the end Julia understood that her mother meant well, and her mother understood that Julia genuinely wanted to be healthier. Although there continued to be a lot of tension in the relationship, Julia understood her mother's concerns, and her mother tried to be more supportive.

Applying the Mind–Body Paradigm to the Patient's Experience

Psychotherapy referrals can result in the patient feeling blamed or pathologized by the medical professional. The proverbial question, "Is it more in the head or in the body?" perpetuates this dichotomous thinking. It can be difficult to convey to a patient that there is an appropriate role for a psychotherapist, even in the most artful of referrals. To be helpful, psychotherapists must address this concern early so the patient accepts the expansion of the treatment system. They must stress that mental health services are in addition to, not instead of, their medical care.

There are numerous ways to address the mind–body link depending on the patient's acceptance and or ability to understand this complex interactive process. Some patients prefer a more scientific explanation of the impact of stress on neurotransmitters and decreased immune function. Others will relate to a more general explanation with examples from their life. The Harvard Mind/Body Institute uses the image of the three-legged stool to talk about addressing chronic pain conditions (Benson, 1996).

Surgery and medications make up two legs of the stool and are described as incomplete without the third leg of patient self-care. This image can be helpful to patients in understanding their role in the coping–healing process. Psychotherapists can ensure that the patient understands the roles of all professionals involved as well as the patient's own role in coping and healing. Reading assignments and patient education handouts can be helpful. Appendix D has a list of patient-oriented Web sites to recommend.

Facilitating Coping With Normal Grief Reactions Associated With Loss of Health and Function

Strong feelings and reactions related to the patient's struggle to adjust to the loss of health and physical abilities often reduce treatment effectiveness and create difficult interactions. Psychotherapists can help patients cope with change and loss in their lives. As they listen to the illness story, they can assess emotional reactions to the loss, normalize these reactions, and facilitate growth. They can help the medical professional and patient recognize that recovery is a process that takes time and is unique to each person.

> Julia began to acknowledge that her emotional state and her pain levels were intertwined. Dr. Norwalk emphasized that her physical pain was "real," whether it came from endometrial tissue, surgical adhesions, or sadness. Although Julia couldn't control the growth of her endometrium or internal scarring, she could work to improve her coping and her mood.
> One of Julia's biggest frustrations was her inability to lead a "normal" life. She feared she would never have a boyfriend or husband and understood that the likelihood of infertility was high—a certainty if she underwent a hysterectomy. She envied her healthy peers and at times would become angry with them because they did not understand her problems and give her the support she needed. She spent many psychotherapy sessions discussing her losses and was comforted that Dr. Norwalk normalized her anger and sadness in the context of the many adaptations she had to make to her illness.

Externalize the Symptoms or Disease—Managing Uncle Buck

Patients with complicated medical and psychological problems can develop an identity over time as a "professional patient." They become dependent on the medical team, make frequent visits to the office, and often consider the medical team part of their "family." This dependence is compounded for patients with social isolation secondary to their illness or persistent pain requiring narcotics (or both). Encouraging patients to see their disease as something external to themselves is one therapeutic technique to challenge this patient identity (White & Epston, 1990). The ability to externalize symptoms enables patients to see themselves as more than their illness. It allows them to think differently about managing the problems associated with the symptoms rather than being controlled by them. For example, psychotherapists can use the comedy film, *Uncle Buck* (Hughes, 1989), to facilitate discussion of "putting the illness in its place." In the movie, Uncle Buck, played by John Candy, comes to visit his brother and his family and takes over the house with his boisterous and obnoxious behavior. The patient can be encouraged to use the image of how to get Uncle Buck (the illness) to live in the upstairs room, like a guest who needs some care but is not allowed to take over the house. This metaphor can help patients recover their sense of self, separate from the disease.

> Julia both embraced but also rejected the "sick girl" role. She saw her illness as a defining characteristic and talked about her illness and pain with others at length. At the same time, she became resentful when others defined her this way. Over time, Dr. Norwalk helped Julia realize that her own focus on her illness and primary identity as a "sick person" was not helping her meet her goals. She started to become more accepting of her "bad days." It is interesting that the more she was able to listen to her body and rest on these days, the less often they spiraled into "bad weeks." Also, she learned to pace herself even on her "good days" and stopped trying to make up for lost time when she felt well, which ultimately resulted in her becoming tired and stressed and precipitating a "bad day."

Collaborative Strategies
During Ongoing Psychotherapy

Challenging situations call for more ongoing collaboration than simpler presentations. Psychotherapists and medical professionals can discuss the reciprocal relationship between stress and illness, help the patient make this link, and find goals that reduce stress thereby reducing physical symptoms.

Transitioning to Intensive Collaboration

The need for more intensive collaboration is not always obvious at the outset of treatment. When it becomes clear that more intensive collaboration would be helpful, the psychotherapist should first discuss this with the patient to ensure comfort with the plan. The psychotherapist should then contact the medical professional and renegotiate the collaboration agreement to better meet the patient's needs. The renegotiated plan should be presented to the patient, and the patient should be given the opportunity to discuss any concerns. This is particularly critical when there is conflict between the patient and professionals or the patient is not satisfied with some aspect of treatment.

Comparing Notes

Intensive collaboration allows psychotherapists to serve as a source of information for the medical provider regarding the patient's progress. For example, a psychotherapist might discover that the patient is not taking his or her medication as prescribed or is thinking about terminating a medication without telling the medical professional. The psychotherapist can suggest the patient discuss this plan with the medical professional. This ensures that the patient stops the medication safely and that the medical professional has an opportunity to discuss the termination with the patient. This role is critical with psychotropic medications, particularly in the early phase of treatment. Psychotherapists can monitor positive and negative effects of the medication, and reassure patients that early negative side effects are likely to dissipate just as the beneficial effects of the medication begin. If the medications are being managed by a primary care medical professional and treatment outcomes are suboptimal, the psychotherapist can assist in making referrals for psychiatric consultation for complicated medication situations.

Avoiding Triangulation

Psychotherapists can inadvertently become triangulated between a patient and the medical professional. It is important that psychotherapists elicit patients' concerns and frustrations with their medical treatment. However, this information then should be shared with the patient's medical professional to give him or her feedback and to hear the medical professional's side of the story. When psychotherapists knows the context of the patient's complaints, they can help the patient learn how to make their needs known appropriately or to work more effectively with the system.

When patients have legitimate complaints about the medical care they have received, psychotherapists can coach them in self-advocacy. Even assertive people experience difficulty in the medical system. Asking the medical professional his or her perspective on the issue can reveal the patient's role in the difficulties or result in changing the medical professional's behavior. When the patient's frustrations are based in immutable, unfortunate aspects of the medical system, liberal doses of empathy from both the medical professional and the psychotherapist can help. When complaints reflect a bad match between the patient and medical professional, and if the medical professional is unwilling to collaborate or accommodate the patient, the psychotherapist can help the patient determine the pros and cons of transferring care.

> About 6 months into Julia's treatment, she reported increasing frustration with Ms. Howard. Initially, Dr. Norwalk was not concerned and allowed Julia to vent her frustrations. However, after Julia reported a particularly unpleasant encounter with Ms. Howard, Dr. Norwalk and she agreed he should call Ms. Howard. During the phone call, Ms. Howard acknowledged she was beyond frustrated caring for Julia and wanted

to terminate treatment. She had discussed Julia with a colleague who specialized in treating chronic abdominal pain. Dr. Norwalk encouraged Ms. Howard to discuss her concerns with Julia and broach a transfer of care. Dr. Norwalk coached Ms. Howard how to present the idea and suggested that a joint appointment that included the new medical professional might help Julia make a successful transition.

Conducting a Joint Appointment

Joint appointments can be a critical juncture in particularly complex, challenging psychotherapy treatment. A minority of clinical presentations necessitates a joint appointment, and even fewer require more than one or two throughout the course of treatment. The medical professionals and psychotherapist should discuss the idea of a joint appointment before the idea is presented to the patient. Ideally, both professionals discuss it with the patient, focusing on their desire to work together to optimize care.

The logistics of the joint appointment are important. Typically, the psychotherapist should attend a medical appointment at the beginning of the medical professional's patient care session, because they frequently run late. The appointment should be a minimum of 30 minutes, and the front-office staff should ensure the medical professional is not double-booked. The psychotherapist and medical professional should meet before the appointment to create an agenda and distribute meeting tasks such as time keeping and meeting wrap up. The agenda should first review each professional's care of the patient and the concerns to be addressed in the joint appointment. The patient and family members should have the opportunity to present their questions, and the professionals should ensure that the patient's and family members' concerns are addressed in the treatment plan. The treatment plan should be reviewed at the end of the appointment with assignment of the planned tasks, including the frequency and means of future collaboration.

About a month after the phone consultation between Dr. Norwalk and Ms. Howard, Ms. Howard told Julia that she wanted to transfer her care to another primary care professional. She explained that Julia deserved a level of medical care that exceeded her own knowledge, skills, and expertise. Julia was ambivalent, torn between the hope of a new medical professional and fear and anger about the change. Dr. Norwalk asked Julia if she would like to have a joint appointment that included Dr. Norwalk, Ms. Howard, and the new medical professional. Julia found this reassuring and agreed. The joint appointment was tense. However, by the end Julia agreed to give the new medical professional a chance. She was still angry with Ms. Howard but thanked her for her care and had some appreciation of why Ms. Howard initiated the transfer. Months later, when Julia had transferred to her new medical professional successfully, she told Dr. Norwalk that she felt the joint appointment had been a turning point for her. She felt she entered into her new treatment relationship with more realistic expectations and felt empowered that she could choose a course rather than be at the mercy of her illness and her caregivers.

Conclusion

One goal of collaboration is to create a team atmosphere that reassures patients that their best interests are paramount. Psychotherapy and medical professionals can discuss and together reinforce the patient's effective use of the overall health care system and, when applicable, other support systems in the community. Professionals can strategize together to help the patient use these systems to their best advantage. Many of the patients described in chapter 4 needed a great deal of assistance to optimize their health and well-being. Both the intensity and breadth of assistance they need is often overwhelming to one professional providing care in isolation. Medical professionals and psychotherapists who work closely together can "divide and conquer" the patient's needs. Psychotherapists who understand the specific issues that patients with complex medical illnesses face and who understand how to manage these issues optimally in psychotherapy are invaluable to the medical professional.

6

Colocating With Medical Professionals: A New Model of Integrated Care

To this point, we have focused on how psychotherapists can integrate collaborative practices into their day-to-day practice. In this chapter, we shift our focus to how psychotherapists can transform their practice model toward integration into the medical setting. We describe how the psychotherapist's role, clinical presentations, and interventions change when treatment occurs in the medical arena. We describe different practice models that correspond to differing levels of integration of services and the systemic factors that facilitate or hinder this process. We then describe experiences of psychotherapists who provide on-site care in systems with varying levels of collaboration and integration to illustrate how these models, and the psychotherapists' roles, evolved in various settings.

Although this chapter may seem more theoretical than the pragmatic chapters that preceded it, on-site services are becoming more common—in private settings, the public health arena, and the military (Robinson & Reiter, 2007). This shift expands the opportunities for the collaborative psychotherapist in medical settings, particularly primary care medical settings. We realize that not all psychotherapists have a desire to move toward this model. However, it has been our experience that the transition to on-site care sometimes evolves from an established collaborative relationship between a psychosocially focused medical professional and a collaborative psychotherapist. Not uncommonly, independent psychotherapists who routinely collaborate initially spend limited time in the medical setting and expand their time as the need or opportunity increases. Beginning collaborators may become more interested in these models with experience and may want to expand their roles in medical settings in the future as they develop meaningful and rewarding collaborative relationships with medical professionals.

Models of Colocated Mental Health Service

The movement toward practicing together reflects a commitment to providing whole-person, biopsychosocial care. Doherty, McDaniel, and Baird (1996) described five levels of systemic collaboration between family physicians, psychotherapists, and other health professionals (see Table 6.1). Collaboration on a given case depends on the patient's needs, the professionals' collaboration skills, and the collaboration capacity (or level) of the health care setting. The model assumes that more intensive systemic collaboration more effectively meets the needs of complex patients.

The first section of this book focused on moving from *minimal collaboration* (Level I) to *basic collaboration at a distance* (Level II), both of which occur when psychotherapists and medical professionals are not located in the same setting. Doherty et al. (1996) cited three other levels of collaboration that can occur when psychotherapists and medical professionals are colocated.

Basic collaboration on-site (Level III) occurs when colocated health care professionals have limited communication about shared patients and do not provide care as a team. The psychotherapist generally sees patients in 50-minute sessions. Medical and mental health services are completely separate, including separate charting with an emphasis on patient confidentiality. Level III collaboration occurs most frequently when a system colocates psychotherapists and medical professionals without providing them with training on collaboration, when productivity demands preclude discussion of complex patients, or when neither the psychotherapists nor medical professionals are willing to go beyond basic collaboration. Systems issues such as the relative location of the psychotherapists and medical professionals' clinical space and regulatory issues can also result in Level III collaboration.

Level III collaboration may improve access to mental health services because patients do not have to go to a separate location, and patients may inherently trust the psychotherapist because he or she works in the same office with their trusted medical professionals. However, Level III collaboration does not ensure that medical professionals will know the outcome of their referrals or psychotherapy. Psychotherapists may not be aware of the patient's relevant medical issues or any other important information the medical professional has to offer. In many situations, this type of arrangement can be a missed opportunity.

Professionals in a setting with *close collaboration in a partly integrated system* (Level IV) communicate regularly and coordinate treatment plans for patients facilitated by regular meetings. Psychotherapists often spend most of their time in traditional mental health service provision. The medical professional may refer patients by encouraging the patient to call the psychotherapist or by referring directly with the expectation that the psychotherapist will initiate contact. Professionals often strive for a *warm handoff* (Robinson & Reiter, 2007) in which the patient meets the psychotherapist before referral. These prereferral meetings range from a brief contact in which the patient simply meets the psychotherapist to an extended joint appointment reviewing care history and reasons for referral and setting treatment goals and collaboration guidelines.

Levels of postreferral communication tend to be higher in Level IV collaboration. Medical professionals and psychotherapists informally consult each other in *hallway consults* facilitated by shared office space. Because this type of communication can be happenstance, professionals may have regular meetings to discuss all shared patients, not just those who are needy. Written communication varies from completely separate charting to a shared medical record with a separate section for the psychotherapy notes. Some psychotherapists will e-mail or write notes to the medical professional depending on institutional rules.

The advantages of Level IV integration include ease of referral, ease of sharing information, and teamwork facilitating better outcomes. The psychotherapist's presence facilitates episodic use of

TABLE 6.1

Levels of Systemic Collaboration

	I: Minimal collaboration	II: Basic collaboration at a distance	III: Basic collaboration onsite	IV: Close collaboration in a partly integrated system	V: Close collaboration in a fully integrated system
Model characteristics	Separate practice sites Little to no communication about shared patients No active referral linkage	Separate practice sites Periodic communication driven by patient issues Active referral linkage	Same practice site, separate practice management system Regular communication about shared patients No team based care structure	Same practice site Some operational overlap and differences (e.g., charting, scheduling, fees) Scheduled collaboration meetings Med provider initiates MH involvement	Same practice site and operational system Shared care paradigm Providers and patients view MH as part of care team MH and Med providers initiate MH involvement

Patients best served by this model	Routine medical and psychosocial issues with little biopsychosocial interplay and few management difficulties	Routine issues and minimal biopsychosocial interplay and management issues	Minimally complicated presentations, with some biopsychosocial interplay Case management ongoing, but not central to care	Moderately complicated presentations, with significant biopsychosocial interplay Case management issues are ongoing and significant	Patients unable or unwilling to access traditional MH treatment, challenging and complex biopsychosocial interplay and management issues

Note. Med = medical; MH = mental health. From *Five Levels of Primary Care/Behavioral Healthcare Collaboration,* by W. J. Doherty, S. H. McDaniel, and M. A. Baird, 1996, *Behavioral Healthcare Tomorrow, 5,* pp. 25–28. Copyright 1996 by Medquest Communications. Adapted with permission.

mental health services as the patient's needs and readiness to change evolve. The disadvantages of Level IV integration include access-to-care issues because the psychotherapist may quickly be overwhelmed with referrals, necessitating a waiting list. Lower barriers to mental health care may result in patients entering psychotherapy with inadequate motivation and readiness to change. When the psychotherapist initiates the referral at the medical professional's request, patients may make the intake appointment to avoid an awkward interaction and then fail to follow through. Although colocated medical professionals and psychotherapists continue to work together with patients who are not ready to change, some psychotherapists find this work challenging as they attempt to learn the best ways to triage and customize strategies on the basis of the patient's level of readiness to change.

Close collaboration in a fully integrated system (Level V) is the most integrated treatment model. Ideally, the team provides a seamless web of biopsychosocial services (McDaniel, Hepworth, & Doherty, 1992). Psychotherapists work side by side with medical professionals, meeting with patients during their regular medical visits. Patients are advised that a psychotherapist may meet with them at any time to ensure that their care is appropriately comprehensive and are encouraged to see the psychotherapist as part of the health care team. Psychotherapists provide screening, brief consultations, and interventions at a moment's notice. When patients acknowledge symptoms of depression or anxiety on a screening tool, the psychotherapist assesses the severity of the problem and relevant life stressors and support systems and may offer further mental health services. However, the focus is on managing the patient's concerns in the moment with problem-focused interventions aimed at improving management of medical issues, managing life stressors, increasing personal support, and averting mental health crises. The psychotherapist communicates directly with the medical professional, and they collaboratively plan next steps in the patient's care. The interested reader is referred to Behavioral Consultation and Primary Care (Robinson & Reiter, 2007) and Primary Care Consultant: The Next Frontier for Psychologists in Hospitals and Clinics (James & Folen, 2005) for an in-depth description of integrated mental health services and the role of a behavioral health consultant.

Level V collaboration has many advantages. It provides access to immediate mental health care and reaches patients who are not amenable to the traditional psychotherapy model through the use of screening and brief interventions. The immediacy of the assistance helps patients slowly move toward behavior changes over time, particularly as they benefit from multiple consultations with a psychotherapist regarding situational stressors and illness management. Screening and brief interventions reach a much higher proportion of patients than traditional referral-based interventions. The overt teamwork between the medical professionals and psychotherapists (or behavioral health consultants) gives patients a clear message that emotional and relational issues are central to their overall health. This model most likely improves professional satisfaction for medical professionals because it eases time pressure and reduces frustration in caring for challenging patients. However, there are several potential cons of this model as well. Not all psychotherapists want to alter their practice from traditional psychotherapy to brief interventions because they may feel that it does not allow them to use all of their skills or does not lead to meaningful change for patients. Despite a great deal of research evidence to the contrary (Crits-Cristoph, 1992; Escobar et al., 2007; Leichsenring, Rabung, & Leibing, 2004), some psychotherapists continue to question the efficacy of brief interventions. Also, if medical professionals expect psychotherapists to manage all patients who present emotionally, they can inadvertently fragment their interactions with patients by involving the psychotherapist whenever patients present with emotional issues, rather than only when a situation exceeds their expertise and time constraints.

Each of the five levels of collaborative care has its advantages and disadvantages. Future research may reveal which model works best in which settings and with which patient presentations. Overall, these models differ along three continuums: the degree of colocation (where the professionals practice), the degree of collaboration (how well the medical professional and psychotherapist work as a team), and the degree of integration (Is the psychotherapist considered part of the team by medical professionals and patients? Are larger system issues such as charting systems and fee structures consistent between medical and mental health provision?; Strosahl, 1998). As reflected in Exhibit 6.1, psychotherapists who work on-site with medical professionals will have different responsibilities and levels of autonomy, depending on the level of integration.

EXHIBIT 6.1

Primary Care–Based Psychotherapist Collaborative "Job Descriptions" From Least to Most Integrated

---

The psychotherapist's primary clinical activity is

— Traditional psychotherapy with little to no communication (Level III).

— Traditional psychotherapy with collaboration based on patient necessity and convenience of communication such as "hallway consults" (Level III/IV).

— Traditional psychotherapy with dedicated time for regularly scheduled collaboration meetings to discuss shared patients (Level IV).

— Mix of traditional psychotherapy with other consultative/brief interventions for patients as referred by medical professional. This brief intervention may coincide with a medical appointment, and serving to diffuse the patient's distress before the medical encounter (Level IV).

— Mix of traditional psychotherapy with time scheduled for consultative/brief intervention appointments for patients as determined collaboratively by the psychotherapist and medical professional (Level IV/V).

— Decreased time devoted to "scheduled" and "referred" patients and increasing time devoted to screening and brief interventions with patients as determined by "in the moment" need. Psychotherapist can initiate services without input of medical professiona (Level V).

Systems Factors That Facilitate Integration

As the previous description of collaboration models illustrates, various levels of collaboration depend a great deal on logistics, professional attitudes and roles, and patient expectations. Multiple researchers have examined the systemic and professional elements needed for successful collaboration and integration. We present these variables for readers who are interested in changing their roles or who serve as administrators and desire to increase collaborative care in their systems. Larry Mauksch (personal communication, October 2005) compiled the following list of elements for the 2006 Collaborative Family Healthcare Integration Summit:

1. The health care professionals must receive training in how to work together productively (Cameron & Mauksch, 2002).
2. The health care professionals must work toward developing interdisciplinary relationships.
3. System leaders must support a move toward greater collaboration and integration (Wagner et al., 2001).
4. Patients and their families have input and influence on the design and implementation of collaborative care models (Pyne et al., 2005).
5. Medical professionals provide evidence-based care (Katon et al., 1997).
6. The system's operational and structural features support collaboration (e.g., colocation, unified medical records).
7. Patient status and progress is tracked (Wagner et al., 2001).
8. The system has treatment protocols and progressive levels of care for patients with various levels of need and complexity (Katon, Von Korff, Lin, & Simon, 2001).
9. Funding supports collaborative care, uncoupled with clinical service reimbursement when necessary (Grazier, Hegadus, Carli, Neal, & Reynolds, 2003; Peek & Heinrich, 1995; Wagner et al., 2001)

Few health systems are able to optimize all of these variables, resulting in combinations that create unique arrangements and degrees of success. The unique combination of variables in each system results in myriad combinations of practice patterns that fall all along the continuum described by Doherty et al. (1996).

The Experiences of Primary Care–Based Psychotherapists

Psychotherapists who work in traditional mental health settings may find it difficult to imagine working in a primary care setting. In this section, we provide a snapshot of primary care–based psychotherapists by describing their roles and experiences. These descriptions are based on individual and joint interviews of multiple primary care–based mental health professionals, including psychiatrists, psychologists, social workers, and licensed professional counselors. The first section describes the experiences of a psychologist who transitioned from separate private practice to on-site collaborative private practice. The second section describes the experiences of psychotherapists in the Salud Family Health Centers, part of the public health sector.

We do not present the full interview texts here. Rather, we summarize the professionals' responses and occasionally quote them directly to highlight specific issues. In contrast, the interviews presented in Part IV of this book include more specifics, edited from the full dialogue of each interview. In Part IV, we also interview two psychologists who practice in primary care: Dr. Driscoll in the private sector and Dr. Altum in the public sector.

Integration in the Private Sector: Dr. Vincent Scalese

Dr. Scalese has practiced as a solo psychologist in Plymouth, New Hampshire, for 30 years. Years ago, Dr. Scalese started working collaboratively with Dr. Fred Kelsey, an internist who directed a primary care practice in the area. They dreamed about developing a truly integrated practice, to move beyond the relatively common model in which the medical professional owns the practice and the psychotherapist rents or contract for space. Toward this end, they formed Mid-State Health Center in 2004, and by June 2005 their practices had merged into one entity. At Mid-State, the 3 psychologists and 11 primary care medical professionals are equal participants in the health of enrolled patients and work under the same administrative structure. The financial model is based on the productivity of all professionals. The psychologists conduct a full range of consultative, evaluative, and treatment services based on the patients' needs.

When Dr. Scalese first started working on site at Mid-State, he spent 1 day a week at the practice. He risked 25% of his income by not accepting appointments for part of his schedule to make himself available for immediate consultation with patients and integrated consultations. Within a year, he started to spend all of his clinical time at the Mid-State practice, seeing between 6 and 12 patients each day, with varying appointment durations depending on patient need. Most of his patients are referred by the medical professionals in the office. Dr. Scalese and his colleagues provide traditional treatment and assessment for mental health issues, as well as therapy focused on coping with a medical illnesses and lifestyle-change counseling. They provide both brief and longer term interventions.

In further efforts to reach patients who might be missed when medical professionals must identify the issue and generate a referral, Dr. Scalese trained the office staff to conduct a brief two-question depression screen of all patients before their medical visit. Patients who screened positive briefly met with Dr Scalese before meeting with the medical professional. Although Mid-State's professionals hoped to screen all patients, they fell short of this goal because of staff training issues and limited psychotherapist availability. They plan to have more psychotherapists in the future to implement depression screening and appropriate follow-up for all patients.

There were numerous other key steps toward integration. The health care professionals worked together to develop an informed consent process to explain the integrated practice model to patients. This helped them clarify their own understanding of the model and how best to present its benefits to patients. They also implemented an electronic medical record with integrated behavioral health diagnoses and treatment plans, allowing all professionals access to both the biomedical and psychotherapy records. Staff training regarding appropriate use of the psychologist was also critical. The psychologist further solidified his relationship with the support staff by developing training to help them manage difficult patient personalities. This program had a tremendous positive impact on staff members and their impressions of the psychotherapists, which also greatly facilitated the process of integration. These joint projects served as extremely effective "team builders" between the professionals of various disciplines and the support staff.

Dr. Scalese advises psychotherapists transitioning to this type of model to recognize the shift in thinking necessary to create an integrated model. The psychotherapist must shift from autonomous practice to being part of a bigger health care team. Although this reduces autonomy, it increases access to various specialties and enhances patients' health care experience. Second, Dr. Scalese stressed the importance of significant staff training to increase awareness of mental health issues. These factors greatly enhanced his experience as an integrated, collaborative psychotherapist.

Integration in Public Health: The Salud Family Health Centers

The second set of interviews provides a brief overview of the experiences of psychotherapists who work in the Salud Family Health Centers in Colorado. Salud Family Health Centers is a federally qualified community health center consisting of 14 health care centers in six counties in north-central Colorado. It was established in 1970 as a migrant health center to meet the needs of farmworkers and their families. In 1972, they added community health center status. Salud focuses on the needs of the medically indigent, uninsured, and underinsured patients. It serves as a safety net for north-central Colorado, providing services regardless of a patient's insurance coverage or ability to pay. In 2005, Salud served more than 65,000 patients, in more than 250,000 visits. Approximately 4,000 of their patients are migrant and seasonal farmworkers. Approximately 65% of their patients are Latino, many of whom speak only Spanish. Salud attempts to reduce barriers to care by employing bilingual, bicultural professionals and staff and providing mobile outreach services. Dental services and mental health services are available at most sites.

Salud is an interesting study in integration, because the evolution toward integration has taken different paths at different sites. The psychotherapists' experiences illustrate how larger system issues affect collaboration and how an integrated psychotherapist functions.

Tillman Farley, MD, the medical director of Salud, has been a driving force behind the inclusion of mental health services into the medical setting. Dr. Farley has been practicing as a family physician since 1990 and has practiced collaborative colocated care in the past. However, he wanted to move beyond a partially integrated system (Level IV) into a fully integrated system (Level V). He feels that practicing alongside psychotherapists in an integrated model facilitates optimal management of mental health issues in primary care. Before having a psychotherapist available to see patients immediately, he felt that he did not always have the time or expertise to manage patients' needs optimally. In the past, he tried to convince his patients to see psychotherapists, or he tried to manage situations himself despite his limitations. Patients often did not follow through on referrals, even when the psychotherapist was on site. When the on-site psychotherapists practiced in a 50-minute hour psychotherapy model, their schedules quickly filled, resulting in a waiting list. In contrast, he feels integrated primary care mental health allows him to "meet patients where they are" and to get help when it is needed to optimize a window of opportunity that would be lost if the patient were asked to come back at another time. He has found that integrated mental health services also avoid psychotherapy waiting lists. He noted that the screening services catch patients in emotional distress who would otherwise remain unnoticed. He stated emphatically that he "wouldn't want to go back" to providing health care any other way.

Having a psychotherapist available to patients in need has obvious advantages to medical professionals, saving them time and frustration; but how do the psychotherapists feel about their role and its impact on patients? The following section presents summaries of interviews with providers at four Salud sites. The sites vary in their level of integration because of a variety of factors, yet the psychotherapists themselves have similar goals and impressions of their work in primary care.

Commerce City, Colorado, Branch: Luis Diaz, MSW

Mr. Diaz has worked previously in a variety of mental health settings but stated that he is "attracted to and fascinated by the medical system." He enjoys working in a primary care setting because "Patients' needs get met immediately—it is one-stop shopping." Although he has worked in a traditional community mental health center, he stated, "I don't think I'd ever go back to that model ever again . . . it is so mental health focused, and the medical gets ignored. I think working in the extreme, either focused solely on the medical or the mental health issues, isn't optimal. I believe patients are served better when we work together." Mr. Diaz splits his time between providing traditional psychotherapy in a collaborative colocation model (Level IV) and integrated screening and brief interventions in the medical setting (Level V). One barrier to further integration is that his office is a short walk from the medical site rather than next to the medical examination rooms.

Longmont, Colorado, Branch: Richard Lowinger, MA, LPC

At the time of the interview, Mr. Lowinger spent a majority of his time in colocated traditional psychotherapy (Level III/IV) but was in the process of transitioning to an integrated model. He acknowledged that he was more comfortable providing traditional psychotherapy but also recognized that integrated work had the potential to meet many patients' needs. From his experience Mr. Lowinger felt that brief interventions helped patients by giving them support when they need it and that he saw many patients make lasting change or seeking psychotherapy after repeated brief interventions. He enjoys working in primary care because "There are people that need a certain type of attention at their medical appointments" and because he feels his assessment skills facilitate earlier detection and treatment of emotional issues. He also feels his presence helps medical professionals better understand how patients' stressful life situations affect their health and well-being: "I do believe that our role here in a primary care setting is to help everyone be more open to the psychological aspects of patient care. Many medical professionals are good at preparing patients to speak with a psychotherapist, but with time constraints and other factors, some patients can't get their needs met."

Ft. Lupton, Colorado, Branch: Susana Gonzalez, MA

Ms. Gonzalez completed a clinical placement at the Longmont Salud center during her training and transferred to Ft. Lupton upon graduating approximately 9 months before the interview.

She spends almost all of her time conducting screening and brief interventions in the medical setting. Her office is a former examination room, making her extremely accessible to medical professionals when they are seeing patients; this has its pros and cons. Like Luis Diaz, Ms. Gonzalez feels that she is able to meet the needs of patients who otherwise would not access mental health services and that her integrated work helps patients get "the right kind of help" rather than continuing to seek medical care for psychosocial problems. However, she notes that medical professionals can become a bit dependent on her presence, having her intervene in situations they would otherwise manage. "Sometimes a patient is crying, and they call me like it's an emergency. They get scared, and they love that they can just call me in. But I'm working with them to remind them that they can manage those situations without my help." Ms. Gonzalez also noted that she sometimes feels isolated as the lone psychotherapist in her office. She and the psychotherapists from other Salud sites meet monthly for peer supervision and professional development. Although she enjoys the camaraderie with other health care professionals, she does not have daily contact with other psychotherapists with whom she can share the specific rewards and frustrations of her job.

Mr. Diaz, Mr. Lowinger, and Ms. Gonzalez are all employees of Salud. They do not have clinical quotas or direct service requirements because grants fund their salaries. They keep records of patient contacts in the medical chart, as well as separate records of psychotherapy contacts. These factors all facilitate greater integration because these psychotherapists can provide services independent of insurance reimbursement structures and outside agency constraints and pressures.

Fort Collins, Colorado, Branch

In contrast to the psychotherapists just discussed, those at the Salud clinic in Fort Collins are not employed directly by Salud. They work for various agencies and thus have different roles, agendas, job requirements, and, more specifically, different productivity goals for services that must be reimbursed under the current fee structure. Therefore, they have far fewer degrees of freedom in how they provide services. The experience of the psychotherapists who practice at the Fort Collins branch illustrates many of the challenges that mental health and medical systems can face when attempting to implement collocation and integrated services. However, these professionals have a strong commitment to collaboration and integrated services and have tried to work creatively to overcome the challenges posed by multiple system constraints. The larger system and their home agencies are also committed to providing integrated care and continue to work toward this ultimate goal.

A brief rundown of the professionals, their home agencies, and their job descriptions reveals the complexity of the situation:

☐ Earl Rendon, MSW, and Martha Ratliff, LCSW, of the Larimer Center for Mental Health care for a subset of Salud patients who meet criteria for inclusion in a program for chronically mentally ill patients. They provide home- and health-center-based services. They do not provide integrated services (Level III).

☐ Richard Oddy, MD, is a psychiatrist who consults with the primary care medical professionals 2 days a week, with an office located in the medical setting (Level IV/V). He is employed by the Health District of Larimer County Integrated Care Program. Much of his time is spent in direct patient care appointments for medication management, but he also consults directly with the primary care medical professionals.

☐ Catherine Watson, MS, LMFT, and Ginger Benson Ross, LCSW, are medical social workers who are employed by Salud to provide medical social work services. They provide almost no traditional psychotherapy and only limited brief interventions in the medical setting. Their offices are in the medical practice setting.

☐ Laura Schwartz, LCSW, CACIII, is a psychotherapist and case manager employed by the Health District of Northern Larimer County Integrated Care Program. She provides primarily traditional psychotherapy and case management in collaboration with the medical professionals (Level III).

☐ Scott Wylie, PsyD, is a psychologist who practices at Salud 3 days a week. He is employed by the Health District of

Northern Larimer County Integrated Care Program. Two of his three days focus on traditional psychotherapy and evaluation provided in his office one floor above the examination rooms (Level IV). One day is devoted to the initiation of a pilot "Behavioral Medicine Provider" program (Level V). For half of this day, he conducts brief (30-minute) consultation and intervention appointments with patients referred by medical professionals. The other half is unscheduled so he can see same-day referrals and conduct consultation with medical professionals. Dr. Wylie stresses that he is "interruptible" while in the Behavioral Medicine Provider role and provides these services in the medical setting.

☐   Malinda Trujillo, MS, is a practicum student from the doctoral program in counseling psychology at Colorado State University. She sees patients primarily in traditional psychotherapy on the 2 days a week she is at Salud (Level III/IV).

During a group interview, the psychotherapists at Fort Collins acknowledged it can be difficult to traverse their various commitments and home system requirements to work with the general Salud population. They each have clinical quotas and have to follow the documentation, service inclusion, and other regulations of their home system. As one psychotherapist remarked, "We all come from different systems and have different rules that we have to follow that affect patient care. Different systems have different mandates."

Despite these challenges, the Fort Collins staff echoes many of the benefits that other psychotherapists noted about practicing collaboratively. One psychotherapist stated, "There is cross-pollination between medical professionals and psychotherapists. Everyone teaches, everyone learns." Another psychotherapist stated, "When I practiced traditionally, I felt like I was missing something, and this is the missing piece. This is more holistic and dynamic. We can do a lot more preventative work." Many of the psychotherapists noted that they enjoyed the variety of patients they see in a primary care setting, the sense of sharing care with another professional, and the opportunity to fulfill different roles in helping patients achieve wellness.

Some of the psychotherapists had little opportunity to integrate themselves into medical care because of their various responsibilities. Even so, they noted that they have altered their psychotherapy mind-set and techniques to work more effectively in primary care. One psychotherapist noted, "I've had to change my conceptualization of therapy. I had to change my expectations of where people are, what I can do. It is totally different than a campus counseling center where people are more introspective." Generally the psychotherapists felt their work was briefer than traditional psychotherapy and more solution focused. The psychiatrist noted that he is "interruptible" at Salud. He noted that the situation sometimes "flies in the face of analytic training and a focus on the therapeutic relationship. It can be a sacrifice, but in the long run, you do more real-time care that really helps people."

The interview with the Fort Collins psychotherapists illustrates that it takes hard work and flexibility for public mental health and medical systems to create a collaborative environment. Unfortunately, many larger system issues such as separate funding streams and system rules can interfere with truly integrating services. At the same time, their words illustrate just how rewarding these psychotherapists find the work they do in the medical setting and how this paradigm shift affects mental health services. Although these psychotherapists have encountered obstacles to integration, they have worked through many issues to the benefit of both patients and the health care delivery system as a whole.

Conclusion

Most psychotherapists in private practice or traditional community mental health settings may have difficulty imagining how their work and role would change if they were to practice in a medical setting. For the uninitiated, this chapter outlined various levels of collaboration and integration that can occur in colocated practices and the pros and cons of each. We reviewed the larger system factors that can facilitate or impede intensive collaboration and integration of services, so psychotherapists who want to change their system's level of integration have information about the work that must be done before implementing an integration project. We reviewed the experiences of psychotherapists who have attempted to shift to integrated services in both the private and public health sectors. These experiences highlight the mindset and role changes integrated psychotherapists must make to optimize integration and how larger system issues can facilitate or interfere with this process. Finally, these psychotherapists share their impressions of the differential effect of integrated and traditional psychotherapy practices and the characteristics of integrated care they enjoy and find challenging.

III

Clinical Examples of Collaboration

How does collaborative care work in the real world? The cases discussed in the chapters that follow illustrate collaborative approaches between psychotherapists and medical professionals that altered the course of psychotherapy and medical treatment. In each case, the professionals communicated, shared care, and consulted with each other as they attempted to provide optimal patient care.

Although the care provided is not the norm, the patient's stories and presentations are common. These are not one-in-a-thousand cases in which collaboration was a key element to success. They are the types of patients and problems that are seen regularly in both medical and mental health settings. The levels of collaboration vary, depending on the needs of each patient and the preexisting relationship between the psychotherapist and medical professional. The variation illustrates how the level of collaboration changes according to patient needs.

The first case illustrates collaborative treatment for severe recurrent depression, a common scenario in primary care. Christine had a history of multiple depressive episodes when she came to see her physician regarding chronic medical conditions. Her physician detected a recurrence of her depression but recognized that Christine needed treatment beyond her expertise. Fortunately for Christine, her physician had an established relationship with a psychotherapist. Her story illustrates how collaborative care can facilitate care of a patient struggling with dysthymia and depression.

The second case focuses on pediatric-based care. Many parents bring their child to a primary care medical professional first for evaluation of attention-deficit/hyperactivity disorder (ADHD). As with many other challenges of childhood and child rearing, parents turn to their trusted pediatrician or family doctor to help them discern the appropriate level of concern and how and when to intervene. The story of Kevin and his family demonstrates how disruptive ADHD can be and how families can become mired in problematic interactional patterns and roles. In this case, Kevin's pediatrician recognized that family therapy was the best modality to target these patterns. She used her established relationship with a family therapist to facilitate his care.

The third case illustrates a team approach to treating a patient with anorexia nervosa. Anorexia is potentially fatal and can have devastating psychological and physiologic effects. Early detection is key. Most patients with eating disorders, and often their families, are in denial of the problem, which complicates the mental health referral. Medical professionals often are the first to evaluate the patient for weight loss and "eating problems." They must work with patients to convince them that they have a problem and need to seek mental health services. Postreferral the various medical professionals must work collaboratively and function as a team. A team approach can strengthen recommendations that may be difficult for the patient or their family to accept. It also allows the professionals to share the burden and anxiety associated with treating a patient with a potentially life-threatening disorder. Sureka's story of anorexia treatment illustrates these points.

The fourth case illustrates intensive collaboration to meet the needs of a patient with complicated, chronic problems. It tells the story of Sergio, a lawyer forced to stop practicing because of chronic pain and poorly controlled diabetes. Chronic lower back pain and diabetes are two of the most common chronic concerns in primary care. Each has been associated with increased symptoms of depression and anxiety, decreased functioning and quality of life, and a high level of general psychosocial distress (Bair et al., 2004). These patients can be difficult for primary care medical professionals to refer to a psychotherapist for a variety of reasons. Patients feel blamed for the way they feel about their medical concerns and for their difficulty managing the demands of their disease. They may feel that the medical professional does not appreciate the impact of illness on their life. They may even fear that acknowledging the role of psychological factors will reduce the medical professional's motivation to relieve their physical symptoms. Finally, when chronic pain is treated with narcotic medications that can lead to dependence or addiction, the potential for conflict and miscommunication is high. This case is an excellent example of the interplay of chronic illness, chronic pain, and the role and identity loss that can occur when illness intrudes on a person's life.

We invite the reader to consider how the collaboration affected the patient, psychotherapist, and medical professional. How might the story have unfolded differently without this communication, sharing, and consultation? Beginning collaborators might consider what they would do in similar circumstances or how they can apply these techniques with current patients.

7

Too Many Stressors: A Case of Major Depression at Midlife

Jan Downs-Barrett, MS, APR, is a licensed marriage and family therapist in private practice. Julianne Lucco, MD, is a family physician. Ms. Downs-Barrett's practice is a few miles away from the health center where Dr. Lucco sees patients. As a result of this proximity, Ms. Downs-Barrett receives many referrals from the health center and over time has developed relationships with a number of the physicians who practice there. Julia Hanson, MD, is a psychiatrist who works for the outpatient mental health services arm of the hospital to which Dr. Lucco admits patients. Dr. Hanson was relatively new to the hospital, and did not have an established relationship with either Dr. Lucco or Ms. Downs-Barrett.

Case Background

Christine was a 58-year-old woman who had struggled with mild to moderate depression throughout most of her adult life. Despite her "down times," she was quite successful in her job as a real estate agent. She had been a patient of Dr. Lucco for many years, and had been maintained on a low-dose course of antidepressant medication. Christine saw Dr. Lucco somewhat regularly for monitoring of some minor chronic conditions, including hypertension and obesity.

Christine was a divorced mother of two grown daughters. One of her daughters had a history of addiction but had successfully attended rehabilitation. She had positive relationships with her daughters but did not see them on a day-to-day basis.

Christine scheduled an appointment with Dr. Lucco in early January for a mild physical complaint. When Dr. Lucco saw Christine, she immediately knew that she had slipped into a significant major depressive episode. Christine was tearful as she discussed a stressful situation at work in which she felt the new management was asking her to behave in an unethical manner. Dr. Lucco assessed Christine's level of depression and found that she was not sleeping well, had difficulty concentrating, and often felt tearful. She had been isolating herself socially outside of work. She denied having thoughts of suicide but acknowledged that she wished "[she] could just stay in bed and sleep all of the time." She felt completely overwhelmed by the demands of her job and put so much energy into functioning at work that she had little energy left for anything else. She was fearful that she was going to lose her job, in part because of the specific ethics concerns and in part because she recognized she was not performing at her typical level. She felt she was "at the end of [her] rope."

Christine felt she needed short-term disability from work and needed Dr. Lucco's help to obtain it. She felt a break from the stressful work environment would make her "feel better." Although Dr. Lucco acknowledged that Christine needed a break from work, she also strongly encouraged Christine to increase her antidepressant medication and to see a psychotherapist. Christine was willing to increase her medication but was resistant to psychotherapy. She did not feel that talking to someone would help. She described a negative experience with couple's therapy when she and her ex-husband were divorcing and did not want to risk another negative experience. Dr. Lucco gave Christine a new prescription and suggested a follow-up appointment in 1 week.

The Collaborative Effort

A week later, Christine was clearly worse. She had been unable to sleep and looked a bit disheveled and extremely depressed.

Dr. Lucco again suggested psychotherapy, and Christine now was willing to take a chance. Dr. Lucco suggested that Christine see Downs-Barrett, emphasizing that she trusted her and felt strongly that the therapy would be helpful to Christine. She obtained a release of information to Ms. Downs-Barrett. She encouraged Christine to continue to take the higher dose of medicine, reminding her that the dosage change would take several weeks to take effect.

Christine called Ms. Downs-Barrett the following day. Fortunately, Dr. Lucco had spoken with her about the need for Christine to be seen as soon as possible. Ms. Downs-Barrett made room for Christine in her private practice within a week. Dr. Lucco was worried about Christine. She knew in her gut that she was sinking much faster than Dr. Lucco's training had equipped her handle. She was relieved that Ms. Downs-Barrett made room for Christine in her schedule immediately.

When Christine arrived for her appointment, Ms. Downs-Barrett understood why Dr. Lucco had been so worried. She knew from Dr. Lucco's description that Christine was a professional woman who was usually well groomed and polished. Christine presented as downtrodden and tired looking. She had difficulty maintaining concentration, seeming distracted and nervous during the appointment. Christine stated that the only reason she agreed to come was because she trusted Dr. Lucco and felt so miserable that she had little to lose. She said she came to the appointment partly out of a sense of loyalty to Dr. Lucco and to reassure her because she knew her doctor was concerned.

Initially, Christine said she felt the primary cause of her depression was her stressful work situation. She would answer questions about her social situation and family history but then state, "I don't want to talk about all of that." She would then tell stories about her family that were clearly connected to her lifelong struggle with depression. Throughout the course of therapy, Christine maintained that she did not want to discuss long-term issues, in part because she believed that her depression was due to her current situation. Yet she tended to talk at length about her history, needing to share it. Only later was she able to see the discrepancy between her stated desire to focus on the present and her tendency to focus on the past.

As Christine began to trust Ms. Downs-Barrett, she disclosed a painful family history of emotional deprivation in the context of great material wealth. She had been born long after her siblings, and her mother made little effort to hide her dismay at having a baby late in life. Christine's father doted on her until his untimely death when she was 4 years old. Her mother experienced serious depression as well, often requiring months of hospitalization. Because of the family's wealth, Christine's mother often stayed at private long-term care psychiatric hospitals. Christine was shuffled from relative to relative. Her siblings were old enough to be independent, so she suffered this fate alone, with no constants in her life. She vividly remembered hearing family members argue over who would take her next and feeling deeply unloved and unwanted.

Ms. Downs-Barrett encouraged Christine to share some aspects of her childhood history with Dr. Lucco to help her understand the depth of her sense of loss and deprivation. As she had with Ms. Downs-Barrett, Christine would state a desire to avoid talking about her painful past then would be almost compelled to tell Dr. Lucco stories that illustrated her deprivation. Christine understood that Dr. Lucco and Ms. Downs-Barrett discussed her and expressed a sense of being taken care of by them. She overtly stated on numerous occasions that it meant a great deal to her that the two professionals helping her were working as a team. Only later did she understand that Dr. Lucco and Ms. Down-Barrett's caring and teamwork was in stark contrast to her disjointed childhood and the lack of harmony and teamwork among the people who parented her.

Ms. Downs-Barrett noted that although Christine was bright and insightful, she avoided discussion of her past as it related to the current situation, perhaps because it was so painful to her. Ms. Downs-Barrett was thankful that Dr. Lucco so actively supported the psychotherapy process because it motivated Christine to work through her fears and reassured her that both professionals were there to support her and to work toward her best interest.

Despite weekly psychotherapy and ongoing collaboration between Dr. Lucco and Ms. Downs-Barrett, Ms. Downs-Barrett was not satisfied with Christine's progress. She and Dr. Lucco agreed that Christine needed a psychotropic medication consultation. Dr.

Lucco regularly referred patients to the psychiatric services affiliated with the hospital to which she admitted patients. Dr. Lucco called Dr. Hanson to arrange the referral and provide background information.

Christine was reluctant to see a psychiatrist, in part secondary to her mother's long psychiatric history and a fear that she was going to follow her mother's sad path. Once again, Dr. Lucco used her relationship with Christine to convince her to follow through on the referral. Christine ultimately saw Dr. Hanson in midsummer. She did not immediately connect with the psychiatrist and did not want to return. However, when Christine learned that Dr. Hanson had called Dr. Lucco to discuss her impressions and recommendations, Christine felt some sense of trust in Dr. Hanson. Again, she expressed a sense of being cared for when the professionals worked together to help her.

Because Christine's depression had not responded to various selective serotonin reuptake inhibitors prescribed by Dr. Lucco, the psychiatrist started her on an antidepressant and a stimulant medication. Combinations of medications were far beyond Dr. Lucco's comfort zone when prescribing psychotropic medications. The quick referral to a psychiatrist and the relatively quick entrance into psychiatric care in a nonemergent situation was one factor that set the stage for Christine to begin the road to recovery.

Dr. Lucco appreciated the psychiatrists' communication for two important reasons. First, it helped her coordinate care and support the work that Christine needed to do with Dr. Hanson. Second, the fact that Dr. Hanson reached out to Dr. Lucco to support a team approach reassured Christine that Dr. Hanson would be helpful. The collaboration superseded Christine's lack of connection to Dr. Hanson during the initial interview, setting the stage for her to continue her psychiatric care.

Through the fall, Christine saw Dr. Lucco, Ms. Downs-Barrett, and Dr. Hanson on a regular basis. She slowly started to feel better. She ultimately decided to leave her firm, feeling that she could not compromise her ethics. Her work and relationship to her customers had always been a source of great pride and satisfaction to Christine, and she struggled to maintain her sense of self-worth and identity without her job.

With Ms. Down-Barrett's support, Christine brought her daughters to a few psychotherapy appointments. The dialogue focused on issues in their relationships and helping Christine's daughters to understand their mother's difficulties. Again, this was in sharp contrast to Christine's experiences of her mother's depressive episodes. No one had ever explained her mother's depressions to her, so Christine always felt she was to blame. It meant a great deal to Christine that her daughters understood her experience and knew they were not to blame. This was particularly important in the context of her daughter's history of substance abuse. During these appointments, Ms. Downs-Barrett had the opportunity to educate Christine's daughters about depression, given their vulnerability. One of her daughters accompanied Christine to a few medical appointments and helped Dr. Lucco assess the affects of the interventions.

Christine stopped seeing Ms. Downs-Barrett about 10 months after the initial referral. Throughout the therapy, Christine expressed a desire to focus on the present but would frequently talk about her painful childhood experiences. She did begin to understand that the rejection and emotional deprivation she experienced as a child were not a rejection of her as a person but a consequence of her mother's emotional difficulties, her father's death, and the circumstances of her birth. She came to some peace with the situation. She understood that her mother did the best she was able to do, albeit with painful consequences for Christine.

Dr. Lucco continues to see Christine and to monitor her level of depression. Approximately 18 months after her initial presentation with more severe depression, Christine decided to return to a simpler antidepressant regimen. With Dr. Lucco's close monitoring, she has been able to maintain a high level of functioning and with relatively little depressive symptomology for over a year. Dr. Lucco and Christine continue to meet regularly to monitor her chronic medical conditions and depressive symptoms.

Conclusion

Christine's story illustrates numerous benefits of collaboration in providing optimal care. Consider the following:

☐ The shared history and continuous relationship that Christine had with Dr. Lucco facilitated diagnosis of her major depression. If Dr. Lucco did not know Christine well, she probably would not have recognized that Christine's presentation for a simple medical concern was different from her baseline. Also, Dr. Lucco was aware that Christine had struggled with depression in the past and that she had a significant family history of depression, all risk factors for a major depressive episode.

☐ Christine probably would not have followed through on the referral to Ms. Downs-Barrett if she did not know and trust Dr. Lucco and if Dr. Lucco did not know and trust Ms. Downs-Barrett. In this situation, Dr. Lucco served as a connector between Christine and Ms. Downs-Barrett. Christine had a stated mistrust of the mental health field because of her own and her mother's experiences with psychiatric treatment. Christine's trusting relationship with Dr. Lucco set the stage for her to be willing to see a psychotherapist. This may not have occurred without Dr. Lucco's encouragement and direct recommendation of a specific person.

☐ Christine's request for a disability allowance from work could have posed a significant challenge for Dr. Lucco. Primary care medical professionals often provide patients with the necessary documentation for short breaks from work when they are either too ill or too stressed to perform their work. However, work release request negotiations between medical professionals and patients can often become contentious. It would have been difficult for Dr. Lucco to continue to justify work release for a mental health concern if Christine had been unwilling to obtain mental health services. Fortunately, because Dr. Lucco's preexisting relationship with Ms. Downs-Barrett facilitated the referral, Dr. Lucco never had to give Christine an ultimatum about seeking psychotherapy.

Unfortunately, physicians often feel backed into a corner when a patient requests documentation for a work break secondary to mental health concerns but will not accept a psychotherapy referral. In the context of disability issues, medical professionals must force the issue of mental health treatment for patients because they cannot continue to sign work release papers for emotional disability if the patient does not seek psychotherapy. More unfortunately, many patients experience such ultimatums negatively, harming the medical professional–patient relationship at a time the patient most needs support and understanding.

☐ The relationship and collaboration between Dr. Lucco and Ms. Downs-Barrett gave Christine a sense of comfort that the professionals caring for her were working as a team. This was likely comforting to Christine on multiple levels. Her loss of function secondary to her severe depression was frightening to her and left her feeling extremely vulnerable. Her treatment team was like a safety net waiting to catch her if she fell farther. In addition, the collaboration and teamwork was the opposite of the parenting she had received. Many patients who have experienced abandonment resist referral to psychotherapy because they fear they will lose the support and relationship with their medical professional once they connect with a psychotherapist. Their fear of being "punted" to another professional sometimes interferes with connecting to a psychotherapist. Christine was reassured that Dr. Lucco would still be involved in her care, and still "cared for" her, even if other professionals were working with her. This connection was reinforced when Christine consulted with a psychiatrist. Although she did not immediately like the psychiatrist, she was reassured that Dr. Hanson involved Dr. Lucco in her decision making and recommendations. Again, the psychiatrist's connection and relationship with Dr. Lucco gave her credibility and created an expectation for Christine that she would receive excellent care.

☐ Both professionals found it comforting to know that they were working with another professional whose clinical judgment they trusted. Christine was severely depressed and did not immediately respond to treatment. Although she denied suicidal ideation, both Dr. Lucco and Ms. Downs-Barrett noted that they were concerned about Christine throughout the course of treatment. They each were reassured when they knew Christine would be seeing the other professional, both for the extra support it provided to Christine and because they then could com-

pare impressions and ideas for future treatment. Dr. Lucco
noted that she would have felt overwhelmed by caring for
Christine on her own but found it far less stressful because
of Ms. Down-Barrett's and Dr. Hanson's involvement.

☐ Christine needed medical treatment that was outside the
expertise and purview of her family physician. She likely
would not have continued working with the Dr. Hanson
if she had not practiced collaboratively with Dr. Lucco.
Often, when patients do not follow up on treatment, psychotherapists believe the patient either improved, pursued
another referral, or "wasn't ready" for mental health intervention. In reality, patients lost to mental health follow-
up often turn to their primary care medical professional.
Sometimes they may get suboptimal care because their
needs exceed the expertise and time constraints of the primary care medical professional. If Dr. Hanson had not initiated contact with Dr. Lucco, this is likely the course that
Christine's treatment would have taken.

☐ Christine needed long-term monitoring but was not willing to stay connected to the mental health treatment system. Because Dr. Lucco was directly and closely involved
with Christine's mental health treatment, she was comfortable, and prepared, to help Christine self-monitor after mental health treatment terminated.

Most patients do not receive the kind of team treatment that
Christine obtained. However, the collaboration was a critical element in her decision to begin and maintain mental health care
and in helping Christine come to peace with her history of emotional deprivation and disengaged family relationships.

8

The Underachieving Son: A Case of Attention-Deficit/ Hyperactivity Disorder

Joni Haley, MS, is a marriage and family therapist who has been in private practice for more than 10 years. Suzanne Boulter, MD, is a pediatrician in a group medical practice in the same building. Ms. Haley and Dr. Boulter first met when Ms. Haley referred a young patient to Dr. Boulter for medical evaluation after another patient of Ms. Haley's told her about positive experiences with Dr. Boulter as her children's pediatrician. Since then, the two professionals have had the opportunity to collaborate successfully on several other pediatric cases.

Case Background

The current case collaboration began with Dr. Boulter's recent appointment with Richard, a 14-year-old boy, who was having continuing behavioral problems resulting from attention-deficit/ hyperactivity disorder (ADHD), developmental issues involving Richard's short stature, and family dynamics. Dr. Boulter has known Richard and his younger brother, Randy, since birth. She was well acquainted with Richard's parents.

The family was upper middle class, and the parents modeled and valued high achievement. The father, Carl, traveled often for his job as vice president of operations for a local company. The mother, Linda, worked part time, but her priority and the majority of her time was invested in staying at home to take care of Richard and Randy.

Several years before this most recent appointment, Dr. Boulter had diagnosed Richard as having ADHD. At that time, she was aware of the family dynamics that indicated she should refer the family for family therapy in addition to prescribing medication for ADHD. However, when she broached the topic, the parents adamantly refused to consider this. They were willing to try medication for ADHD, so she decided to bide her time and try referring the family again later for family therapy.

Richard, according to his parents, had never quite lived up to the high expectations his parents had for him. He struggled in school and barely made passing grades. He had physical problems, including an awkward gait and short stature, that prevented him from participating in sports. Randy, however, was described by his parents as gifted, both academically and athletically. His parents were as proud of Randy and his accomplishments as they were frustrated and disturbed with Richard's problems and lack of progress in overcoming them.

The parents first met Dr. Boulter as their pediatrician when Richard was born and continued his and later Randy's pediatric care with her. They had come to trust her a great deal as a physician over this long period of time. Dr. Boulter reviewed some of the history of her involvement with Richard and his family. She noted that Richard's long history of ADHD had intersected with his being of short stature. She also believed, from her observation of Richard and his family, that the parents treated the two boys differently, favoring Randy, which complicated the family dynamics and contributed to Richard's behavioral and academic problems.

Despite these factors, Richard had been doing well on stimulant medication for ADHD until a few years before the current crisis. At that time, he began to have behavior problems at home and at school. She had adjusted his medications, and he improved. Then, after a yearlong period of improvement, Richard's attention difficulties in school were again hampering his academic progress. At that time, his father was traveling more for work, and this was particularly hard on Richard, who felt closer to his father than to his mother. His father changed his work schedule to be home more, and Richard improved.

The Collaborative Effort

Before this, as noted previously, Dr. Boulter had encouraged the parents to pursue family therapy, but they had consistently refused. She thought that they had not wanted to admit there were any problems in their family. It was hard for her in these situations because she could see the tension building within a family, contributing to a patient's problems, and she felt responsible for doing something about it. However, she knew that her time was limited and that her skills were not those of a family therapist. Fortunately she had good referral relationships with psychotherapists in the community, including one who worked for the mental health center in her building. However, she knew that the family had to be willing to take the elevator to a different floor. In such cases, motivating them to do so was no small feat.

When Richard entered middle school, his concentration and difficulty in completing homework increased. The tension within the family also increased, and Richard was enrolled in a private tutoring program. The following year Richard's behavior significantly deteriorated both at home and at school. At the same time, Richard received testosterone shots from the pediatric endocrinologist to jump-start puberty and increase height. The pediatrician and endocrinologist met to discuss Richard's case and agreed that the testosterone was at least partially to blame for the changes. Richard's parents stopped the shots about halfway through the full series.

Because Richard's behavior was still extremely problematic, his parent's reluctantly accepted a referral for family therapy. Because Ms. Haley was out on temporary medical leave, Dr. Boulter referred the family to a community mental health center with which she had had a positive experience. An intern saw Richard and his family for four sessions over the summer. However, the family did not make much progress and terminated in August. The problems escalated with the start of the school year, and the parents again were reluctantly willing to try therapy again. Given the difficulty in engaging the family in therapy and one false start, Dr. Boulter was relieved that Ms. Haley had returned from medical leave and she could be more sure of the quality of treatment the family would receive. After Dr. Boulter met with the family in September, she called Ms. Haley and described the case, with the parents' permission. Ms. Haley agreed to see the family for an evaluation visit and, if appropriate, would make time in her schedule to see the family on an ongoing basis.

Dr. Boulter faxed over her case note from the September meeting:

> Patient returns for follow up of ADHD, behavior problems, and poor school performance. Patient now attends private high school and his progress reports indicate poor performance. Mother and patient interviewed separately today. Mom was teary and reports that the patient has no friends, is lazy with both schoolwork and physical activities, and does not comply with family expectations for even simple chores. He is not eating a lot and sleeps a lot. He reportedly has asked to move out and go into the foster care system. Father travels a lot with his job, leaving mother to run the house and boys. Sibling Randy has no issues with learning, ADHD, or behavior. Patient himself reports constant yelling in the household. He admits to doing little schoolwork. He does feel sad some of the time and was surprised to learn he had lost four pounds in weight. He finds schoolwork hard but admits that he is not really trying. Both patient and mother are willing to accept another counseling referral. Goals would be to sort out questions of significant depression plus start to deal with family interaction issues. Will try to arrange.

The situation within the family had reached a critical point. Richard was threatening to walk out or be transferred to another family. His mother, Linda, was overwhelmed and reported considering leaving the family. Systemically, Richard was an underfunctioning 14-year-old in a family of high achievers. Richard's parents had, at his request, enrolled him in a local private high school well known for its high standards. All hoped he would thrive in the smaller classes and attention. His behavior at home was marked by passive aggression (e.g., saying he would do something but waiting for his mother to do it) and outright defiance. He also showed symptoms of depression: difficulty getting motivated, losing weight without trying, low energy, and poor concentration. His affect was flat, and he displayed psychomotor retardation. He reported having few friends.

Richard's parents were disappointed in him. In particular, Linda had become increasingly furious with him, to the degree that she admitted that she could not find one thing that she liked about him. Linda and her husband, Carl, had attempted to impose restrictions on Richard, and they had become increasingly punitive and harsh. He was not allowed to spend time watching favorite television shows with the rest of the family as punishment. His mother locked him out of the house until "his attitude improved," and he stayed outside in November for three hours. The level of conflict in the home had increased significantly, not only between Richard and Linda but between Linda and Carl as well. Linda was resentful of Carl's travels and felt as if she was dealing with Richard on her own much of the time.

Haley initiated the therapy by meeting with Richard and his family. Although the family remained skeptical about the efficacy of therapy, their trust of Dr. Boulter's opinion that it could help motivated them to try again. Ms. Haley assessed Richard for depression and felt that he could benefit from an antidepressant in addition to family therapy. She assisted in setting up a visit to Dr. Boulter to prescribe Zoloft. She describes the therapy process and outcomes.

> My first task was to decrease the tension in the home. Linda, in particular, was feeling very responsible and blamed, so when I met with Richard's parents alone, I allowed them to express their disappointment about Richard—to grieve that they did not have a perfect child. Only after they were allowed to grieve were they able to accept Richard for who he is. I encouraged Linda to look for one positive thing to compliment Richard on every day, acknowledging that she may have to stretch to find something. I also supported their efforts to limit Richard's television viewing but encouraged them to allow Richard to participate in family viewing time, as well as finding other activities in which Richard could join.

When I met with Richard alone, my first priority was to give him a positive experience with an adult so that he might be more open to looking at his part in the negativity that was swirling around him. He definitely felt as if everyone was out to get him, and nothing he could ever do would make a difference. He initially denied fearing his mother or being sad but was able to acknowledge that he wished it could be different. This gave me some leverage to start to think about what he could do differently.

When I met with them as a family, which was part of every session, we focused on areas of concern and strategies for making changes. One of the biggest areas of conflict was around Richard's homework. Linda's efforts to organize Richard were increasingly met with opposition. In fact, this was isomorphic with other areas in their relationship: to the degree that Richard did less, Linda became more controlling, which caused Richard to either withdraw further or to become hostile and aggressive. Particularly when Carl was away, it was hard for Linda to let go of even the smallest transgression from Richard. In an effort to take some of the pressure off, I tried to engage the guidance counselor in setting up a system for Richard's work to be monitored at school rather than at home. In addition to getting more support from school, I encouraged Carl to find ways to be "more present in his absence" while he was away on business. He phoned every night and spoke with Richard and problem solved some areas of concern with him.

After a few weeks of relative success with homework and behavior at school, the tensions in the family were remarkably decreased. Richard expressed the wish that his parents would back off even further, but they were concerned that he would not follow through. I suggested an experiment; Richard arrived home from school before Linda got home from work 2 days a week. Typically Linda would call Richard and instruct him to do his homework, yet he rarely did so. She agreed not to call, and he agreed to do his homework without a reminder. If he had not completed it by the time she got home, then he would have to sit down and do it right away. The next session, they reported success, as well as decreased tension.

There was a real turning point in therapy after the Thanksgiving holiday. When the family visited Linda's family, her sister asked Richard to live with them. They came to therapy saying that Richard was considering it. Oddly enough, Linda and Carl felt as if they should allow this to be Richard's decision—a sharp contrast to their previous attempts to control even small areas of his life. They told him they did not want him to go. During the session, Richard asked them why. It was a breathtaking moment in therapy. Linda said, "Because we love you, Richard. We always wanted you, and we want you still."

After this session, Linda and Carl were more clearly "on Richard's side." They realized that the private high school was not as supportive of Richard as they claimed to be. They felt the school was trying to edge Richard out without kicking him out because of the financial implications. They struggled with keeping Richard accountable for his behavior while supporting him if he was being treated unfairly. They decided to investigate enrolling him in the local public high school. This was initially going to be Richard's decision to make. However, after a discussion, they realized that this was their decision. In the end, Richard was enrolled in the public school and did well there. He joined the band and reconnected with friends. He was evaluated for special education services and received assistance with his academic subjects.

Throughout the therapy, Ms. Haley communicated with Dr. Boulter about the family's progress. She sent copies of the initial meeting and updated progress notes. Because they had worked together previously, Ms. Haley knew that Dr. Boulter wanted to be involved in the treatment. Richard saw Dr. Boulter four times for medication management during the therapy, and she was able to support the themes and progress in therapy during those visits.

Conclusion

Collaboration may have altered the course and outcome of this case in a number of ways.

- [ ] Dr. Boulter recognized that Richard's problems were unlikely to recede unless family interactional patterns changed. Rather than focusing on finding a "silver bullet" medication to solve all the problems, Dr. Boulter assessed the context of the problem and its effects on everyone in the family. Her familiarity with various psychotherapy modalities helped Dr. Boulter refer the family to the appropriate intervention. Many medical professionals are not as savvy as Dr. Boulter, in part because of a lack of exposure to different professionals and modalities. Also, Dr. Boulter may have been more motivated to pursue these issues because she knew she could easily refer the family if necessary. Many medical professionals are hesitant to "go fishing" for problems when they are afraid they can't manage the "fish" once they find it. Dr. Boulter knew she had accessible backup that would help her manage what she found.

☐ The advantage of the long-term relationship with the pediatrician enabled the initial and follow-up referral. This family, like many individuals and families, did not want to start therapy. Dr. Boulter had to work hard and wait for a crisis to create the opportunity to press the referral. The initial false start and poor connection with the first therapist could have derailed this process completely. Rather, the relationship between Dr. Boulter and Ms. Haley enabled the pediatrician to promote the psychotherapist to the family as someone who could help them with their difficulties. It seems highly unlikely that the family would have sought therapy again if this aspect of the case had been missing.

☐ Provision of antidepressants to teenagers is controversial. Pediatricians are reluctant to initiate this treatment without having a psychotherapist involved. In this case, Haley was able to assess Richard and suggest consideration of antidepressant medication. She also helped the family watch for any troubling side effects of the medication.

☐ The psychotherapist was aware that Dr. Boulter wanted to be kept informed about the therapy. The communication enabled Dr. Boulter to talk about the therapeutic goals during medical visits. Dr. Boulter's familiarity with the family dynamics helped her monitor their functioning posttherapy. In addition, her appreciation of the high stress levels in the family may have spurred her to assess other members for stress-related disorders.

The Best Little Girl in the World: A Case of Anorexia Nervosa

Deborah Wheeler, MD, is the medical director of a school infirmary at a prestigious independent boarding high school. She is a psychiatrist who is also trained in adolescent medicine. She is responsible for all aspects of the students' health. She works with a multidisciplinary team, including nurse practitioners, registered nurses, a nutritionist, and several psychologists. She frequently consults with psychologists and psychiatrists outside of the school when specialists are required.

Jane King, RD, is a nutritionist in private practice in the community. She frequently collaborates with Dr. Wheeler and other members of the treatment team. Her expertise is working with adolescents with eating disorders and with adolescent athletes.

Irene Ellis, PhD, is a clinical psychologist in private practice in the community. She works with adolescents and adults specializing in eating disorders. She is frequently referred patients from the school and sees them either at the school infirmary or, if possible, in her office.

Case Background

Sureka Shah was a 15-year-old Pakistani American who left her home in Los Angeles during her freshman year of high school to attend a prestigious boarding school in Connecticut. She was the older of two sisters. They were the first generation born in the United States. Sureka's father and mother were born in Lahore, Pakistan. Her father was an international investment banker, and her mother came from a wealthy family of philanthropists. Both parents traveled almost constantly to Asia and Africa for their work. They had family living all over the world, many of whom were quite accomplished in their fields. They communicated with their children and each other using e-mail and mobile phones. Both parents were frequently on different continents from each other and their children. The family had homes in Los Angeles, Paris, and Karachi but rarely spent time at any of them.

Sureka seemed to make a good transition to boarding school life and was doing well academically and socially in her freshman year. She was outgoing and involved in school activities. She had high academic aspirations and hoped to attend an Ivy League university. She was taking difficult courses, including two languages. She was working on several time-consuming community service projects that she planned to work on until she graduated. She had a strong ethic of social responsibility from both her parents, but particularly from her mother. Every summer while she was in middle school, she and her mother had gone to Africa and worked on humanitarian projects.

In September, Sureka returned to school for her sophomore year after spending the summer in Africa working with young girls who were pregnant after being raped. She had been sick for several weeks with diarrhea and decreased appetite. She decided to run cross-country track and began training with her team, even though she did not feel well. In November, Sureka was asked by her house master to go to the school health center because of weight loss that had become noticeable to her track coach, teachers, and peers. She looked tired and depressed. She was 5 foot, 9 inches, tall and weighed 115 pounds with her clothes on. She had arrived at school in September weighing 125 pounds. This was a 10-pound weight loss from her freshman year when she had been a healthy weight of 135 pounds. Dr. Wheeler did a thorough assessment considering anorexia, as well as other medical problems, in her differential diagnosis. She was concerned that Sureka might have contracted a gastrointestinal problem in Africa. She initially focused on the medical complications of altered nutrition. All of Sureka's medical tests were ultimately normal.

Dr. Wheeler knew Sureka from treating her for allergies and colds during her freshman year. She was struck by how an adolescent who had been cheerful and outgoing was now pale, guarded, and withdrawn. She spent considerable time talking to Sureka to understand the context of this weight loss that was beginning to look like anorexia. Sureka denied feeling anxious or depressed. She did admit to being irritable and annoyed with her friends and preferring solitude. She did acknowledge lethargy, dizziness, and missing menstrual periods. Sureka expressed surprise that she had lost 25 pounds since her freshman year. She talked about eating "healthy" and had become a vegan over the summer. She minimized her weight loss throughout the interview and denied that she was trying to lose weight. She was participating in cross-country track and sometimes ran by herself "to get in more miles." Sureka thought she was "too heavy" to be a successful cross-country runner and was intent on making her father proud of her.

Sureka told Dr. Wheeler that both her parents were "very healthy." The family had participated in various runs and bike rides to benefit social causes and was excited that she was running track. She said that she and her father "loved to eat, too much" but noted her father's recent intentional weight loss of more than 30 pounds. She did not know of anyone in the family with eating problems, except she thought her cousin may have had some "eating issues" while attending an Ivy League university.

By the end of the appointment, Dr. Wheeler felt reasonably certain that Sureka had symptoms consistent with anorexia. She told Sureka that she would call her parents and let them know about her weight loss. She restricted her from exercise or sports participation until her weight stabilized. Sureka was upset and angry that Dr. Wheeler was calling her parents and tried to convince her not to restrict her exercise. However, she did not seem worried or concerned about her health.

The Collaborative Effort

Dr. Wheeler called Sureka's mother the next day to get more history and discuss her assessment and diagnostic impressions. Mrs. Shah was surprised that her daughter had lost weight but did not seem particularly concerned. She focused on her daughter's efforts to eat only healthy food. Dr. Wheeler told Mrs. Shah that Sureka's weight loss and body image distortion were serious symptoms consistent with an eating disorder. She recommended that Sureka see Dr. Ellis as soon as possible. She explained that Dr. Ellis specialized in eating disorders and stressed that she trusted her on the basis of her past successful care of other students. She explained that psychotherapy was the cornerstone of treatment and would be necessary for Sureka to stay in school. She also recommended that Sureka see Ms. King for further evaluation of her eating patterns. Initially, Mrs. Shah resisted the psychotherapy referral but accepted the nutrition evaluation. Eventually, Dr. Wheeler was able to convince Mrs. Shah to agree to the psychotherapy referral as well.

Several days later, Sureka met with Ms. King. Her assessment was that Sureka was eating between 500 and 700 calories a day. Sureka described gradually withdrawing any food items that contained fat, including nuts, cheese, chicken, meat, and dairy products. At the time of the evaluation, Sureka was eating few food items with little variety from day to day. Sureka's weight was 113 pounds on the day of her evaluation. Ms. King's impression was that Sureka was restricting her caloric intake and had an intense fear of food, but especially food that contained fat. She recommended that Sureka complete a diet diary and follow up with her weekly. She reiterated that Sureka needed psychological evaluation because Mrs. Shah had not contacted Dr. Ellis. Ms. King called Mrs. Shah to tell her that she agreed with Dr. Wheeler's assessment of anorexia, primarily the restricting type.

Dr. Wheeler called Mrs. Shah again to tell her that Sureka had lost 2 more pounds in just 3 days. She emphasized that early intervention and individual and family therapy were important for recovery from anorexia. She stressed again that she and Dr. Ellis had successfully helped other students with eating disorders. Mrs. Shah reluctantly agreed to call Dr. Ellis. Mrs. Shah and Sureka signed a release of information so that Dr. Wheeler could discuss Sureka's situation with Dr. Ellis.

Dr. Wheeler called Dr. Ellis and discussed her assessment and plan. Dr. Wheeler faxed a copy of her evaluation, lab results, tests, and the nutrition evaluation. Several days later, Mrs. Shah finally called Dr. Ellis, who had the advantage of knowing a great deal about Sureka before the phone contact. This helped her to organize her interview efficiently and prepared her for Mrs. Shah's minimization of the weight loss. Mrs. Shah focused on Sureka's healthy diet and blamed the "bad food" at the cafeteria. She was not concerned about Sureka's weight loss, stating that she looked "fine" when she saw her 2 weeks earlier. She did acknowledge that her sister's daughter had anorexia in her freshman year at Harvard. Dr. Ellis recommended a psychological assessment and faxed Mrs. Shah a consent form for treatment and release of information.

Dr. Ellis met with Sureka a few days later at the boarding school. She did a detailed history and evaluation and worked to develop a rapport with Sureka. Dr. Ellis agreed with Dr. Wheeler and Ms. King that Sureka was struggling with anorexia in the early phase and was not stable. Sureka was losing weight and had no insight into her difficulties. She did agree to meet twice weekly with Dr. Ellis for psychotherapy. Dr. Ellis called Mrs. Shah and shared her clinical impressions and recommendations for treatment, which had been formulated collaboratively by Dr. Wheeler, Ms. King, and Dr. Ellis. They recommended Sureka meet with Ms. King weekly to be weighed and to discuss her diet diary. They established an initial weight goal of 125 pounds. Dr. Ellis would initially meet with Sureka twice a week until her weight stabilized. Dr. Wheeler and Ms. King recommended that Sureka have nutritional support of a high calorie shake between meals to be consumed at the health center. Sureka's blood pressure and pulse were monitored weekly, and she saw Dr. Wheeler as needed. Sureka was restricted from sports until her weight stabilized.

Dr. Ellis met with Sureka weekly until Christmas break. Sureka initially lost more weight. Her lowest weight was 109 pounds. Dr. Ellis became increasingly uncomfortable with the lack of family involvement. She and Dr. Wheeler agreed to continue to work with Sureka but felt that family involvement was necessary despite the logistical barriers. The parents agreed to a weekend visit before the Christmas break. Sureka was anxious to see her parents and reported that she had experienced an "epiphany" about her eating patterns and "understood" that she was restricting. Although her diet diary indicated increased caloric intake, she continued to lose weight. Two weeks before her parent's visit, Sureka began to gain weight slowly.

Sureka's parents attended a family therapy session in early December. It was a difficult session because the family dynamics supported Sureka's eating disorder. During the session, Sureka's father was focused on their "healthy eating." He reported losing a significant amount of weight through dietary changes and rigorous exercise after his father died suddenly from a heart attack 1 year earlier. Mr. Shah kept saying he "just didn't understand what was going on" with Sureka and made numerous dietary suggestions to her. Sureka sat mute most of the session, smiled, and tapped her foot nervously. Her father asked her to stop tapping her foot because "it makes you look nervous." The parents met with Dr. Wheeler and Dr. Ellis later that day to discuss the treatment plan because she would be going home for a 3-week break in 2 weeks. They agreed to make appointments with Sureka's pediatrician and a local psychotherapist who specialized in eating disorders. Mrs. Shah seemed to understand the seriousness of Sureka's weight loss, but Mr. Shah seemed puzzled. They spent the weekend with Sureka taking her to restaurants and dinners with friends. She lost 3 pounds that weekend.

Sureka returned to school and gained back the 3 pounds before going home for the holiday. During the break, Sureka communicated with Dr. Ellis by phone and e-mail, and Dr. Ellis spoke with Sureka's parents, who assured her that Sureka was doing well. Sureka gained 4 pounds over the vacation.

During the rest of the academic year, Sureka met with Dr. Ellis, Ms. King, and Dr. Wheeler. Sureka continued slowly to gain weight and weighed 123 pounds in April. Her mood brightened, and she reported increased energy and decreased food and weight obsession. She was feeling less isolated from her friends. She did express the fear that she would eventually become overweight, but her body image was more stable and realistic. In May, she reached her goal weight and was able to play a sport. She no longer needed to drink shakes between meals because she added her own snacks. She began to develop insight into her fear of leaving home and the link to her grandfather's death. She disclosed that she had always hoped to be a fashion model in Paris, a goal her mother had supported. She understood that striving for a body "like the models" had been part of her eating disorder. She continued to be ambivalent about her body and was uncomfortable when she began to fill out and regain her breasts and hips but didn't lose weight. She continued to compare herself with her mother who was very thin and petite. Over time she became more accepting that she had a different type of body.

After several more family sessions, both parents seemed to understand the factors that precipitated Sureka's eating disorder including leaving home, the death of her overweight grandfather, her father's health anxiety, and a family culture that valued thinness. They understood that her perfectionism, low self-esteem, and difficulty expressing negative emotions were factors that made her vulnerable to developing an eating disorder. They also understood that they had communicated both verbally and nonverbally to her that she should be exceptional, accomplished, and very thin. Their expectations of Sureka gradually became more realistic. Her father stopped discussing Ivy League universities and shifted his focus to her overall well-being. He encouraged her to express her opinions even when they differed from his. There was no longer talk about Sureka modeling in Paris.

Sureka went home for the summer and saw a nutritionist several times. She continued to gain weight slowly, and when she returned to school in September she weighed 130 pounds. She met with Dr. Ellis several times in the fall and winter terminating after Christmas break. Dr. Wheeler continued to meet with Sureka regularly in her junior year to monitor her weight and provide support when needed. They met less and less frequently as Sureka's weight and body image remained stable.

Conclusion

This case illustrates many benefits of collaboration with a multidisciplinary team.

☐ A successful referral is the first step toward treatment and recovery. Dr. Wheeler could not have convinced Sureka and her parents to meet with Dr. Ellis and Ms. King if she did not have an established collaborative relationship with them.

☐ Treating eating disorders and other serious mental illnesses in isolation can be anxiety producing for psychotherapists. Dr. Ellis, Dr. Wheeler, and Ms. King functioned informally as a treatment team. They provided each other with support and consultation, especially at difficult points in the treatment. They had regular face-to-face interaction and periodic team meetings. Although she is in private practice, Dr. Ellis never felt isolated or alone in her treatment of Sureka. The team's support helped Dr. Ellis manage her apprehension about continuing outpatient care for Sureka when her weight dropped after the family therapy session and may have averted a hospitalization.

☐ A high level of collaboration is necessary and effective when the patient has significant biopsychosocial interplay. Sureka was experiencing a disorder that has serious psychological and physical consequences if treatment fails. Shared information helped Dr. Wheeler, Dr. Ellis, and Ms. King provide effective assessment develop a family-based treatment plan. They modeled a team approach to a family that was frequently disrupted by geography and high-pressure professions.

☐ Collaboration requires power sharing. Dr. Wheeler diagnosed Sureka, but despite her comfort helping students with eating disorders, she still consulted a psychologist and a nutritionist. Each member of the team had her own area of expertise. This multidisciplinary approach required them to seek consensus about treatment goals. Power sharing enabled them to disagree with one another and problem solve creatively.

☐ The collaborative relationship between Dr. Wheeler and Dr. Ellis provided the family and Sureka with a sense of security. Poor or absent team coordination could have caused mixed or confusing messages to the family, exacerbating any denial of the problem they might be experiencing.

Anorexia is difficult to treat even under the best of circumstances. In this case, it was particularly difficult because the family lived at a great distance and was unable to participate in ongoing family therapy. Sureka's treatment succeeded despite these barriers. Early identification and intense intervention avoided hospitalization and allowed Sureka to continue in school. The process was slow and gradual but ultimately successful, and Sureka maintained her weight gain. The collaborative approach that Dr. Wheeler, Dr. Ellis, and Ms. King had to Sureka's treatment is unfortunately fairly unique in many outpatient settings. However, this case dramatically demonstrates the power of working collaboratively and providing "a seamless web of biopsychosocial services" (S. McDaniel, personal communication, November 9, 2007).

10

A Man Loses His Identity: A Complex Case of Chronic Pain, Disability, and Depresssion

Frank Burns, MD, was a primary care physician who worked in a small rural community near Concord, New Hampshire. Dominic Geffkin, MD, worked at a larger clinic in the city. The two physicians knew each other and served on several hospital committees together. William Gunn, PhD, one of this book's co-authors, was a psychotherapist who worked in the same clinic as Dr. Geffkin, and the two of them had collaborated on several difficult cases together. At the time of this particular collaboration, Paul Arnstein, PhD, a nurse practitioner and pain medicine specialist, was providing case consultations in the same clinic as Drs. Gunn and Geffkin.

Case Background

Sergio was a 54-year-old single man living in a rented apartment in a rural area in New Hampshire. He grew up in a metropolitan area, one of three children, the other two a set of female twins 2 years older. His father worked construction and valued physical prowess and a strong work ethic. He believed and taught Sergio that if you were hurt, sick, or in pain, you just worked through it. Sergio's mother stayed at home and took care of the family.

Sergio was an intelligent, compassionate man who enjoyed music, gardening, reading and writing poetry, and learning in all forms. It was clear from an early age that he had the intellectual ability to develop a professional career. He did well academically in college and was in the first class of a "radical" law school just starting in the Northeast. He claimed he had never had been comfortable in the mainstream and had always been attracted to the fringe. After graduating from law school, he became the lead attorney of a rural legal aid law firm. This work reflected his strong belief in helping the less fortunate and in ensuring everyone had a fair chance in legal proceedings. He held this job for 20 years and was proud of his accomplishments. Unfortunately, growing health issues forced him to stop working and apply for disability.

Sergio had been married twice, each marriage producing a daughter. At the time of treatment, he had frequent contact with his younger daughter but had been estranged from his older daughter for several years after she cut off all contact. This estrangement had been extremely difficult for Sergio, and he frequently wondered why she abandoned their relationship and how he could build a bridge back to her. Sergio and his health care team believe that this "chronic emotional pain" directly related to his physical problems. Despite this, Sergio had never sought or received any consistent mental health treatment; perhaps little value was put on such treatment within his family.

Sergio had multiple complex medical problems. He had Type II diabetes that required daily insulin shots. He had degenerative disc disease secondary to a 1979 falling accident in which he sustained injuries that required six surgeries over the next 10 years. He continued to work through the pain and experimented with many pain relief regimens for severe, chronic, low back pain. Sergio took high doses of methadone, prescribed by his family physician to control his pain. The combination of side effects from his pain relief regimen and his diabetes took its toll in peripheral foot and joint pain and erectile dysfunction.

When Sergio was in his mid-40s, his physician, Dr. Burns, convinced him to apply for disability and leave the workplace. Sergio and Dr. Burns had developed a significant positive relationship because of their frequent visits and ongoing dialogue regarding his use of narcotic pain medications. However, over time the relationship had deteriorated. Ultimately, Dr. Burns dismissed Sergio from the practice, stating that he felt Sergio used narcotic pain medications inappropriately. Sergio believed the fact that he owed the physician a great deal of money and was now on disability also played a role. Sergio felt betrayed and abandoned by this dismissal and subsequently sought care at a safety-net clinic. Said Sergio,

> It is impossible for someone who has not been through this to understand the feelings that go on when your life dramatically changes. I was a working professional with financial resources and the ability to live a comfortable middle-class life. As my medical condition deteriorated and my emotional state worsened, I went from this position in life to losing 75% of my income and being dependent on the welfare system. I found myself begging for sympathy and support to pay the bills and hating myself for it. I did not have any family financial support and had to manage completely on my own. One of the hardest parts of this transition was dealing with the reactions of well-meaning professionals. When my chronic pain required methadone treatment, I had to go to a clinic that primarily treated heroin addicts and face the condescending stares of others. Having to face the reality of the situation, my self-perception changed in such a way that has continued to cause my thinking and my mood to be negative. In addition, I found myself completely dependent on my primary care doctor to understand my situation and prescribe the amount of pain medication that allowed me to function. I felt I had to be a "good patient" and do what I was told to continue to receive good treatment, particularly for my pain.

The Collaborative Effort

Dr. Geffkin now provides Sergio's medical care in a family health center. He began working with Sergio 2 years ago. He talked briefly to Dr. Burns when Sergio first came to him, a conversation that served to make him wary of Sergio initially. Early in their relationship, Dr. Geffkin discussed the need to engage a psychotherapist to assess and treat the depressive symptoms. However,

Sergio resisted all efforts in this direction. In 2004, Sergio was hospitalized for cellulitis in his leg, a complication of diabetes. When the inpatient team felt Sergio was ready to leave the acute-care setting of the hospital to go "home," he did not feel he could manage his own care. The inpatient team's use of "home" meant only he was able to leave the hospital to a rehabilitation center. In contrast, Sergio's image of "going home" was to his apartment, difficult to access in winter, and to a situation in which he would be isolated and unable to care for himself. Dr. Geffkin advocated for Sergio and extended his hospital stay a few days. Dr. Geffkin's decision to advocate for Sergio was not a popular intervention for the inpatient team members because they felt Sergio was ready to leave the hospital.

Dr. Geffkin was insightful about his desire to advocate for Sergio. He described a commonality with Sergio on their views of the world because they had both chosen their profession out of a desire to help the "underdog." In addition, Dr. Geffkin was impressed by how articulate Sergio was about the effect of the chronic pain on his life and recognized he may have treated Sergio differently and minimized how all of the situations in his life were contributing to the problem secondary to his sophistication.

At the time of Sergio's hospitalization, Dr. Geffkin asked for a behavioral health consultation because he felt that Sergio needed more resources than he could to provide. He convinced Sergio to engage in a consultation with Dr. Gunn, who was colocated in his practice. Dr. Gunn saw Sergio for the hospital consultation and then began to see Sergio for psychotherapy. Dr. Gunn explored how depression affected Sergio's ability to keep a proactive focus in his life and to take care of the complications of his disease. Sergio spoke at length about the estrangement of his daughter and the loneliness he felt in general. He did have a close female friend who helped him organize his home, with whom he hoped to pursue a relationship in the future. However, he felt he had nothing to offer someone because of his job loss, financial status, and physical problems, including erectile dysfunction. His view of himself as a competent man had been severely altered. Although Sergio was able to describe some limited personal goals for the future in the area of writing and gardening, he felt helpless in pursuing them because of his health issues.

The context of the inpatient psychological consultation helped the medical team understand Sergio's perception of "home" as his apartment and his fears of falling and being unable to take care of himself. Sergio realized that he needed to take increased responsibility for his care and that the acute care hospital was not the best place to do so. The team worked together to implement a viable plan using visiting nurse services to relieve Sergio's anxiety about being alone. During the last 3 days of his hospital stay, the plan was solidified and expanded to include outpatient psychotherapy visits.

After this hospitalization, Dr. Geffkin continued to see Sergio on a regular basis to monitor diabetic control and the chronic pain syndrome. Neither issue was under control. Sergio's depression and hopelessness affected his motivation and ability to follow through with the complicated regimen to control his diabetes and chronic pain. Both Dr. Geffkin and Sergio found the medical visits frustrating because they were never able to cover all the issues both patient and physician wanted to discuss. Sergio felt that he "was at the mercy" of Dr. Geffkin because he controlled access to pain medication and saw the physician as "in control." Dr. Geffkin also felt powerless in the face of Sergio's difficulty following through on recommendations. He was worried about addressing the pain and use of the narcotic medication in a responsible and ethical fashion. He found that Sergio was intellectually able to understand the mind–body connection and have constructive dialogue about the issues this created for him.

Although Sergio continued to feel he had little control over his life, he enjoyed and reported benefit from weekly concurrent psychotherapy visits that focused on his ability to take a proactive stance in his life. Sergio struggled to cope with the estrangement from his daughter. Dr. Gunn reached out to his ex-wife to try to engage his daughter in treatment, but she was unable to attend an appointment. Sergio began to recognize how his mind-set and identity as chronically ill patient exacerbated both his physical and psychological pain.

At one point in therapy, Sergio was able to discuss his frustration in his medical visits with Dr. Geffkin. Although Sergio saw Dr. Geffkin as extremely caring, patient, and attentive, he was still annoyed by his sense that their visits focused too much on the high doses of pain medication to the neglect of other aspects of his health. Sergio noted the following:

> I did not feel like I could talk about the larger stresses I faced in the visits to my doctor. I knew by now that each visit would contain some discussion of the pain medication and that most of my symptoms would be attributed to the high doses of narcotics I was taking. It seemed like my body had completely turned against me, and I have many symptoms that I'm worried about. However, I did not feel I could bring them up. I did not think I controlled the process of the visit and what we talked about.
>
> It also affected my relationship with my psychotherapist, Dr. Gunn. I knew the two of them were talking about me, and, for the most part, I think that is a good thing and they have positive intentions in doing this. However, I worry, for instance, that talking to Dr. Gunn about my drug use as a teenager will somehow cause my medical doctor to not prescribe the narcotics that I need to get through the day.

Dr. Gunn spoke directly with Dr. Geffkin about Sergio's frustrations with his medical care. Dr. Geffkin stated that he wanted to treat Sergio humanely and compassionately but was fearful because Sergio's dose of methadone was exceptionally high and because Sergio used both short- and long-acting pain medication. Dr. Geffkin's discomfort was exacerbated by the complicated documentation and contracting that is necessary whenever a medical professional prescribes opioid pain medications for a patient. Although Dr. Geffkin did not believe Sergio was selling his medication, he did worry that the pain management regimen was aiding a physical or psychological dependence (or both). When Dr. Geffkin broached these issues with Sergio, he was open to the discussion, in contrast with other patients who became angry. Yet Dr. Geffkin worried when Sergio would request increased opioid medication rather than exploring other pain management modalities.

Dr. Gunn helped Dr. Geffkin focus on his role as a teacher in caring for Sergio. He encouraged him to challenge Sergio's thoughts and beliefs about his powerlessness to improve his own health, to help him transform his life for the better. Dr. Geffkin needed support to take on this role, because he found it distressing to confront and challenge Sergio in this way. Dr. Geffkin wanted to talk about other events and frustrations in Sergio's life but felt like he had to keep focused on the medical issues.

After hearing both perspectives, Dr. Gunn arranged a conjoint visit to help Sergio and Dr. Geffkin clarify expectations for the medical visits. Sergio and the team agreed to have one visit at least quarterly to review the pain medication regimen. This agreement increased Dr. Geffkin's comfort in addressing Sergio's other agendas, because he knew the narcotic medication issues would be reviewed regularly. Both patient and physician benefited from this joint visit.

Before selecting Dr. Geffkin as his physician, Sergio had been to a number of pain clinics and specialists. Each had offered recommendations, resulting in his current medication regimen, which allowed Sergio to function. Although Dr. Geffkin respected previous treatment, he also wanted to explore other options and consultation. The clinic had recently contracted with Dr. Arnstein, a nurse practitioner specializing in pain medicine to provide consultations 1 day a week. Dr. Arnstein met Sergio and reviewed his history and current medication list. He was able to reassure Dr. Geffkin that the pain medication regimen was appropriate. He supported planned quarterly medication review meetings and recommended that each visit address four general questions to avoid conflict:

1. Is the medication improving Sergio's activity level and functional status?
2. Are there adverse side effects to the medication?
3. Is aberrant behavior occurring (e.g., abusing the medication or diverting it to others)?
4. Is the medication controlling the pain in the way it is designed to do?

Expanding the team to include this pain specialist helped Sergio feel he is a respected member of his own pain management team and relieved Dr. Geffkin's discomfort in treating Sergio's chronic pain.

Although Sergio found psychotherapy helpful, he had been dealing with his condition for a long time and was not open to major changes. Over time, Dr. Gunn and Sergio developed a rapport and focused on two themes in therapy. Sergio agreed to seek ways to be proactive in his life while accepting his limitations. Each psychotherapy session comprised a check-in on the medical conditions, his adherence to his medical regimen, and any adverse side effects to share with Dr. Geffkin. Next, he discussed what his life goals would be if he could put the "illness in its place." Dr. Gunn used the strategy of "externalizing the illness" (see chap. 5) to help Sergio separate himself from his disease and recognize what he can control. Finally, Dr. Gunn and Sergio negotiated a "homework assignment." Sergio sometimes accomplished the homework but often felt that he was in too much pain and too overwhelmed by depressive symptoms to follow through. In these circumstances, Dr. Gunn informed Dr. Geffkin using internal electronic communication. (Although the two professionals shared an office and discussed shared cases, they often used clinical notes and internal e-mail correspondence.)

Conclusion

This case illustrates how collaboration can improve care for a complicated patient and help the professionals involved support each other to manage their own reactions. This section highlights aspects of the collaboration that maximized these benefits.

☐ One of the most effective times to begin a collaborative effort is when a patient is hospitalized. Patients are vulnerable and may be more open to psychological intervention during a hospitalization. Psychologists and other psychotherapists can gain privileges at hospitals to see patients during this time.

☐ Medical language can interfere with effective communication. For example, negative results are good, and positive results are usually bad. *Unremarkable* is a good thing, and "this won't hurt much" increases patient anxiety. In Sergio's case, the use of the word *home* and the different perceptions of that image by the patient and medical team created unnecessary conflict. Dr. Geffkin and Dr. Gunn worked together to help the medical team understand this and to change the image to something that was acceptable to the Sergio.

☐ In this case, conjoint visits with the physician and the psychotherapist were helpful. Although Sergio was somewhat concerned about the professionals sharing information, he was reassured that both were in the same building and shared an office. Dr. Gunn reassured Sergio by clarifying what information would be shared and having joint appointments with Dr. Geffkin.

☐ Collaboration with a pain specialist who could outline treatment options and make recommendations was helpful in this case. Cases with this degree of complexity often benefit from consultation by multiple professionals. It is most helpful to frame these consultations as expanding the treatment system rather than sending the patient away from the primary care team.

☐ Treatment of chronic pain with high doses of narcotics is often anxiety producing to the medical professional. This anxiety often translates to the patient. Sergio certainly felt this transferred anxiety at times. His questions about his symptoms resulted in dialogue about his narcotic use. Medical professionals often wonder whether the narcotics are doing more harm than good because narcotic side effects often limit the patients' functioning. They also worry about scrutiny from colleagues or the regulatory agencies. Discussing these concerns through a mediated conversation often helps mitigate these concerns. Working collaboratively can help to alleviate this anxiety tremendously.

☐ When complex patients have few social supports and live alone, they often feel more dependent on and connected to the medical system. This can present a challenge to the medical professional to respond to this need while setting appropriate limits. Involving two primary professionals can spread the sense of responsibility and give such patients more ways to have their needs met without overwhelming any one provider in the system.

Sergio was overwhelmed by how illness took over his life. In a parallel fashion, his health care professionals were overwhelmed by the task of caring for him. Just as Sergio often felt powerless to improve his own life, his health care professionals feared they could do more harm than good. In this situation, it is often helpful to expand the treatment team, as Dr. Geffkin did for Sergio, first by consulting Dr. Gunn and then by consulting Dr. Arnstein. These consultations and the ongoing collaboration relieved both the professionals' and Sergio's sense of helplessness and fear as they worked to improve his life.

IV

Collaboration in the Real World: Interviews With Collaborative Health Care Professionals

The case material illustrates how collaboration alters the clinical course of psychotherapy and medical treatment. However, it may not have clarified how collaboration can transform the practice of psychotherapy. Psychotherapists who increase their level of collaboration necessarily change the way they function day in, day out.

The following interviews with expert collaborators demonstrate the impact of collaboration on practice. These collaborative psychotherapists were chosen for interviews because their practices occur in various types of settings, and they represent a full spectrum of backgrounds and experience levels.

The first interview is with David Driscoll, PsyD, an experienced psychologist in private practice. After decades in traditional practice, he recently expanded his practice to provide services in a private pediatric office. In this interview, he discusses the reasons for this change and how it has invigorated him to take on a new role.

The second interview is with Deborah Wright, MD, a family physician in a small group private medical practice. She is a psychosocially oriented physician but does not have an on-site psychotherapist. She reflects on her experiences attempting to collaborate with psychotherapists in the community and to provide comprehensive biopsychosocial care to patients with little support from the mental health community.

The third interview is with Michael Hoyt, PhD, a senior staff psychologist who practices in a managed care setting at Kaiser Permanente. Dr. Hoyt has practiced collaboratively throughout his career and has played an important role in the evolution of collaborative and integrated health care at Kaiser. He is the 2007 recipient of the American Psychological Foundation Cummings PSYCHE Prize for promoting the roles of psychologists in organized behavioral health care and fostering the further integration of mental health and medical care.

The fourth interview is with Shari Altum, PhD, a psychologist who works for a community mental health center but practices in a primary care office. She has been practicing for approximately 5 years, all in the primary care setting.

Finally, the fifth interview is with Albert Bassetti, MA, the director of a crisis services unit. Mr. Bassetti's experiences reflect both his roles as a clinician and administrator and how both have evolved in his work to create a crisis service that best meets the needs of patients and community-based primary care medical professionals through collaborative care.

The interviews themselves have some common elements and questions, as well as some questions tailored to the specifics of that psychotherapists' practice. In each, a collaborative psychotherapist shares his or her expertise in altering practice patterns to increase collaboration and describes how routine collaboration has changed clinical care. They also discuss their views of the pros and cons and barriers to practicing collaboratively. Each has adapted his or her practice in different ways depending on the needs and requirements of their settings and larger systems. Despite these differences, there was one interesting constant in all of the interviews: All of the experts agreed that psychotherapists who want to become more collaborative must broaden the scope of treatment to focus on the patient's context and support systems. They must value a team approach over an intense, exclusionary psychotherapist–patient relationship.

These experts illustrate how their practices in various settings are different from the norm because they collaborate. Their experiences can help psychotherapists who are new to collaboration prepare themselves for changes they may need to make to integrate collaboration into their practices successfully. As these health care professionals discuss, becoming collaborative alters mindset, daily practice patterns, patient interactions, and support systems for the professionals in multiple ways. These professionals have enjoyed their experiences with collaboration and feel that it enhances their practices in multiple ways. As psychotherapists move toward greater collaboration, they must determine how to make these changes in a way that is consistent with their own practice environment and professional beliefs.

11

Collaborative
Private Practice

Dave Driscoll, PsyD, is a psychologist in private practice in Rochester, New York. He has been in private practice for more than 20 years. Over the last 10 years, he has focused on increasing his collaboration with medical professionals. This interview highlights how his collaborative style evolved over time and how he integrates collaboration into his everyday practice.

How would you describe your psychology practice?

I run a longstanding private practice. My time is split between independent outpatient practice, consultation, and teaching at the University of Rochester. One day a week I provide consultation to a community mental health center, which is also where I provide psychotherapy supervision to family therapy trainees from the University. I am part of a group practice, and we all spend some of our time in a pediatric practice of physicians with whom we've been collaborating for some time.

How do you collaborate with primary care medical professionals?

Virtually all of my referrals come from primary care physicians. My referral network has just evolved over time; as primary care physicians have liked the services they and their patients received from me, they referred more and more patients.

Collaboration starts before I even see a new patient. When patients call to make a first appointment, I get their permission to communicate with their primary care physician. Before the patient comes in, I notify the physician that the patient followed through on the referral by sending them a brief handwritten note, fax, or e-mail. Because I have established relationships, I have everyone's contact information, which makes this a lot easier. When the patient will be seen in the pediatric practice, I have group messaging with them, so I contact the physician that way.

We include a written release of information to the physician in our initial packet of forms for the patient to complete before or at the first visit. Also, we include an explanation of the way we practice, highlighting the goals of collaboration and setting the expectation that we'll be communicating. Our process is transparent to the patient from the very beginning.

After I've seen the patient for three or four appointments, I forward a summary to the physician. The summary is usually a one-page, handwritten form that I fax. The form includes space for my initial assessment, a brief summary of treatment direction. As treatment progresses, I do periodic updates driven by the duration of treatment, any significant shift or development in the case, or suspension of treatment. When a patient stops attending therapy, I let the physician know. We share anything we think they need to know to provide optimal treatment and follow-up.

I do some phone-based collaboration, as needed. I find it is sometimes difficult to connect by phone, so I use that only when there is something significant or time urgent that the physician needs to know. Again, because of my relationship with the physicians, they take a phone message from me seriously, because they know I call only when necessary. I also do some face-to-face collaboration, but this is really only with the pediatricians with whom I practice on-site.

What do you consider the "nuts and bolts" of your collaboration with medical professionals? How does collaboration fit into your daily routine?

At this point, collaborating is so second nature, it is automatic. Within every patient encounter there is an implicit question about the need for communication with other team members. I have an automatic thought process about how to proceed with the collaboration, just like I do with how to proceed in the psychotherapy. When I have breaks in my schedule, I use that time to maintain the structure of the collaborative communication. Once the model evolved the collaboration occurred seamlessly. I just automatically use any free time I have to pick up the phone and make a call, write a note, or whatever.

We've evolved to the point that the physicians who refer to us assume collaboration will occur. They expect to be contacted and trust that I'll reach out to them at the appropriate time. They trust my judgment as to how and when collaboration will occur. If they need to know, they'll know. I also make myself available to them. The physicians who refer to me regularly have my cell phone number, and they know how to contact my answering service.

How did your collaborative relationships evolve?

My practice became more collaborative over time because I really enjoyed the experience of collaboration and because I found collaborative relationships satisfying professionally. I developed a whole new set of colleagues and believe I'm providing better patient care.

There is a subset of physicians with whom I have not been able to develop successful collaborative relationships, and subsequently I do very little business with them. There definitely is a compatibility factor. Physicians have to be receptive. Their belief system about behavioral health is important. If they want me to be the expert to take over so they can be done with it, we can't be collaborative. It isn't going to work if physicians view me as a servant who has to check in with them every two visits to get their approval. I've found it difficult to establish collaborative relationships with physicians who are extremely hierarchical, so at a certain point I don't pursue it anymore. Fortunately, this is a minority of physicians. Most of them want to create a relationship with a psychotherapist similar to those they have with other specialists, in which there are both a sense of give and take and of shared responsibility of patient care.

Were you anxious when you started to collaborate?

Honestly, no. I found medical professionals to welcome my communication, so there really wasn't anything to be anxious about.

How do patients respond to the collaboration?

The majority of patients don't respond in any way. The modal response is to view it as natural expectation that we would communicate. Occasionally, a patient has questions about the flow of information among professionals, but they rarely have concerns about communication with their primary care physician. Their questions are usually about communication with schools and other systems, such as drug and alcohol treatment, probation, or social services.

Occasionally, patients express reluctance to sign a release to their primary care physician. I try to explain the rationale to them, in case their reluctance is based in misinformation or fear. Also, the fact I negotiate the information to be included in collaborative contacts often helps. However, if a patient doesn't want me to talk to his or her physician, I respect that and continue without the collaboration. It really is pretty rare, though.

How has practicing collaboratively changed your practice?

One of the unanticipated developments as we've started to practice on-site is the permanence of the relationship that exists with patients. When you practice independently of the physician, patients come and go, some satisfied some not, some truly helped, some not. When they stop coming to your office, they go away and fall off your radar screen. When you practice collaboratively, you realize all of your patients continue to exist because they're linked to you through your relationship with the physician. Less than satisfactory outcomes don't just disappear into the ether, because you hear about them from the medical staff or see them in the waiting room for our on-site patients. I became aware of that through experience. The longer I've collaborated, I've had to contend with some tough cases that didn't work out that well, and now I'm not off the hook just because they stopped coming to therapy. It is an unanticipated challenge. I guess they never really went away; they just became someone else's problems and got even less optimal care.

Another change is how I manage my time. As I said, any breaks I have I use to collaborate. Also, the 50-minute hour is no longer sacrosanct. I interrupt medical professionals, and they interrupt me. If someone needs to talk to me about a patient, I'll excuse myself and make the contact. It doesn't happen all the time—maybe once a week—but that is what it takes. When I'm practicing on site at the pediatric office, I do a lot more abbreviated appointments. A lot of the work happens in the collaborative contacts, reducing the demand to accomplish everything in the 50-minute hour.

We have become their first responders for mental health crises in the pediatric practice. We respond to these situations to the best of our ability, generally with an immediate evaluation appointment and triage to appropriate service. We ultimately serve as a conduit to the larger mental health system when we can't meet their immediate needs. This is a role that I wouldn't have in a traditional private practice. Again, I think it allows us to meet people where they are and provide a higher level of care than they would receive without the collaboration.

I would have to say that practicing collaboratively is compatible with my epistemology of the nature of behavioral health issues. Collaboration has been a natural extension of the relational model I use to help me understand people and their challenges because it extends the relational model to the professional level. Patients' relationship to their medical professionals and my relationship to their medical professionals are an important contextual element to understanding them and their challenges. Collaboration is simply isomorphically extending the relational model to the professional context—a natural outgrowth.

What do you consider the potential advantages of and barriers to collaboration between psychotherapists and medical professionals?

In my experience, patient outcomes are better. The therapy moves along better when the patients trust me because their physician trusts me and when I can learn about the context and issues from someone who knows them. Everyone talks about the time collaboration takes away from practice, but I think the time is well spent. The face-to-face work is easier and faster because so much work happens outside the psychotherapy relationship.

Collaboration reduces the burden I feel in the patient care. I have a sense of professional integration and teamwork with the physician—we are there to back each other up. Because the physician and I share care, patients with urgent needs reach out to their physician in addition to calling me. It is not uncommon that the physician has already managed an urgent issue in the 20 minutes it takes me to get back to the patient.

I've found collaboration to be very compatible with independent practice. It has a positive impact on patient outcome and satisfaction. Medical professionals, all of whom can be referral sources, appreciate that I communicate with them and also benefit from the sense of shared care. Pediatricians say, "We send patients to you because things get better." They tend to be outcome-driven individuals, and they want to see their patients get better. They respect the psychotherapeutic process to a point, but that wears thin quickly if they do not see and hear about functional improvement in the patients that they refer.

Recent contact is a critical element to physicians as they make referrals. The last name they've seen come across their desk may be the first one they think of when they encounter the next problem. Collaboration helps build and maintain an independent practice. More referrals are a significant side effect—you become the go-to person for their patients with mental health or stress issues. Primary care practices have thousands of patients in their practice—if they refer 2% of their patients to you, you're full. I hope people don't collaborate just to market themselves—it is more than that, but it does lead to more referrals.

What advice would you give to psychotherapists who are considering or are just beginning to collaborate with medical professionals?

Be true to yourself. You have to assess your own professional attitudes and beliefs carefully to understand how well a collaborative practice fits within that framework. Self-assessment is key. There are a variety of belief systems and epistemologies about the genesis of mental health that can be consistent or inconsistent with collaboration. If you believe that mental health difficulties stem solely from internal psychological dynamics, it's going to drive a certain type of practice, which is unlikely to include collaboration. If you believe that biology is an important factor in mental health, than you're going to practice a different way and have a different intervention continuum. Psychosocial perspectives that focus on the patient's context and relationships make you more open to collaboration. It is easiest to collaborate with medical professionals who share common beliefs about the genesis of mental illness. You evolve treatment options that are consistent with your beliefs about the causes—if you focus on psychosocial issues, then incorporating others and expanding the people you work with just makes sense. You have to examine your core beliefs—some core beliefs aren't consistent with collaboration.

This self-assessment leads to a basic question: Where do you want to be on the spectrum of collaboration? I'm at a pretty extreme end of the collaborative continuum, because I'm in a pediatric office and because I focus on relational and contextual factors in mental health.

When we started to implement collaboration in my practice, three psychotherapists were on board, and two weren't. The two who weren't on board saw collaboration as burdensome rather than as an opportunity to practice more effectively and efficiently. If you aren't committed to collaboration, you can find all kinds of barriers such as confidentiality that extend from core-belief issues. Also, if you don't feel collaboration is valuable, it is hard to set aside the time and make it a priority. If you don't believe that collaboration is a necessary, core process in optimally effective services, you will find these "challenges" insurmountable rather than something to be overcome toward an important goal.

Communicate, communicate, communicate. That's really what collaboration is all about, whether it's by phone, e-mail, or fax. Take advantage of easy communication strategies, balanced with confidentiality, and go from there. Examine your comfort level with having a transparent practice. You have to build structures in your practice to maintain the boundaries of the therapy while communicating the correct type and level of information to the patient's physician. Collaboration introduces shades of gray of which you have to be constantly mindful, whereas practicing in a vacuum is very black and white (see also *Primary Care Psychology* by Frank, McDaniel, Bray, & Heldring [2004]).

12

Collaborative Primary Care Medical Practice

Deborah Wright, MD, is a family physician who sees patients in a group practice with two other physicians, both internists. She has been practicing for more than 15 years. She treats patients 12 years of age and older. Dr. Wright provides women's health services but does not practice obstetrics. Her practice is a typical, suburban private medical practice in Pennington, New Jersey.

How do you integrate psychosocial issues into the medical care that you provide?

I think I have become better at it over the years. My family medicine residency did train me to address emotional issues. I am much more comfortable dealing with anxiety and depression than my colleagues who are internists and were trained to work in hospitals. Sometimes my colleagues come to me, because they are not sure how to manage a patient with anorexia or depression. I am more comfortable talking to people. I see a lot of people with eating disorders. I have become more comfortable working with these patients, especially when I am working with a team, a psychotherapist and a nutritionist. But sometimes it is hard not to get very behind in my schedule.

I find that identifying psychosocial issues is not difficult. I try to understand the patient's agenda from the beginning of the appointment, but sometimes these issues do not come up until the end. Patients say, "There is just one more thing," when I thought I was finished. Sometimes I can ask the patient to come back, but sometimes I have to just accept that I am going to be behind schedule the rest of the day.

Just today, a young woman came in with a cold. At the end of the visit, she said, "There is just one other thing." Then she told me she had been irritable and agitated and not enjoying things she usually enjoys. Her family was worried about her not seeing friends. I thought "Oh boy, I am so far behind." I treated her infection, talked to her about her symptoms, and told her I thought it sounded like depression and anxiety. She agreed to come back in a couple weeks to talk more about it. I brought up the idea of medication but did not go into details. I have found that if you bring up too much the patient is overwhelmed, especially with new patients. In this case, I knew she was safe; she was not suicidal. We said we would meet in a few weeks. I might have talked to her longer, if she needed medication right away.

How does the psychotherapy referral process work in your practice?

I start by talking with patients about their symptoms and normalize the experience of anxiety and depression. This seems to help them consider psychotherapy. Sometimes patients are resistant to referral because they have had a bad experience with therapy in the past. I encourage them to try again with someone different.

I think being a woman helps. Most of my patients are women, and they generally are very open to considering psychotherapy. I would say 90% of them agree that it might be helpful. When they are not open to it, I just keep bringing it up. Every time I see them I just check in with how they are doing and if they have changed their mind. I will discuss it in different ways. Over time, they usually come around.

I generally will not suggest therapy to a patient I am seeing for the first time. It helps to get to know a patient unless it is urgent. I have better luck with patients who I have known for years. It is like a colonoscopy, if they do not want to do it I just keep bringing it up in different ways.

Do you have established referral relationships with specific psychothera-pists?

I really have no way to find good psychotherapists or psychia-trists unless they make contact with me. If I share a patient with a psychotherapist, then I get impressions from that patient's expe-rience. When a patient reports a good experience, then I try to make a note and refer to that person in the future. I definitely try to refer patients to psychotherapists who work with me and share information, but there are not very many out there.

What are the barriers to referral?

I think the biggest barrier in primary care is time. Second is lack of reimbursement for talking to patients and collaborating with psychotherapists. Time and lack of reimbursement are num-bers one, two, and three.

The insurance companies have really complicated the referral process. Patients have to find a psychotherapist in their network, and these provider lists shift constantly. I cannot always provide them with a name because I do not know who will be covered. The patient has to call the insurance company to get names, and it cuts me out of the process. They can spend the whole day on the phone trying to find an in-network psychotherapist who will see them in any timely manner. Most patients find it is just too expensive to see a psychotherapist outside their insurance net-work. The whole process is very difficult and discouraging for patients to manage, especially if they are depressed and anxious, and not functioning well.

If you broke your leg, I would have a group of orthopedic sur-geons to refer to. I see a lot of patients with depression and anxi-ety, but I cannot direct the referral and do not feel like I know a lot of good psychotherapists to refer to.

How do you communicate with psychotherapists who see your patients?

I would say less than 10% of them communicate with me. Usu-ally they will contact me when there is a crisis or they need help with something like short-term disability. I never know what is going on, and it is really frustrating, particularly if I am prescrib-ing the psychotropic medication. It would be helpful to hear from them about symptoms and side effects, but it rarely happens.

What kind of information would be helpful to you?

An update once a month or when things change would be good. The psychotherapist has more time with patients and sees them more frequently, so they know a lot more about patients' functioning. It helps me to give patients better care when I know if someone is having a problem in his or her family or marriage. The gestalt, family issues, target symptoms, and therapy progress are important, especially if I am prescribing the psychotropic medications or the patient has a chronic illness. I need to know if patients have an abuse history, because it is very important to their health care.

What is the best way for psychotherapists to contact you?

I know that the phone is difficult because it is so hard to connect, but when I have never talked to a specific psychotherapist, it helps to hear a voice and make a connection. Also, it can be helpful to share information and ideas at the beginning of treatment. I like it when psychotherapists send faxes to update me on patients. Letters and faxes are great!

How do you manage information that you receive from psychotherapists?

When I talk to psychotherapists directly, I write a note in the chart. I may leave out exquisitely personal details. I try to write as much as I can to jog my memory the next time I see the patient. Sometimes I see 75 patients in 1 week, and I only work part time! I could not possibly remember everything if I didn't write it down.

Any written or faxed information from a psychotherapist goes into the chart. We have a special section for all of the correspondence we receive from specialists.

How do patients respond to the collaboration?

Most patients do not have a problem with my talking to their psychotherapist or documenting it in the chart. They sign a release. Sometimes there will be a specific piece of information they do not want me to share with their psychotherapist. Usually after I explain the importance of sharing the information, they give me permission.

It is amazing what people tell me. Sometimes they tell me about abuse issues, affairs, marital problems, substance abuse. People do not hold back, maybe because I have seen them for a long time. They see me as someone who understands and will not judge them.

What situations do you try to manage in primary care, rather than referring to a psychotherapist or psychiatrist?

I treat a lot of patients with depression and anxiety. I start with medication, but I always recommend therapy, too. I would guess 60% of the patients I refer actually go to psychotherapy. When they have not improved after trying a few medications, I refer to a psychiatrist. Unfortunately, patients do not like to see psychiatrists, so this can be a hard.

Suicidal thoughts are red flags. This has to be evaluated. I remember a man who said he had a loaded gun in his car. He needed to be inpatient. Then you get into the whole insurance problem, the patient's options are really limited. They need to be seen right away. I knew what needed to be done medically, but it can be very difficult and time-consuming to get patients what they need.

I recently saw a patient I have known for years. Her husband died of liver cancer about this time last year. I knew it was the anniversary of his death, so I asked her about coping with the holidays, and specifically about depression symptoms. When I asked her if she ever felt suicidal she said, "I was not going to tell you, but since you asked, yes." She wanted to commit suicide without her daughter knowing it was suicide. She thought about getting a rabid bat bite so she could die and her daughter would not know that she had "killed herself." I evaluated her further, and she agreed to restart an antidepressant that she had used successfully in the past. She felt that she was safe, and so did I. When we made the follow-up appointment, I told her to call me if she found herself thinking about rabid bats. We both laughed, and she felt a lot better after talking. She is doing better now.

Sometimes a patient has been on every medication and refuses to see a psychiatrist. As I get older and more experienced, I realize that some people just do not get better. Some people will not, as in do not want to, get better. When people have multiple medical problems and anxiety and depression, I cannot prescribe the best medication because they are already on so many medications with so many interactions. Sometimes the goal is to just help make the patient's life livable.

Would you consider having a psychotherapist in your office?

It would be fabulous! I think the internists would be asking them to see their patients a lot. I think having a psychotherapist on site could help with the referral process. Patients would really like it. They already know how to get to the office and feel comfortable there. The biggest problem would be dealing with the insurance companies. It would be difficult to get on all of the insurance panels, and some of them are difficult to deal with.

Would you agree that you are more psychosocially focused compared with other medical professionals? If so, how do you think less psychosocially focused medical professionals would respond to a psychotherapist who contacted them about a shared patient?

Yes, I would say I am very psychosocially focused. I think that less psychosocially focused medical professionals would feel pressured when a psychotherapist contacted them about a shared patient because of time constraints. They might not immediately recognize the potential benefit but would hopefully experience the consultation as helpful for their patients and be more open in the future.

Do you have any final words of advice to psychotherapists who are trying to become more collaborative?

Be persistent, try different methods of contacting primary care medical providers, and realize that even if the collaboration is not successful 100% of the time, many patients will still get better, more coordinated care which is what is important.

13

Collaborative
Managed Care

M ichael F. Hoyt, PhD, is a senior staff psychologist with Kaiser Permanente in Northern California, which is perennially highly rated among the best health maintenance organizations (HMOs) in the United States in terms of various measures of quality and patient satisfaction. He is the author of a number of books, including *Brief Therapy and Managed Care* (1995), *Some Stories Are Better Than Others: Doing What Works in Brief Therapy and Managed Care* (2000), and *The Present Is a Gift: Mo' Better Stories From the World of Brief Therapy* (2004). Dr. Hoyt is the 2007 recipient of the American Psychological Foundation Cummings PSYCHE Prize for promoting the roles of psychologists in organized behavioral health care and fostering the further integration of mental health and medical care.

How would you describe your psychotherapy practice?

I am a licensed psychologist. I work full time as a staff psychologist in the outpatient psychiatry department at the Kaiser Permanente Medical Center in San Rafael, California, a suburb north of San Francisco. Each week I have approximately 30 to 32 clinical sessions, including intakes, return appointments, crisis intervention meetings, and visits with inpatients in our medical hospital. In addition, I supervise postdoctoral psychology residents, attend staff meetings, and frequently consult with colleagues both within my department and throughout the medical center.

Beyond my direct patient care and teaching duties at Kaiser, I do some writing and editing, and for 20 years have also taught numerous continuing education seminars, both across the United States and internationally, on making therapy more efficient and effective.

How did you first become interested in collaborative care?

Serendipitously. I fell into it. After I received my PhD, I did a 2-year postdoctoral fellowship. Although I had some family therapy experience, most of my formal training was in psychodynamically oriented individual therapy. Near the end of my postdoc, I was looking for a job. Someone told me that Kaiser was expanding mental health services, so I applied and got hired at the large Kaiser Medical Center in Hayward, California. That was back in 1979! I've been with Kaiser ever since.

Fortunately, the service chief who first hired me, Norman Weinstein, MD, who was a psychiatrist, had great respect for psychologists and other psychotherapists such as clinical social workers and psychiatric nurses. He envisioned psychiatry and behavioral medicine as part of the overall health enterprise, not simply some specialty department to which neurotics, psychotics, and the chemically dependent could be sent.

We did a lot of outreach, especially at the beginning. We walked the halls of the hospital medical floors and contacted every outpatient medical department, asking what psychiatry could do to help them. Over time we developed relationships with various medical professionals. We got invited to their staff meetings to discuss managing difficult patients, promoting adherence to medical regimens, and recognizing symptoms of depression and anxiety. These meetings gave us the opportunity to remind them of the research showing that up to half of medical visits yield no organic etiology. The problems are often essentially manifestations of psychological issues such as stress, depression, and relationship conflicts. We also educated them about the efficacy of brief psychotherapy in reducing unnecessary medical use; a finding first documented by Nicholas Cummings and William Follette in the 1960s and replicated many times since, and suggested that they refer to us those very patients who made them feel frustrated.

This outreach helped integrate Psychiatry into the overall health care provided at Kaiser. Some patients did not want to "go to Psychiatry," however, so after a few years, we began to experiment with placing psychotherapists at primary medical stations. In essence, if the patients wouldn't come to Psychiatry, we took Psychiatry to them. The medical professional could walk the patient down the hall and hand them to the colocated psychotherapist.

As I've written elsewhere (Hoyt, 1995, 2000), there are eight characteristics of managed behavioral health care:

1. Specific problem solving to help the patient identify and achieve measurable goals
2. Rapid response and early intervention
3. Clear definition of patient and psychotherapist responsibilities, with an emphasis on patient competencies, resources, and involvement
4. Flexible and creative use of time
5. Interdisciplinary cooperation that blends medical and psychological perspectives and interventions into a more holistic view of the patient
6. Multiple treatment formats and modalities, including individual, group, and marital or family therapy, in sequence or concurrent combinations, as well as the use of various community resources
7. Intermittent treatment or a family practitioner model
8. Results orientation and accountability

These dovetail nicely with my interest in brief, time-sensitive therapies. Both the HMO environment and brief therapies focus on the development of a collaborative alliance and an emphasis on patients' strengths and competencies in the service of the efficient attainment of cocreated goals.

How do you collaborate with primary care medical professionals?

For the past 6 years, it's been my privilege to work at the Kaiser Permanente Medical Center in San Rafael, California, which is much closer to my home. I'm not speaking here as an official Kaiser representative, but for me it helps greatly that Kaiser Permanente is organized as a staff-model HMO providing comprehensive services. We have in-house clinicians serving a prepaid membership population. The word *collaboration* means "working together." I think it starts with a mutual understanding that we are all, including the patients, on the same team with the same goal: high-quality, affordable health care. When it's done right, we're talking about managed care, not just managed costs— some companies that only worry about their mental health budget may be more interested in getting rid of the patient. The right mission is to care for the whole person.

What do you consider the "nuts and bolts" of your collaboration with medical professionals? How does collaboration fit into your daily routine?

The first thing I do when I get to my office in the morning is to turn on my computer. We have a new electronic information management system that allows all clinicians to see the patient's entire medical chart including history, diagnoses, medications, procedures, and so on. It's easier to collaborate if you know what your coworkers are doing. I can put confidential psychiatric information in a file that is only available to psychotherapists, but all health care professionals in our system can see what appointments are being made, whether they were kept or not, what medications may have been prescribed, for example. Patients are aware of this through our informed consent procedures.

Working within a psychiatry department that is part of a full-service medical center that includes outpatient departments, an emergency room, and medical hospital floors helps keep me tuned in to the opportunities and advantages of collaboration. It's good to be mindful that most psychiatric medications, particularly antidepressants and anxiolytics, are prescribed by primary care physicians and nurse practitioners, not by psychiatrists. I spend some time virtually every day calling primary care physicians and nurse practitioners and talking with them about their patients' medications, their responses, and the like. When I speak about a patient with a colleague, especially someone who doesn't work in my department, I tend to say "our patient, Mrs. Jones" rather than "your patient" or "my patient." When I get a call from a colleague,

I try to be user-friendly. What kind of help does my colleague need? What can I do so my colleague will feel that our contact was useful?

When I see medical patients in the hospital or psychiatric patients in the emergency room, during the day or after hours, I need to understand their concurrent medical and psychosocial situations. The medical professionals welcome our involvement and can be useful sources of information. I also check with the on-duty nurses when I want to know what's "really happening." Such cases involve careful consultation and collaboration as we identify complicating issues and oftentimes multiple diagnoses on the way to an appropriate treatment plan.

Even within our psychiatry department, collaboration is the norm and very different from the daily life described to me by my friends in independent private practice. Referrals go back and forth—to other psychotherapists for one-on-one therapy, to various therapy groups, to our intensive outpatient program, and to psychiatrists for medication evaluation. We also have staff meetings, consult with one another regarding cases, sometimes do cotherapy, supervise postdoctoral psychology residents, share day and night call responsibilities, and participate in a labor-management partnership in which union members and administration work together to make decisions affecting our mutual interests.

Are there certain types of cases that particularly lend themselves to a collaborative approach?

Certainly. Having psychotherapists, known here as *behavioral medicine specialists,* available in primary care make it easier to see a patient if there are questions about anxiety, depression, or unusual mental processes. Medical problems such as irritable bowel syndrome, headaches, chronic pain, diabetes, or coping with cancer are often exacerbated by psychological issues. Illness and intervention occur within an interpersonal context. A cerebral stroke or developing dementia affects all the family members, not just the person with the damaged brain. Caregivers sometimes need support dealing with both acute and chronic conditions. Primary psychiatric issues such as eating disorders, panic attacks, and obsessive-compulsive disorder may also require coordinated psychological and medical treatment. Even those situations that one might think of as traditional psychotherapy cases involving anxiety, depression, grief, and marital or family problems can result in concomitant medical issues if not handled properly.

You mentioned earlier having "fallen into" collaborative work when you took a job at Kaiser. How do you think that affected your development as a clinician?

At the risk of oversimplifying, I think psychotherapists may have more of a tendency to conflate understanding a problem with solving it, whereas in my experience, medical professionals are more directly focused on figuring out what to do to make a difference. I had to become a very pragmatic interventionist. What would work best with this patient with this problem in this situation to bring about symptom reduction or resolution? Most of my initial training was psychodynamic. Although "insight" can be interesting and awareness of relationship dynamics can be invaluable, what are we actually going to do and have the clients do? I needed to learn ways to connect quickly, to build a therapeutic alliance and motivate patients rapidly, and to have specific ideas about what I was hoping to accomplish to help them. This led me into learning more about both medicine and the world of brief therapy, especially Ericksonian, cognitive–behavioral, family systems, solution-focused, and narrative approaches. I call these approaches *constructive therapies* because of both their emphasis on how people construct their realities and the connotation of empowerment and forward movement.

What do you see as special problems for psychologists and other psychotherapists working collaboratively?

Psychotherapists who have chosen to work in a group medical setting may already especially value teamwork and social interaction with other people, but there are still potential problems. There is an inherent "pecking order" in medical settings. When collaborating with psychiatrists and other physicians, it is important that the patient doesn't get the message that the prescribed medication is the "real treatment" and that what we're doing is just "holding hands" or filling time until the medication kicks in. To help obviate this potential splitting, when I'm making a referral for a medication evaluation, I like to introduce the patient in person so that I can explain the referral and shape the patient's and medical professional's understanding of our roles. I might say something such as, "I've been working with Mrs. Smith, and I think her depression is interfering. If medication could help with her mood and energy, she'll be better able to do what she needs to do to get better and stay better." Even if I'm making the referral through our newfangled computer system, I can easily read to patients what I want them to know so that they understand that pharmacology will augment, not replace, the work of psychotherapy.

Collaboration takes time and space. A lot can be done quickly, on the telephone or in the hallway, although sometimes a multidisciplinary meeting may be needed to coordinate care in a particularly challenging case. Appropriate provisions need to be made for when and where to communicate with colleagues, including building some time into one's schedule.

In all collaboration, good people skills are essential. You must be able to build alliances, communicate respectfully, be helpful, and have a sense of humor. It is important that we psychotherapists conduct ourselves as coequals, bringing our special expertise. "You're not a 'real doctor' " can be addressed lots of ways. Sometimes I smile and say, "I know what you mean, that I'm not a medical doctor. My doctoral specialty is in thinking and emotions and human relationships and how those can affect your health. Maybe that's why the head is on top of the body."

To interact well with medical professionals, we need to speak some of their language. They view their clinical work through the lens of the medical model, treating "patients" not "clients." We need to know some medical jargon such as *titrate*, for example, and a bit about diseases, common medications, and medical procedures. It's important to ask for information when ignorant and to provide psychological information and explanations when appropriate.

How is the presentation and subsequent psychotherapy process different for patients seen in psychiatry versus those who receive their mental health services in a primary care setting?

Patients seen in primary care usually initiate their contact through their physician or nurse practitioner, so they may begin with more of a belief that there is something physically wrong that is causing their distress and may be hoping just a simple "pill" needs to be prescribed to fix things. Some of these patients need help accepting the idea that there is a significant psychological, behavioral, or emotional component, whereas others may be relieved that their problem is not entirely medical. Primary care patients may prefer to frame their problems as "stress" rather than "anxiety" or "depression." When patients are treated in a group, they may refer to it as a "class" rather than as a "therapy group." Understanding of the concept of mind–body medicine is growing, and using terminology that engages patients is important because getting them to participate actively in their care produces better results.

How do you hire and train staff to work collaboratively?

Generally speaking, we look for people who have demonstrated skill in working with others or who have had prior successful experience working in a collaborative setting. Graduate school courses in health psychology and continuing education classes on working with medical patients can be helpful. We also train postdoctoral fellows by having them observe and participate in a panoply of collaborative ventures including cotherapy, supervision, staff conferences, and working with medical doctors on cases that involve cooperation across disciplines.

For many years, when I was the director of adult psychiatric services at the large Kaiser Medical Center in Hayward, California, I was part of the hiring process. We hired collaboratively. Various staff members would interview a prospective new hire, and then we would discuss and give input to the chief of service. By the time I interviewed a candidate, I trusted that others had assessed his or her skill level, motivation, relevant experience, and the like. I would often ask something such as, "If you had a colleague with a patient who had committed suicide, what would you do?" The answer that made me feel I'd want this person as a colleague on my team was something along the lines of, "That would be terrible! Gosh, I'd ask my colleague out to lunch and see how he or she is doing and offer support."

What advice would you give to psychotherapists who are considering or just beginning to collaborate with medical professionals?

Collaborative care, whether done on an occasional basis or more intensively, is an excellent opportunity for psychotherapists to serve the best interests of patients. Practicing in isolation leaves care plans fragmented, whereas sharing the work across discipline lines allows us to bring complementary skill sets to bear; it promotes improved outcomes and can reduce practitioner frustration and burnout. I appreciate this opportunity to encourage my colleagues to work collaboratively.

14

Collaborative Primary Care Mental Health

S hari Altum, PhD, is a psychologist who works for community mental health center in Lawrenceburg, Indiana. She has held this position since receiving her doctorate in clinical psychology, with an emphasis on health psychology, approximately 5 years before this interview. She primarily provides services at Rising Sun Medical Center, a primary care medical clinic about 15 miles from the community mental health center. Rising Sun serves primarily rural, low-income patients, with one family doctor and one family nurse practitioner. It is a typical family practice.

Dr. Altum's presence within the Rising Sun Medical Center is one way the community mental health center has worked to bring services to the patients who need them. The following excerpts from an interview with Dr. Altum illustrate the experiences many psychotherapists have had as they transition to a different care model.

What is your current role in providing mental health services?

I am employed by the community mental health center (CMHC). All of my paperwork and billing goes through the CMHC, but I'm almost always working at Rising Sun. At Rising Sun, I do traditional mental health services, seeing patients for 1-hour intake and assessment with follow-up as indicated. Most of my work is in the 50-minute-hour psychotherapy format. I schedule 30 patients a week and generally see about 22. All of my patients are patients of Rising Sun and are referred by the medical professionals here. When I'm at the CMHC, I coordinate student intern placements, drop off my paperwork, and attend agency meetings.

How do you collaborate with primary care medical professionals?

My office is right beside one of the physicians' offices, so whenever he's there, we'll consult on shared patients. Also, we'll often talk during lunch or when we see each other in the hall, especially if there is something of particular concern. Sometimes the medical professionals will talk to me before they refer a patient, particularly if they have specific concerns.

Before I see a patient, I usually review the most recent medical chart note to understand the issues of concern and his or her medical problems. Because of regulatory issues, my mental health notes don't go into the medical chart. We find other ways to communicate. Sometimes I leave a Post-It note on the most recent medical note so the medical professional has specific information the next time he or she sees the patient. The note isn't part of the patient's permanent medical record and might review the patient's compliance and response to medications, any significant events in the patient's life, or questions or concerns that the patient has expressed that I think the medical professional should know. It isn't a psychotherapy note, just critical information that the medical professional needs. When I see patients on psychotropic medication, I always ask whether they're taking their medications, check on side effects, and get the patient's or patient family member's impressions of the medication effects. I often include this information on a sticky note to the medical professional, especially if there are any issues.

I do some crisis intervention work. When patients are in crisis, I see them right away and try to connect them with the mental health system. When appropriate and possible, I see then for ongoing psychotherapy. The medical professionals really appreciate this. It makes it easier for them to ask about patients' emotional functioning during medical visits because they know they have backup and don't have to fear that they'll uncover some mess and not be able to manage it in the time they have.

Finally, we have a formal venue for collaboration. We have a monthly meeting to discuss shared patients, as well as any issues in our collaboration and working together. It is really helpful to have this time set aside. Our monthly meetings help me teach them and vice versa. The medical professionals give me family background and health information. I inform them about their patients' diagnoses and how these are relevant to medical care. I try to help them have realistic expectations based on the whole picture. We also decide together which patients need certain kinds of interventions such as seeing only one medical professional, having longer appointments, drug contracts, and so forth.

How does collaboration affect patient care?

When patients are reluctant to follow through on the referral to mental health, I meet with the patient and the medical professional to ease the way. We call it a *warm handoff* because the patients really seem to be comforted by meeting me ahead of time and are much more likely to come for their intake when they've met me.

I have ongoing relationships with many patients. They fall in and out of seeing me, but we have a lasting connection. They know they can come back when they are in stress or need support. It really meets them where they are, rather than making them go back on a long waiting list when they're under stress. It is a much more realistic flow. Many patients have chronic problems that are exacerbated during times of increased stress. Our goal is to develop an effective management plan to reduce the intensity, duration, and frequency of exacerbations and the disruption in their lives. These are not patients whose problems will be forever resolved after one episode of brief psychotherapy. They benefit from an ongoing relationship with both a medical professional and a psychotherapist.

Our level of collaboration varies depending on the patient. There are some patients who we'll just discuss occasionally. On the other end of the continuum, we have monthly joint appointments with certain patients. We make sure that they see the medical professional regularly rather than making symptom-contingent appointments. I see them just before their medical appointment, in the regular 50-minute-hour psychotherapy format. One goal of the psychotherapy session is to prepare patients for the following medical appointment. We focus on the links among health concerns, emotional functioning, and relationship issues. Most of the patients who need this level of intervention have a hard time identifying and sharing their emotions directly but can discuss how their physical health affects relationships and how relationships affect health. That is the main role I play with those patients, because they often aren't amenable to traditional psychotherapy.

These preappointments also reduce the extent to which patients spend their entire medical appointment venting about the troubles in their life. This makes it much easier to focus on the medical issues at hand. I'm able to summarize the psychosocial issues that may be affecting a patient and influencing his or her medical treatment. We've also found that having concurrent appointments reduces logistical barriers for people. They don't have to make two visits, don't have to find transportation or pay more, so they are more willing to come.

We've noticed that when patients who were previously overutilizers of care have a venue on a regular, monthly, basis and get a lot of our time and attention when they're here, they stop being as desperate and needy. Of course, they still have their crises and seek medical care more than the average person, but the regular concurrent visits help get them into a pattern that is easier to manage.

You've mentioned patients with chronic medical problems, somatization, and pain all seem to benefit from this model. Are there any other patients whom you feel benefit from a collaborative model of care?

Patients with anxiety problems also really benefit from collaboration. Patients who present with anxiety and want benzodiazepines are a big challenge. We try to provide better care that minimizes the role of medication and ultimately dissuades drug-seeking behavior. All patients who present with anxiety are given a handout that describes our anxiety management plan. If they insist on medications or appear really to need them, the medical professionals prescribe a long-acting anxiolytic, and they are referred to me for psychotherapy. Patients are required to see me at least twice across a 1-month period, and then their medications are reevaluated. If the patient is still struggling after 1 month of psychotherapy and medication, the medical professionals will consider other medications. If patients do not follow through with therapy appointments, they may continue on the long-acting medication but will not be considered for a benzodiazepine. Our protocol puts some responsibility on the patients and encourages them to make changes to help themselves; it also helps us determine whether they are drug seeking. It is really helpful to make that differentiation early, because patients with substance abuse issues are highly unlikely to improve when getting better means they will lose their drug supply. Also, we can start working toward appropriate referral for substance abuse treatment, rather than realizing the problem too late, after we've made it worse by enabling the patient's problem.

I also think we're able to intervene more successfully with women in abusive relationships. They tend to be very reluctant to go to the CMHC. We've had a few cases in which I've been able to see a battered woman with the medical professional right after the patient was injured. I use a supportive approach to assess her readiness for change and provide her with education and resources. It often takes a few drop-in visits like this, and eventually, in some cases, the woman finally agrees to a few visits with me and makes a move to leave the relationship.

Do you find that the patients are different from those you would see in a community mental health center?

There is a significant contingent of patients who have been to our mental health center and refuse to go back or who have never gone there and will not go there because they're too fearful. Some patients just can't get there because they're too anxious or too chaotic. Some of the patients just don't function well enough to navigate the system and get services at the mental health center.

Many of the patients I see at the health center are still in early stages of recognizing that they have a mental health or emotional issue relevant to their health care. They're in precontemplation. They come to see me because their medical professional asked them to, and, because I'm in the same office, it is pretty easy for them to make an appointment and meet with me. They may only see me for one or two visits, but it's a start for them in their recognition and awareness that they may be dealing with a long-term problem. In some cases, they return to see me for more intensive treatment a few months or years later.

I see a lot of really young kids, ages 2 through 6, because their parents need assistance with parenting skills and behavior management. I help identify speech delays and refer parents to the local resources that address developmental delays. In most cases, I ultimately treat the parents, giving them additional support, behavioral strategies, and anger management skills. The intervention is often brief but effective.

How do patients respond to the collaboration?

Patients don't seem to worry about the sharing of information. Ninety-nine percent of patients haven't batted an eye when we've presented how we practice. A few patients have wanted specifics about how we communicate, but I've never had anyone refuse to allow us to do so. Patients always seem to think I should share more with the medical professionals and are surprised that there are things I don't share. Because we all work in the same office, they think we're all privy to everything. They are surprised when I don't know medical issues and the medical professionals don't know mental health issues. It is a division that professionals have made that just doesn't make sense to patients.

How do you collaborate with other types of health care professionals?

The nursing staff is critical to creating an atmosphere of collaboration. There are key nurses who are on the lookout for patients who need my services, who are attuned to mental health issues. Some of them will initiate the warm handoff themselves. One nurse, in particular, comes to find me when a patient's chief complaint is mental health related. If I'm available, I see the patient before the medical professional and provide a brief assessment. With this information, the medical professional is equipped to address medication decisions and can reinforce the need for psychotherapy. The nurses know the patient population well and may also know when patients are in crisis from their frequent calls and visits. They will let me know when those patients are scheduled to come in. Sometimes they'll prod the other medical professionals a bit to make referrals.

Do you find that the services you provide are different from what you would provide in a community mental health center?

I see a lot more people for one or two visits than I would at the community mental health center. I do an assessment and provide diagnostic feedback, including a review of how psychotherapy might progress and how it might help them. Unfortunately, because they are earlier in the readiness to change continuum, sometimes they're just not ready to follow through. Now that I've been here for a number of years, I see a pattern in which people obtain brief treatment repeatedly, slowly moving toward real change. We just get them earlier in the process. I tend to think many of the people who need that continuity of services wouldn't be able to get their needs met in a mental health center. They would have to go through the waiting-list process multiple times, possibly see multiple therapists over time, and would likely be lost to follow-up.

What do you consider are barriers to collaboration?

Being colocated reduces a lot of the barriers. Even so, I often find that we communicate in notes a lot because we don't have the chance to talk to each other. I think there are some cultural barriers in that I'm viewed as a psychotherapist who manages the mental health issues. I'd love to see more patients with medical problems, to help patients make lifestyle changes and improve coping with medical problems. I don't often get the opportunity to apply my expertise to traditional health psychology issues.

At the mental health center, there is very limited contact with medical professionals. I recognize that it is difficult to reach the medical professional, and collaboration takes time. When collaboration does occur, there is little professional-to-professional contact, which decreases the richness and detail of the interactions. It is harder to establish relationships among professionals. Collaboration between CMHC-based psychotherapists and medical professionals tend to focus on medication issues and current symptoms, rather than dialogue about the patient's background.

Were you anxious when you first tried to collaborate with medical professionals?

When I first started at Rising Sun Medical Center, I was anxious because I realized that the development of the collaboration started before I was hired and was discussed only by the administrators of the mental health center and the medical center. The doctor whom I would be working with was not approached at all. I made the assumption he knew and scheduled an appointment to meet him. Thankfully, he was gracious about it and was interested in what I might offer. The uncertainty about how I would be received by the whole staff also created some anxiety.

How did you work through your anxiety to make contact?

At that point in my training, I was well versed in the change process and knew how to identify readiness for change. My first task was to interview each member of the medical team and determine what problems they had experienced with mental health patients and the mental health system. That helped me get to know them and start to see ways that integration could help. I wasn't sure how beneficial it would be to interview every person individually, but it actually helped a great deal. It helped me learn more about each person individually, and it helped to distinguish the problems the receptionists might have, compared with the nurses, compared with the office manager.

How do your colleagues at the mental health center view what you do?

I think they see it as a positive thing. I don't know that they completely understand it, and some of them aren't sure they'd want to practice in a medical setting. Their comparable process is collaboration with other types of programs such as school-based services programs or drug court programs. So they do have some sense of how working with other professionals affects mental health care. They seem to be interested in the relative simplicity of my collaboration compared with the complex array of services and systems that come with a large community mental health center.

What do you consider the advantages about practicing in a primary care setting?

The physician I work with has known a lot of these patients for 30 years or more. He knows their families and their life situation and has a lot of shared history with them. He is a wealth of information. He recognizes personality disorders and family dynamics that might be relevant to a patient's presentation. He doesn't use formal mental health terms for these issues, but he tells me things before I begin to see a patient that help me in my assessment and in joining with the patient.

In my training I intentionally worked in medicine. I provided mental health services in a chronic pain center, a brain injury rehabilitation hospital, and in a primary care clinic at a Veterans Administration hospital. I really enjoy the variety of working in a medical setting and the convenience of the collaboration. I feel like I can provide a different level of care, because I know so much more about the patient and because I can make sure the medical professional and I are working together toward the best interest of the patient. I also really enjoy my ongoing relationship with the medical professionals.

There is another advantage to working in a medical setting. It is nice to know that a patient having physical symptoms in my office can be evaluated. I've had a few times that this was very reassuring. One time I was seeing a patient with panic symptoms, but it turned out that the patient was in the early stages of a heart attack in my office.

I think I've been interested in the mind–body connection for a very long time. Even in high school, I taught relaxation techniques and was curious about how our health was affected by our emotions.

What advice would you give to psychotherapists who are considering or just beginning to collaborate with medical professionals?

It is really helpful to find medical professionals who are psychologically minded. You have to pick and choose. To be fair, I think it takes the right psychotherapist as well. My training in various medical settings not only prepared me to work on a team, it also gave me a good foundation of medical knowledge—from diseases, to treatments, to medications. I've found all that information to be very useful.

It's important to make sure your suggestions are pragmatically helpful but also stay within your scope of expertise. Medical professionals can be territorial, so you have to listen and learn from them and allow them to get to know your expertise over time. They will respect you more once you've helped them with a difficult case, rather than trying to convince them that you're knowledgeable and useful. It helped me to shadow a medical professional to learn more about what they could do. The conversations we had during these experiences also helped the professionals understand what I could do and facilitated a respect for each other's expertise.

I've had to adapt how I talk about patients. Because I work in a medical setting, I now follow the medical model for case presentation. You have to start with a brief description because the medical professionals have so many patients, they don't know who you're talking about if you don't tell them the patient's name, age, demographics, symptoms, diagnoses, and medical issues. Also, I have to be brief in my discussion and get to the point quickly.

I've found working in a medical setting very rewarding. I reach patients that would never come see me at the CMHC and enjoy the colleagueship that has developed with my medical colleagues. I think that the minor changes I've had to make in how I practice have been well worth the benefits of being in a medical setting.

15

Collaborative
Crisis Services

$\mathbf{M}$r. Bassetti is the director of psychiatric emergency services at Hunterdon Medical Center in Flemington, New Jersey. He strives to achieve collaborative care for all patients who receive crisis services. Medical professionals are often the first to intervene in mental health crises. Patients not uncommonly present with suicidality, domestic violence, substance abuse crisis, and psychosis. Unfortunately, medical professionals are ill suited to cope with these mental health emergencies and must rely on psychiatric crisis services to assess their patients and facilitate engagement in mental health services.

It is in the patient's best interest if there is coordination between the crisis services unit and the medical professional whom the patient first contacted. In a coordinated system, when medical professionals determine that the patient needs psychiatric crisis services, they will know how and when to contact the crisis services professional. In response, the crisis services professional will trust the medical professional's assessment of the situation and will facilitate the patients' immediate transfer to care. In addition, the psychiatric crisis services professional will communicate the case disposition and follow-up plan to the medical professional. The medical professional can then ensure the patient gets follow-up care, rather than waiting until the next crisis to repeat the cycle.

Excerpts from an interview with Mr. Bassetti illustrate the benefits of a collaborative model, the challenges of providing collaborative psychiatric crisis management, and the methods he has used to create a collaborative atmosphere and esprit de corps in the service that he manages.

How does collaboration affect the mental health care that you provide?

We are really committed to keeping patients in the least restrictive environment possible. Involving the primary care medical professional often prevents a hospitalization. We can observe the patient in the emergency department for 24 hours, start a medication, and arrange linkage to appropriate medical and mental health services. This is particularly true with patients who come in often. We know their history and can plan their treatment on the basis of what has worked for them before.

Also, we operate our screening service differently. We see ourselves as consultants to the medical professionals. Basically, if medical professionals refer a patient, we accept their definition of "crisis" and will try to help. Sometimes we help medical professionals and patients with end-of-life issues, helping a child getting stitches, drug and alcohol presentations—people who may or may not have mental illness. The fact that we accept their definition of a crisis encourages the medical professionals to see our staff members as resources. They seek us out. I think this is different from many psychiatric crisis services that will only accept evaluations for mental health issues that involve immediate danger. We're an emergency service. We're the only ones in the county. There is nowhere else for people in crisis to go, so someone has to address these issues. Granted, we can't do ongoing therapy, but we can do what we can do. We can provide immediate evaluation, assessment, brief therapy, and linkage to appropriate services.

How else do you try to assist medical professionals?

I find that medical professionals sometimes struggle with behavioral health issues. They aren't sure what to do when there isn't a test you can run to figure out what is causing the problem and what to do about it. Usually the patients who get referred to us are not your standard patient. They are high utilizers of service and really burden an emergency department. For example, a patient who arrives intoxicated often waits in the emergency department for 12 to 15 hours before an evaluation can be done, which means there is one less bed available for that time. In the emergency department, there is a natural tension between providing treatment and discharging the patient quickly. We often are able to assess the patient, determine that close follow-up is an appropriate option, arrange that follow-up, and help get the patient on his or her way.

The floor consults on the inpatient services are the best. You have the opportunity to talk to the medical professionals who have requested your expertise, and they are really grateful for the assistance. They appreciate when you can link patients with the appropriate services. Also, we begin to get to know the medical professionals, and they get to know us. It is a lot easier when we have a relationship with the referring medical professional, because then we aren't just faceless people on the other end of the phone. We develop trust over time.

How do you collaborate with primary care medical professionals?

We have a mobile outreach grant that pays for someone to be available 24/7 to go out into the community to provide assessment and linkage to services. We also have a psychiatric advanced practice nurse who can go to outpatient offices to evaluate patients with specific medication needs. Providing real-time evaluation often saves the patient a trip to the emergency department. The medical professionals also help us. Sometimes the advanced practice nurses can't provide close follow-up because of time constraints, but they may manage the medication through the consultation with the primary care medical professional. We also have a postpartum depression program. The medical professionals know we will immediately evaluate their patients and make recommendations regarding medications and other issues to get the mother on the road to recovery.

How do you create a collaborative environment with your staff?

It starts with who you hire. I hire for two things—intelligence and motivation—because we can train for the rest. I tell people in the interview that our philosophy may be different from other places. I have prospective employees meet with current employees to learn about our culture. If an applicant doesn't want to work collaboratively, the person is likely to self-select out of the interview process.

When we hire new employees, they undergo a training process that emphasizes collaboration. They spend at least 80 hours in training, being paired with seasoned staff and documenting cases separately to help the new staff learn how to document correctly. We emphasize the importance of assessing family, social, and medical factors and integrating them into a coherent assessment. The treatment plan should come organically out of assessment. We also emphasize follow-up to ensure the patient actually attends the linkage appointment, ending our involvement only once the patient has connected with services or refuses further intervention.

We also support collaboration at the larger system level. Basically, collaborative care is our standard of care, a part of our treatment process. We don't "make time" for it. When our staff gets a call for a consult, the first step is to discuss the situation with the referring medical professional to get the context of the referral and understand the reasons for it. After the evaluation, our staff members report their findings and treatment plan to the referring medical professional. The discharge summary is always faxed to the medical professionals so that they know their patients were in the emergency department, the course of their stay, and the discharge plan. We also negotiate which professional is going to implement what parts of the treatment plan and how the various professionals will communicate about the plan. Collaboration is an integral part of the process.

What do you consider to be the barriers to collaborative psychiatric crisis services?

Unfortunately, a direct referral to outpatient mental health services may not be communicated to the primary care medical professional. The behavioral health system is insulated from the primary care medical system—more by default than by design—to detriment of the patient. All psychotherapists are supposed to contact referring medical professional and have a dialogue about the patient, but it doesn't always happen.

There are a lot of reasons psychotherapists don't communicate. Often, it is the sheer volume of patients with needs. However, it doesn't take a whole lot of time to leave someone a voicemail. With technology there is no excuse not to communicate with all of the professionals involved in a patient's care.

Another issue is training people to practice collaboratively. New clinicians have a lot to learn, and we try to integrate collaborative practice into their learning curve to avoid overwhelming them with too much, too fast. As a supervisor, you have to pick your training battles, realize when someone just can't integrate the collaborative piece yet, and let it go for a bit. I've found that different mental health disciplines have different levels of training and understanding of collaboration, so I have to begin where their other training leaves off.

Finally, collaboration is difficult and almost impossible when the medical professional doesn't return phone calls and participate in the collaboration. It is a small minority of medical professionals who don't collaborate, but it is very frustrating. It is particularly problematic when a new clinician who is not completely sold on collaboration has this experience.

Were you anxious when you started to collaborate?

No. I had a phenomenal mentor, Rob Lieberman, at JFK Medical Center in Edison, New Jersey. He should be in the annals of emergency mental health services! He was a master's level counselor in the emergency department in the 1970s, so when I came along in the 1980s, his mentorship made the transition painless and seamless. It was second nature to take psychological theory and apply it into practice by working collaboratively with medical professionals. I attribute my comfort level to his mentorship.

What advice would you give to psychotherapists who are considering or are just beginning to collaborate with medical professionals?

I do have one tip regarding communication with medical professionals. Medical professionals want a brief synopsis of the case. They want a very concise message about what is going on, why it's going on, and what you suggest be done about it. If you can't formulate the information in a concise, usable manner, you're lost.

Psychotherapists have to recognize that many medical conditions cause psychiatric symptoms. If psychotherapists have any suspicion that a patient has an underlying medical condition, they're ethically bound to make a referral to a medical professional for assessment. I often refer to medical professionals and really push patients to follow up to rule out my suspicions. These referrals are really just hypothesis testing, which is what a good clinician does anyway.

Everything we've discussed is about human relationships. You do whatever you need to do to build the relationship. You have to invest the time, energy, and commitment to create and maintain collaborative relationships.

Afterword

Most psychotherapists and medical professionals entered their field out of a genuine desire to help people lead happy, healthy lives. Some medical patients have solely an acute biomedical problem such as a sinus infection or a muscle sprain. Some people who seek mental health care have solely psychosocial issues that do not have long-term consequences for their physical health. However, most people experience distress both psychically and somatically. Relationships suffer. Patients with chronic illness must adjust to a "new normal." Patients experiencing a major depression often experience intense aches and malaise that interferes with recovery. Many people do not realize that a biomedical problem may underlie their psychiatric symptoms or vice versa.

Decades ago, medicine started shifting toward biopsychosocial, whole-person care. Many medical professionals focused on people and their context before this "official" shift altered training and expectations. With the advent of the biopsychosocial model, medical professionals' purview grew to include the alleviation of suffering that arose from nonbiomedical causes. Interviewing courses taught them to ask patients about stress and about the impact of their illness on their daily lives. Not all medical professionals "walk the walk," but many, especially those in primary care, do.

In contrast, many psychotherapists still define their purview narrowly. Few would deny that there is a link between our minds and bodies. Yet our practice trails these theoretical paradigm shifts. Many psychotherapists do not ask about physical health. Many psychotherapists never communicate with patient's medical professionals. We do not even "talk the talk," yet alone "walk the walk."

In the beginning of this book, we asked the reader to contemplate how collaboration and a collaborative mind-set might have altered patient care provided in the past. Could underlying physical symptoms related to the patient's psychiatric symptoms have been missed? Did patients struggling with an illness, or the illness of a family member, ever have the opportunity to work with their medical professionals to optimize functioning and coping with the illness? Did the medical professionals of patients with chronic pain or substance abuse problems unwittingly play into these issues because they did not have the information they needed to provide optimal care? How often did psychotherapists and medical professionals fail to work together to provide the best care?

To take this exercise a step farther, contemplate times of distress in your own life or the life of a loved one. Was it solely biomedical, solely psychosocial, or was both physical and emotional functioning affected? Would you have talked to your medical professional about it? Would you have talked to a psychotherapist about it? Would it have helped you to have your psychotherapist and medical professional work together as a team? As a psychotherapist, would you have desired an integrated model of care?

Just as medicine is shifting, mental health must make a shift toward greater contact with the medical world. Separate evolution of the two systems and completely separate training and practice settings makes this difficult. Yet it is common sense that the two "sides of the house" need to work together. Ask someone who does not work in health care if it makes sense to them that a patient's medical and mental health professionals talk to each other. Most people are surprised that we do not.

We can strengthen each other, and create a healing synergy. But we have to go outside our comfort zones, and reach out to our medical colleagues. Recognize that not all medical professionals will be receptive. Be prepared for some rejection, and some contacts that feel awkward. Just as we encourage patients to "try out" a behavior until it begins to feel normal, psychotherapists must "try out" collaboration until it becomes second nature. Those professionals who have made this shift feel it has improved the care they provide and would "never go back" to a separate model of care.

Collaboration and the resulting referral relationships with medical professionals may also reach many patients that would otherwise never darken the doorstep of a psychotherapist. It is hard to argue with the statistics—the vast majority of people who experience emotional distress never get mental heath services. We need to broaden our net to help patients who either cannot use traditional psychotherapy or do not understand what we have to offer. These patients *do* seek help from the medical system. If we choose to meet patients where they are, we can help a much higher proportion of people who could benefit from mental health services.

Beginning to collaborate does not necessitate a practice overhaul. Assess where you are now, and make small changes to implement collaboration. Simply ask patients about their health. Get a release to their medical professional, and send a brief summary letter at the beginning and end of treatment. Make these simple acts part of the daily routine. Over time, it will become clear which medical professionals are willing to collaborate and which have little interest in doing so. Psychotherapists may be surprised how often collaboration affects the course and outcome of medical and mental health care. Collaboration begets collaboration, and patients will reap the benefits.

Appendix A

Medical Problems Associated With Psychiatric Symptoms

Cancer

☐ Pancreatic cancer can present with severe depression.
☐ Lung carcinomas can cause progressive dementias.
☐ Breast and colon cancer is associated with depression.
☐ Hematologic malignancy is associated with depression.

Cardiopulmonary Conditions Associated With Depression and Anxiety

☐ Mitral valve prolapse, arrythmias, and implantable defibrillators are associated with anxiety.
☐ Heart disease is associated with depression and anxiety.
☐ Hypertension is associated with anxiety.
☐ Myocardial infarction is associated with depression and anxiety.
☐ Hypoxia is associated with depression and anxiety.
☐ Hypercarbia is associated with depression and anxiety.

Compiled from Chuang and Forman (2006), Good and Nelson (2005), and Polsky et al. (2005).

Endocrine and Metabolic Diseases

☐ Cushing's disease can lead to a variety of mental status changes, including feeling moody and periods of elation alternating with periods of depression. Exogenous steroids can cause these symptoms.

☐ Addison's disease can present with symptoms of social withdrawal, apathy, and depression. Weight loss and vomiting may resemble anorexia.

☐ Hepatic failure may involve apathy, lethargy, and mood swings.

☐ Hyperthyroidism may lead to hyperactivity, pressured speech, irritability, and impulsivity that may masquerade as "mania." Frequently, patients with hyperthyroidism are very thin.

☐ Hypothyroidism can cause depression in some patients. Apathy, social withdrawal, and lack of interest in previously enjoyed activities are some signs. These patients are usually overweight or obese.

☐ Hypoglycemia can cause anxiety, progressing to various neurologic symptoms. Patients may also have personality changes.

☐ Parathyroid disorders may include symptoms of dementia, depression, anxiety, psychosis, and apathy.

☐ Pheochromocytomas can cause patients to have anxiety or manic attacks (or both).

☐ Porphyria is associated with psychosis.

☐ Carcinoids are associated with depression.

☐ Diabetes Types 1 and 2 are associated with depression.

Infectious Diseases Associated With Depression

☐ AIDS
☐ Epstein-Barr
☐ Lyme disease
☐ Hepatitis
☐ Influenza
☐ Syphilis
☐ Tuberculosis

Neurological Disorders Associated With Depression

- ☐ Stroke
- ☐ Alzheimer's disease
- ☐ Parkinson's disease
- ☐ Head and spinal trauma
- ☐ Multiple sclerosis
- ☐ Wilson's disease
- ☐ Brain tumors
- ☐ Normal pressure hydrocephalus
- ☐ Seizure disorder

Nutritional Deficiencies Associated With Depression

- ☐ Folate
- ☐ Vitamin B12
- ☐ Pyridoxine (B6)
- ☐ Riboflavin (B2)
- ☐ Thiamine (B1)
- ☐ Iron
- ☐ Vitamin D

Others Associated With Depression

- ☐ Anemia
- ☐ Systemic lupus erythematosus
- ☐ Vasculitis

Appendix B

Psychiatric Side Effects of Commonly Used Medications

Antiarrhythmics

- ☐ Lidocaine   Psychosis and anxiety
- ☐ Digoxin   Visual hallucinations, anorexia, and depression

Antihypertensives

- ☐ Beta-blockers   Fatigue, insomnia, lethargy, and decreased libido
- ☐ Alpha-blockers   Depression
- ☐ Thiazide diuretics   Fatigue, weakness, and anorexia

Antituberculosis Therapy

- ☐ Schizophrenia-like syndrome

Antiparkinsonian Agents

- ☐ Depression and psychotic symptoms

Compiled from Chuang and Forman (2006).

Cancer Chemotherapy Agents

- ☐ Interferon   Depression
- ☐ Procarbazine   Confusion

Cimetidine (Treatment for Peptic Ulcer Disease)

- ☐ Depression, toxic psychosis, and confusion

Drugs With Anticholingergic Properties

- ☐ Tricyclic antidepressants   Worsening depression
                                 and psychosis
- ☐ Antiparkinsonian agents   Depression and psychotic
                                 symptoms

Anti-Malaria Drugs

- ☐ Anxiety and psychosis

Oral Contraceptives

- ☐ Depression

Psychoactive Substances

- ☐ Alcohol   Depression
- ☐ Opioids   Depression
- ☐ Amphetamines Toxic psychosis and depression
- ☐ Cocaine   Toxic psychosis and depression

Quinolone Antibiotics

- ☐ Floxin   Toxic psychosis
- ☐ Cipro   Anxiety, agitation, and confusion
- ☐ Levaquin   Insomnia, depression, and toxic
               psychosis

Steroids

☐ Depression, mania, and confusion

Appendix C

The Collaborative
Psychotherapist's Toolbox

Sample Letter of Introduction

Dear (Medical Professional's Name),

I am writing to introduce myself and my practice. I am a (specialty) with expertise in working with (specific population or issue). I have been practicing for XX years. I would describe my practice style as (e.g., solution oriented, family oriented, cognitive behavioral, etc.).

My office is located (location, in reference to the medical office). I see patients (particular days, evenings, weekend days). I accept the following insurance plans:

I am writing to you because I am interested in sharing patient care with primary care medical professionals. I know that many primary care medical professionals are frustrated by a lack of communication from psychotherapists. I understand how important it is to work collaboratively with you. I am happy to discuss patients with you prior to referral and to ensure that you are kept abreast of treatment progress after referral. I will notify you when the patient has terminated treatment.

I hope that you will not hesitate to contact me if I may be of assistance. I have enclosed business cards for your reference. I would be happy to meet with you to discuss my practice and opportunities for working together in the future. I will contact you by phone in the next few weeks to discuss whether you feel this would be helpful to you. I look forward to working with you in the future.

Sincerely,

Name and Title

Sample Integrated Collaboration
Tracking System

PROGRESS NOTE

NAME: _____ DATE: _____

Appearance/Behavior   Sensorium/Intellect:

Thought Process/Content: Insight/Judgment:

Mood/Affect: Suicidal/Homicidal:

Session Content:

_____

_____

_____

_____

_____

Time: Group _____ Individual _____ Collateral _____ Other: _____

Medical professional contact: _____

_____
  Name and Title

Sample Separate Collaboration Tracking System: Collateral Contact Sheet

PATIENT NAME: _____

PATIENT ID#: _____

WITH WHOM CONTACT MADE: _____

DATE	PHONE	E-MAIL	U.S. MAIL	FAX

NOTE _____

_____

_____

_____

_____

WITH WHOM CONTACT MADE: _____

DATE	PHONE	E-MAIL	U.S. MAIL	FAX

NOTE _____

_____

_____

_____

_____

WITH WHOM CONTACT MADE: _____

DATE	PHONE	E-MAIL	U.S. MAIL	FAX

NOTE _____

_____

_____

_____

_____

WITH WHOM CONTACT MADE: _____

DATE	PHONE	E-MAIL	U.S. MAIL	FAX

NOTE _____

_____

_____

_____

_____

Sample Postreferral Letter

Dear (Medical Professional's Name),

Thank you for your referral of (Patient Name). I saw (name) on (date) for an initial appointment. My working diagnosis is (diagnosis). I anticipate that I will work with (name) for (time frame, approximate number of sessions).

In an effort to improve communication, I have enclosed a form that I kindly request you to complete and return. This form helps me understand your concerns and history with this patient. In addition, it would be helpful to know the extent to which you would like to be in contact about this patient and the best way to contact you. I will do my best to keep you informed about your patients' progress in psychotherapy as needed. I will certainly let you know when your patient stops attending therapy.

Again, thank you for the referral. I look forward to collaborating in the care of (Patient Name). I have enclosed a business card for your future reference.

Sincerely,

Name and Title

Medical Professional Communication Preference Form

Patient Name:

Medical Professional Name:

Specific Concerns and Questions:

I prescribe psychotropic medicine to this patient: ___No __ Yes
Medication and dosage: _____

With this patient, I want the following level of communication:

_____ Minimal (critical incidents and termination only, appropriate for most situational, non–health care related issues)

_____ Moderate (monthly updates, appropriate for patients with concomitant medical issues affected by behavioral or mental health issues)

_____ Intensive (weekly updates, appropriate for patients in crisis or whose health is adversely affected by behavioral or mental health issues)

The best way to communicate is (please check all that apply):

_____ Telephone number: _____

Interrupt patient care? Yes/No

_____ Fax number:_____

_____ Pager number: _____ Emergent Only? Yes/No

_____ E-mail address: _____

Thank you. I look forward to working together to provide optimal care to your patient.

PLEASE RETURN IN THE ENCLOSED STAMPED ADDRESSED ENVELOPE.

Sample Termination Notification Letter

Dear (Professional Name),

I am writing to inform you that I have terminated treatment with (Patient Name). Termination was/was not mutually agreed upon. (Patient Name) fully/partially/minimally achieved his or her goals for treatment.

As (Patient Name)'s medical professional, you are in a unique position to help him or her reenter psychotherapy if necessary in the future. (Patient Name) and I have/have not discussed conditions that would indicate a return to therapy is indicated. These include (list):

(For patients who terminated prematurely): I hope that (Patient Name) will seek further psychotherapy. Please discuss options with (Patient Name). I would be happy to see him or her again in my practice, or you may suggest an alternate psychotherapist if (Patient Name) is not willing to continue work with me. Please do not hesitate to contact me if you have any questions or concerns.

(For patients who terminated upon mutual agreement): I hope that (Patient Name) found his or her work with me to be helpful. I would be happy to accept him or her back into my practice in the future, if the need arises. Please do not hesitate to contact me if you have any questions or concerns.

Sincerely,

Name and Title

Appendix D

Additional Resources

Influential References on Medical–Mental Health Cultural Differences and Collaboration

Blount, A. (Ed.). (1998). *Integrated primary care: The future of medical and mental health collaboration.* New York: Norton.

Bray, J. H., & McDaniel, S. H. (1998). Behavioral health practice in primary care settings. In L. Vandecreek, S. Knapp, & T. Jackson (Eds.), *Innovations in clinical practice: A source book* (Vol. 16, pp. 313–323). Sarasota, FL: Professional Resource Press.

Bray, J. H., & Rogers, J. C. (1995). Linking psychologists and family physicians for collaborative practice. *Professional Psychology, 26,* 132–138.

Campbell, T. L., McDaniel, S. H., & Seaburn, D. B. (1992). Family systems medicine: New opportunities for psychologists. In T. J. Akamatsu, M. A. Parris Stephens, S. E. Hobfall, & J. H. Crowther (Eds.), *Family health psychology* (pp. 193–215). New York: Hemisphere Publication Services.

Frank, R. G., McDaniel, S. H., Bray, J. H., & Heldring, M. (Eds.). (2004). *Primary care psychology.* Washington, DC: American Psychological Association.

Glenn, M. L. (1987). *Collaborative health care.* New York: Praeger.

Haley, W. E., McDaniel, S. H., Bray, J. H., Frank, R. G., Heldring, M., Johnson, S. B., et al. (1998). Psychological practice in primary care settings: Practical tips for clinicians. *Professional Psychologist, 29,* 237–244.

McDaniel, S. H., Belar, C., Schroeder, C., Hargrove, D. S., & Freeman, E. L. (2002). A training curriculum for primary care psychologists in primary care. *Professional Psychology, 33,* 65–72.

McDaniel, S. H., Hepworth, J., & Doherty, W. (1992). *Medical family therapy: A biopsychosocial approach to families with health problems.* New York: Basic Books.

Pace, T. M., Chaney, J. M., Mullins, L. L., & Olson, R. A. (1995). Psychological consultation with primary care physicians: Obstacles and opportunities in the medical setting. *Professional Psychology, 26,*123–131.

Rolland, J. S. (1994). *Families, illness, and disability: An integrative treatment model.* New York: Basic Books.

Schroeder, C. (1979). Psychologists in a private pediatric practice. *Journal of Pediatric Psychology, 4,* 5–18.

Wynne, L. C., McDaniel, S. H., & Weber, T. (1987). *Systems consultation: A new perspective for family therapy.* New York: Guilford Press.

Mind–Body Connection Internet Links

☐ *Mind/Body Connection: How Your Emotions Affect Your Health (AAFP):* http://familydoctor.org/782.xml

☐ *The Mind and Body Institute at Harvard University Health Services:* http://huhs.harvard.edu/CWHC/MindnBody/MindBodyInst.htm

☐ *The Benson-Henry Institute for Mind Body Medicine:* http://www.mbmi.org/home

☐ *How Does Stress Affect Your Body? (APA):* http://helping.apa.org/articles/article.php?id=141

☐ *Stress and Disease: New Perspectives (NIH):* http://www.nih.gov/news/WordonHealth/oct2000/story01.htm

☐ *Positive Thinking: A Skill for Stress Relief (Mayo Clinic):* http://www.mayoclinic.com/health/positive-thinking/SR00009

☐ *Relax: Techniques to Help You Achieve Tranquility (Mayo Clinic):* http://www.mayoclinic.com/health/relaxation-technique/SR00007

☐ *Stress and Your Health (http://womenshealth.gov):* http://womenshealth.gov/faq/stress.htm

☐ *Stress: The Mind-Body Connection* (Michael Gerrish, MS): http://www.webmd.com/content/chat_transcripts/2/110852

☐ *Center for Mindfulness in Medicine, Health Care, and Society:* http://www.umassmed.edu/cfm/index.aspx

Appendix E

Questions to Elicit the Patient's and Family's Story

History of the Illness/Problem

☐ How long have you had this problem?

☐ How did you first notice it?

☐ How did family and friends react to changes you were going through?

☐ Who first suggested that you seek medical help?

☐ How many physicians and other health care professionals have been involved in your care? How have they been helpful? How have they not been helpful?

☐ What tests or procedures were needed to diagnose this problem? Have your been hospitalized? What medications are you taking?

☐ What is your understanding of the current status of your health?

Impact of the Illness on the Individual

☐ How has your daily functioning changed?

☐ What do you miss most from before you were ill?

From *Models of Collaboration: A Guide for Mental Health Professionals Working With Health Care Practitioners* (pp. 309–310), by D. B. Seaburn, A. D. Lorenz, W. B. Gunn, Jr., B. A. Gawinski, and L. B. Mauksch, 1996, New York: Basic Books. Copyright 1996 by Basic Books, a member of Perseus Books Group. Reprinted with permission.

- [ ] What have you learned from the illness that has been useful to you?
- [ ] What do you think will happen with the illness in the future?
- [ ] How has your vision of the future changed? What do you hope for?

Impact of the Illness on the Family

- [ ] What changes have occurred in your family since the illness began?
- [ ] How are family members coping with this difficulty?
- [ ] Do you talk about the illness as a family?
- [ ] Who has been most affected? Who has been least affected?
- [ ] Who has the greatest responsibility for caring for the ill family member? How does the primary caregiver get support?
- [ ] In general, how do you support one another? How do you express emotions?
- [ ] Does this experience remind you or your family of other difficulties the family has faced?
- [ ] How well do you feel the family is coping? Is there anything the family members wish they could do differently?

Meaning of the Illness and Family Resources

- [ ] Why do you think this illness has occurred?
- [ ] How long do you think it will last?
- [ ] Are there times when the illness seems stronger than you or the family? Are there times when you or the family system are stronger than the illness?
- [ ] Do you or your family have religious or spiritual beliefs about this illness? Is so, what are they?
- [ ] What are the strengths of your family? What keeps you going?

References

Accreditation Council for Graduate Medical Education. (2005). *The ACGME Outcome Project: An introduction.* Retrieved June 19, 2007, from http://www.acgme.org/outcome/project/OPintrorev1_7-05.ppt

American Association for Marriage and Family Therapy. (2001). *AAMFT code of ethics.* Retrieved November 10, 2007, from http://www.aamft.org/resources/LRMPlan/Ethics/ethicscode2001.asp

American Psychiatric Association. (1998, November 20). Collaboration between psychiatrists, primary care doctors vital in ensuring more mental health care. *Psychiatric News,* p. 9.

American Psychological Association. (2002). *Ethical principles of psychologists and code of conduct.* Retrieved November 10, 2007, from http://www.apa.org/ethics/code2002.html

American Psychological Association Practice Directorate. (2006). [Survey of psychologists' opinions and practice patterns regarding collaboration with medical professionals]. Unpublished raw data.

Ansseau, M., Dierick, M., Buntinkx, F., Cnockaert, P., De Smedt, J., Van Den Haute, M., et al. (2004). High prevalence of mental disorders in primary care. *Journal of Affective Disorders, 78,* 49–55.

Bair, M. J., Robinson, R. L., Eckert, G. J., Stang, P. E., Crogban, T. W., & Kroenke, K. (2004). Impact of pain in depression treatment response in primary care. *Psychosomatic Medicine, 66,* 17–22.

Barsky, A. J., & Borus, J. F. (1995). Somatization and medicalization in the era of managed care. *Journal of the American Medical Association, 274,* 1931–1934.

Bass, C. (1990). *Somatisation: Physical symptoms and psychological disorder.* Oxford, England: Oxford University Press.

Benson, H. (1975). *The relaxation response.* New York: Morrow.

Benson, H. (1996). *Timeless healing: The power and biology of belief.* New York: Scribner.

Benson, H., Beary, J. F., & Carol, M. P. (1974). The relaxation response. *Psychiatry, 37,* 37–46.

Bleijenberg, G., & Fennis, J. F. (1989). Anamnestic and psychological features in diagnosis and prognosis of functional abdominal complaints: A prospective study. *Gut, 30,* 1076–1081.

Brody, D. S., Khaliq, A. A., & Thompson, T. L. (1997). Patients' perspectives of the management of emotional distress in primary care settings. *Journal of General Internal Medicine, 12,* 403–406.

Cameron, J., & Mauksch, L. (2002). Collaborative family healthcare in an uninsured primary care population: Stages of integration. *Families, Systems and Health, 20,* 343–363.

Chantal, M. L. R., Brazeau, C. M., Rovi, S., Yick, C., & Johnson, M. S. (2005). Collaboration between mental health professionals and family physicians: A survey of New Jersey family physicians. *Primary Care Companion to the Journal of Clinical Psychiatry, 7,* 12–14.

Chesney, M. A., & Antoni, M. H. (2002). Translating a decade of innovation into clinical practice. In M. A. Chesney & M. H. Antoni (Eds.), *Innovative approaches to health psychology: Prevention and treatment lessons from AIDS* (pp. 3–12). Washington, DC: American Psychological Association.

Chuang, L., & Forman, N. (2006, April 13). Mental disorders secondary to general medical conditions. *eMedicine from WebMD.* Retrieved February 11, 2007, from http://www.emedicine.com/med/topic3447.htm

Crits-Cristoph, P. (1992). The efficacy of brief dynamic psychotherapy: A meta-analysis. *American Journal of Psychiatry, 149,* 151–158.

Croghan, T. W., Schoenbaum, M., Sherbourne, C. D., & Koegel, P. (2006). A framework to improve the quality of treatment for depression in primary care. *Psychiatric Services, 57,* 623–660.

Cross, N., March, L., Lapsley, H., Byrne, E., & Brooks, P. (2006). Patient self-efficacy and health locus of control: Relationships with health status and arthritis-related expenditure. *Rheumatology, 45,* 92–96.

Cummings, N. A. (2000). The behavioral health practitioner of the future: The efficacy of psychoeducational programs in integrated primary care. In J. L. Thomas & J. L. Cummings (Eds.), *The collected papers of Nicholas A. Cummings: Vol. 1. The value of psychological treatment* (pp. 406–422). Phoenix, AZ: Zeig, Tucker & Theisen.

Dec, E. (2006). Impact of locus of control on clinical outcomes in renal dialysis. *Advanced Chronic Kidney Disease, 1,* 76–85.

DiMatteo, M. (2004). Variations in patients' adherence to medical recommendations: A quantitative review of 50 years of research. *Medical Care, 42,* 200–209.

Doherty, W. J. (2007). Fixing health care. *Psychotherapy Networker, 31*(3), 24–31.

Doherty, W. J., McDaniel, S. H., & Baird, M. A. (1996). Five levels of primary care/behavioral healthcare collaboration. *Behavioral Healthcare Tomorrow, 5*(5), 25–28.

Ellen, A. (2005, December 6). Workouts are potent medicine for the mentally ill. *The New York Times,* p. 1.

Elliot, C., & Chambers, T. (Eds.). (2004). *Prozac as a way of life: Studies in social medicine.* Chapel Hill: University of North Carolina Press.

Engel, G. L. (1977, April 8). The need for a new medical model: A challenge for biomedicine. *Science, 196,* 129–136.

Engel, G. L. (1980). The clinical application of the biopsychosocial model. *American Journal of Psychiatry, 137,* 535–544.

Escobar, J. I., Gara, M. A., Diaz-Martinez, A. M., Interian, A., Warman, M., Allen, L. A., et al. (2007). Effectiveness of a time-limited cognitive behavior therapy-type intervention among patients with medically unexplained symptoms. *Annals of Family Medicine, 5,* 328–335.

Escobar, J. I., Waitzkin, H., Silver, R. C., Gara, M., & Holman, A. (1998). Abridged somatization: A study in primary care. *Psychosomatic Medicine, 60,* 466–472.

Fleet, R. D., Dupuis, G., Marchand, A., Burelle, D., Arsenault, A., & Beitman, B. D. (1996). Panic disorder in emergency department chest pain patients: prevalence, comorbidity, suicidal ideation, and physician recognition. *American Journal of Medicine, 101,* 371–380.

Frank, R. G., McDaniel, S. H., Bray, J. H., & Heldring, M. (Eds.). (2004). *Primary care psychology.* Washington, DC: American Psychological Association.

Funnell, M. M. (2000). Helping patients take charge of their chronic illness. *Family Practice Management, 17,* 47–55.

Future of Family Medicine Project Leadership Committee. (2004). The future of family medicine: A collaborative project of the family medicine community. *Annals of Family Medicine, 2,* S3–S32.

Gallagher, A., Thomas, J., Hamilton, W., & White, P. (2004). Incidence of fatigue symptoms and diagnoses presenting in UK primary care from 1990 to 2001. *Journal of Research in Social Medicine, 97,* 571–575.

Gatchel, R. J., & Oordt, M. S. (2003). *Clinical health psychology and primary care: Practical advice and clinical guidance for successful collaboration.* Washington, DC: American Psychological Association.

Gilbody, S., Bower, P., Fletcher, J., Richards, D., & Sutton, A. J. (2006). Collaborative care for depression: A cumulative meta-analysis and review of longer-term outcomes. *Archives of Internal Medicine, 166,* 2314–2321.

Good, W. V., & Nelson, J. E. (2005). *Psychiatry made ridiculously simple* (4th ed.). Miami, FL: MedMaster.

Grazier, K. L., Hegadus, A. M., Carli, T., Neal, D., & Reynolds, K. (2003). Integration of behavioral and physical healthcare for a Medicaid population through a public–public partnership. *Psychiatric Services, 54,* 1508–1512.

Greer, J., & Halgin, R. (2006). Predictors of physician–patient agreement on symptom etiology in primary care. *Psychosomatic Medicine, 68,* 277–282.

Gunn, W., & Stulp, C. (1989). [A qualitative look at the difficult interaction]. Unpublished raw data.

Haas, L. J., Leiser, J. P., MacGill, M. K., & Sanyer, O. N. (2005). Management of the difficult patient. *American Family Physician, 72,* 2063–2068.

Hahn, S., Kroenke, K., Spitzer, R., Body, D., Williams, J., Linzer, M., et al. (1996). The difficult patient: Prevalence, psychopathology, and functional impairment. *Journal of General Internal Medicine, 11,* 1–8.

Hamilton, N., Karoly, P., & Zautra, A. (2005). Health goal cognition and adjustment in women with fibromyalgia. *Journal of Behavioral Medicine, 28,* 455–466.

Haugg, T. T., Mykletun, A., & Dahl, A. A. (2004). The association between anxiety, depression, and somatic symptoms in a large population: The HUNT-II study. *Psychosomatic Medicine, 66,* 845–851.

Hoyt, M. (1995). *Brief therapy and managed care: Readings for contemporary practice.* New York: Jossey-Bass.

Hoyt, M. (2000). *Some stories are better than others: Doing what works in brief therapy and managed care.* Philadelphia: Brunner/Mazel.

Hoyt, M. (2004). *The present is a gift: Mo' better stories from the world of brief therapy.* New York: iUniverse.com.

Hughes, J. (Writer/Director). (1989). *Uncle Buck* [Motion picture]. United States: Universal Pictures.

Institute of Medicine. (2001). *Crossing the quality chasm: A new health system for the twenty-first century.* Washington, DC: National Academies Press.

James, L. C., & Folen, R. A. (2005). *The primary care consultant: The next frontier for psychologists in hospitals and clinics.* Washington, DC: American Psychological Association.

Jolly, W., Froom, J., & Rosen, M. G. (1980). The genogram. *Journal of Family Practice, 10,* 251–255.

Kahn, A. A., Khan, A., Harezlak, J., Tu, W., & Kroenke, K. (2002). Somatic symptoms in primary care: Etiology and outcome. *Psychosomatics, 44,* 471–478.

Kahn, L. S., Halbreich, U., Bloom, M. S., Bidani, R., Rich, E., & Hershey, C. O. (2004). Screening for mental illness in primary care clinics. *Journal of Psychiatry in Medicine, 34,* 345–362.

Kathol, R., Saravay, S. M., Lobo, A., & Ormel, J. (2006). Epidemiologic trends and costs of fragmentation. *Medical Clinics of North America, 90,* 549–572.

Kato, K., Sullivan, P., Evengard, B., & Pedersen, N. (2006). Chronic widespread pain and its comorbidities: A population-based study. *Archives of Internal Medicine, 166,* 1649–1654.

Katon, W., VonKorff, M., Lin, E., Lipscomb, P., Russo, J., Wagner, E., et al. (1990). Distressed high utilizers of medical care: *DSM–III–R* diagnoses and treatment needs. *General Hospital Psychiatry, 12,* 355–362.

Katon, W., VonKorff, M., Lin, E., & Simon, G. (2001). Rethinking practitioner roles in chronic illness: The specialist, primary care physician, and the practice nurse. *General Hospital Psychiatry, 23,* 138–144.

Katon, W., VonKorff, M., Lin, E., Simon, G., Walker, E., Bush, T., et al. (1997). Collaborative management to achieve depression treatment guidelines. *Journal of Clinical Psychiatry, 58,* 20–23.

Katon, W. J. (2003). Clinical and health services relationships between major depression, depressive symptoms and general medical illness. *Biological Psychiatry, 54,* 216–226.

Katon, W. J., & Walker, E. A. (1998). Medically unexplained symptoms in primary care. *Journal of Clinical Psychiatry, 59,* 15–21.

Katzelnick, D. J., Kobak, K. A., Greist, J. H., Jefferson, J. W., & Henk, H. J. (1997). Effect of primary care treatment of depression on service use by patients with high medical expenditures. *Psychiatric Services, 48,* 59–64.

Kessler, R. C., Demler, O., Frank, R. G., Olfson, M., Pincus, H. A., Walters, E. E., et al. (2005). Prevalence and treatment of mental disorders, 1990–2003. *New England Journal of Medicine, 352,* 2515–2523.

Kessler, R. C., Ormel, J., Demler, O., & Stang, P. E. (2003). Comorbid mental disorders account for the role impairment of commonly occurring chronic physical disorders: Results from the National Comorbidity Survey. *Journal of Occupational and Environmental Medicine, 45,* 1257–1266.

Kleinman, A. (1988). *The illness narratives: Suffering, healing and the human condition.* New York: Basic Books.

Kroenke, K., & Mangelsdorff, A. D. (1989). Common symptoms in ambulatory care: Incidence, evaluation, therapy, and outcome. *American Journal of Medicine, 86,* 262–266.

Kuritzky, L. (1996). Practical tips for dealing with difficult patients. *Family Practice Recertification, 18,* 21–36.

Leichsenring, F., Rabung, S., & Leibing, E. (2004). The efficacy of short term psychodynamic psychotherapy in specific psychiatric disorders: A meta-analysis. *Archives of General Psychiatry, 61,* 1208–1216.

Lewis, E., Marcus, S. C., Olfson, M., Druss, B. G., & Pincus, H. A. (2004). Datapoints: Patients' early discontinuation of antidepressant prescriptions. *Psychiatric Services, 55,* 494.

Lucas, S., & Peek, C. (1997). A primary care physician's experience with integrated behavioral healthcare: What difference has it made? In N. Cummings, J. Cummings, & J. Johnson (Eds.), *Behavioral health in primary care: A guide for clinical integration* (pp. 371–398). Madison, CT: Psychosocial Press.

Luoma, J. B., Martin, C. E., & Pearson, J. L. (2002). Contact with mental health and primary care providers before suicides: A review of the evidence. *American Journal of Psychiatry, 159,* 909–916.

Marvel, K., Epstein, R., Flowers, K., & Beckman, H. (1999). Soliciting the patient's agenda: Have we improved? *Journal of the American Medical Association, 281,* 283–287.

McDaniel, S. H., Campbell, T., Hepworth, J., & Lorenz, A. (2005). *Family-oriented primary care* (2nd ed.). New York: Springer Publishing Company.

McDaniel, S. H., Hepworth, J., & Doherty, W. (1992). *Medical family therapy: A biopsychosocial approach to families with health problems.* New York: Basic Books.

McGoldrick, M., Gerson, R., & Shellenberger, S. (1999). *Genograms, assessment and intervention* (2nd ed.). New York: Norton.

Miranda, J., Hohnmann, A. A., & Attikisson, C. A. (1994). *Epidemiology of mental health disorders in primary care.* San Francisco: Jossey-Bass.

Murtagh, J. (1991). The angry patient. *Australian Family Physician, 20,* 388–389.

National Association of Social Workers. (1999). *Code of ethics of the National Association of Social Workers.* Retrieved November 10, 2007, from http://www.socialworkers.org/pubs/code/code/asp

National Institute of Mental Health. (2006). *Department of Health and Human Services, National Institutes of Health, National Institute of Mental Health FY 2007 budget.* Retrieved July 18, 2007, from http://www.nimh.nih.gov/about/cj2007.pdf

National Institutes of Health. (2006). *Fiscal year 2007 budget request House Subcommittee on Labor: HHS—education appropriations.* Retrieved July 18, 2007, from http://www.nih.gov/about/director/buegetrequest/fy2007directorsbudgetrequest.htm

National Mental Health Association. (2000). *America's mental health survey, May 2000* [conducted by Roper-Starch Worldwide]. Alexandria, VA: Author.

Nyman, K. (1991). The weeping patient. *Australian Family Physician, 20,* 444–446.

Ofri, D. (2005). *Incidental findings.* Boston: Beacon Press.

Ormel, J., VonKorff, M., Ustun, T. B., Pini, S., Korten, A., & Oldehinkel, T. (1994). Common mental disorders and disability across cultures. Results from the WHO Collaborative Study. *Journal of the American Medical Association. 272,* 1741–1748.

Peek, C. J., & Heinrich, R. (1995). Building a collaborative care organization: From idea to invention to innovation. *Family Systems Medicine, 13,* 327–342.

Polsky, D., Doshi, J. A., Marcus, S., Oslin, D., Rothbred, A., Thomas, N., et al. (2005). Long-term risk for depressive symptoms after a medical diagnosis. *Archives of Internal Medicine, 165,* 1260–1266.

Prochaska, J. O., & DiClemente, C. C. (1983). Stages and processes of self-change of smoking: Toward an integrative model of change. *Journal of Consulting and Clinical Psychology, 51,* 390–395.

Prochaska, J. O., Velicer, W. F., Rossi, J. S., Goldstein, M. G., Marcus, B. H., Rakowski, W., et al. (1994). Stages of change and decisional balance for 12 problem behaviors. *Health Psychology, 13,* 39–46.

Pyne, J. M., Rost, K. M., Farahati, F., Tripathi, S. P., Smith, J., Williams, D. K., et al. (2005). One size fits some: The impact of patient treatment attitudes on the cost-effectiveness of a depression primary care intervention. *Psychological Medicine, 35,* 839–854.

Rice, V. (2006, Winter). The tales of residency: Lesson #6: The difficult patient. *Journal of the New Jersey Academy of Family Physicians, 5,* 40.

Robins, L. N., & Regier, D. A. (1991). *Psychiatric disorders in America: The Epidemiologic Catchment Area Study.* New York: Free Press.

Robinson, P. J., & Reiter, J. T. (2007). *Behavioral consultation and primary care.* New York: Springer Publishing Company.

Rost, K., Nutting, P., Smith, J., Coyne, J. C., Cooper-Patrick, L., & Rubenstein, L. (2000). The role of competing demands in the treatment provided primary care patients with major depression. *Archives of Family Medicine, 9,* 150–154.

Russell, A. S., & Hui, B. K. (2005). The use of PRIME-MD questionnaire in a rheumatology clinic. *Rheumatology International, 25,* 292–295.

Schulberg, H. C., Block, M. R., & Madonia, M. J. (1997). The "usual care" of major depression in primary care practice. *Archives of Family Medicine, 6,* 334–339.

Seaburn, D. B., Lorenz, A. D., Gunn, W. B., Jr., Gawinski, B. A., & Mauksch, L. B. (1996). *Models of collaboration: A guide for mental health professionals working with health care practitioners.* New York: Basic Books.

Simon, G., Gater, R., Kisely, S., & Piccinelli, M. (1996). Somatic symptoms of distress: An international primary care study. *Psychosomatic Medicine, 58,* 481–488.

Simon, G. E., & VonKorff, M. (1995). Recognition, management, and outcomes of depression in primary care. *Archives of Family Medicine, 4,* 99–105.

Simon, G. E., VonKorff, M., Piccinelli, M., Fullerton, G., & Ormel, J. (1999). An international study of the relation between somatic symptoms and depression. *New England Journal of Medicine, 341,* 1329–1335.

Simon, G. E., VonKorff, M., Wagner, E. H., & Barlow, W. (1993). Patterns of antidepressant use in community practice. *General Hospital Psychiatry, 15,* 399–408.

Smith, G. R., Monson, R. A., & Ray, D. C. (1986). Patients with multiple unexplained symptoms: Their characteristics, functional health, and health care utilization. *Archives of Internal Medicine, 146,* 69–72.

Strosahl, K. (1998). Integrating behavioral health and primary care services: The primary mental health model. In A. Blount (Ed.), *Integrated primary care: The future of medical and mental health collaboration* (pp. 139–166). New York: Norton.

Van de Putte, E., Engelbert, R., Kuis, W., Sinnema, G., Kimpen, J., & Uiterwaal, C. (2005). Chronic fatigue syndrome and health control in adolescents and parents. *Archives of Disabled Children, 90,* 1020–1024.

Wagner, E. H., Austin, B. T., Davis, C., Hindmarsh, S., Schaefer, J., & Bonomi, A. (2001). Improving chronic illness care: Translating evidence into action. *Health Affairs, 20,* 64–78.

Wang, P. S., Bergland, P., & Olfson, M. (2005). Failure and delay in initial treatment contact after first onset of mental disorders in the National Comorbidity Survey Replication. *Archives of General Psychiatry, 62,* 603–613.

Wells, K. B., Katon, W., Rogers, B., & Camp, P. (1994). Use of minor tranquilizers and antidepressant medication by depressed outpatients: Results from the medical outcomes study. *American Journal of Psychiatry, 151,* 694–700.

White, M., & Epston, D. (1990). *Narrative means to therapeutic ends.* New York: Norton.

Winnick, S., Lucas, D., & Hartman, A. (2005). How do you improve compliance? *Pediatrics, 115,* 718–724.

Zubialde, J., Shannon, K., & Devenger, N. (2005). The quadrants of care model for health services planning. *Families, Systems, and Health, 23,* 172–185.

Index

Cummings, Nicholas, 178, 196
Cummings PSYCHE Prize, 195
"Curbside consults," 36
Curing coping continuum, 102–103
Curiosity, 97
Current Procedural Terminology
    (CPT) codes, 68
Cushing's disease, 225

Defibrillators, implantable, 225
Dementias
    and cancers, 225
    and collaborative managed care,
        199
    and endocrine/metabolic
        diseases, 226
Depression
    and antiarrythmics, 229
    and anticholingergic-property
        drugs, 230
    and antihypertensives, 229
    and antiparkinson agents, 229
    and cancer chemotherapy agents,
        230
    and cancers, 225
    and cardiopulmonary conditions,
        225
    case study, 139–147
    in chronically ill patients, 48, 84
    and cimetidine, 230
    and collaborative primary care
        medical practice, 193
    in complex medical conditions,
        169–171
    and endocrine/metabolic
        diseases, 225–226
    and infectious diseases, 226
    latency between onset/treatment
        of, 47
    medical professionals' treatment
        of, 11–12
    medical recognition of, 18
    and neurological disorders, 226–
        227
    and nutritional deficiencies, 227
    and oral contraceptives, 230

physician's expertise with, 135–
    136
and psychoactive substances, 230
and quinolone antibiotics, 230
screening for, 125
and steroids, 231
Diabetes, 168, 170, 171, 226
Diagnosable mental health
    conditions, 11–12
Diagnostic feedback, 211
Diagnostic process, 48
Diaries, symptom, 103–104
Diaz, Luis, 127–128
Digoxin, 229
Disability, 90, 92, 145, 168, 169
Discharge summary, 218
Disease, illness vs., 102
Distancer–pursuer pattern, 97–98,
    100–101
"Doctor shopping," 49, 57
"Do something" model, 35, 78, 79
Downs-Barrett, Jan, 139, 141–147
Driscoll, Dave, 177, 181–187
Drug-seeking behavior, 208, 209

Eating disorders. See Anorexia
    nervosa
Education
    in collaborative managed care,
        196
    of patients, 84
    psycho-, 14
Electronic information management
    system, 198
Electronic medical record, 125
Ellis, Irene, 157, 160–165
E-mail, 66
Emergency departments, 12, 217
Empathy, 44, 97, 111
Endocrine diseases, 225–226
Environment, for collaborative crisis
    services, 217–218
Epstein-Barr, 226
Exogenous steroids, 225
Expectations, 58–59
"Externalizing the illness," 109, 174

About the Authors

Nancy Breen Ruddy, PhD, received her doctorate in child clinical psychology from Bowling Green State University in Bowling Green, Ohio, in 1991. She served on the faculty of the family medicine and psychiatry departments at the University of Rochester School of Medicine and Dentistry in Rochester, New York, from 1991 to 2000. During that time she completed postgraduate training in family therapy and family therapy supervision. In 2001, Dr. Ruddy joined the faculty of the Hunterdon Family Practice Residency in Flemington, New Jersey. She lives in Lawrenceville, New Jersey, with her husband and two children.

Dorothy A. Borresen, PhD, APN, has been in private practice for more than 20 years, where she practices both psychotherapy and psychopharmacology. She has a doctorate in psychology from Temple University in Philadelphia, Pennsylvania, and a master's degree in nursing, with a specialty in psychiatric mental health, from the University of Pennsylvania in Philadelphia. She is an assistant professor of family medicine at the University of Medicine and Dentistry of New Jersey—Robert Wood Johnson Medical School in New Brunswick and teaches behavioral science to medical students and family medicine residents. Dr. Borresen lives in Pennington, New Jersey, with her husband, Bill Alexander.

William B. Gunn Jr., PhD, received his doctoral degree in family therapy at Virginia Tech in Blacksburg in 1986. Prior to receiving his PhD, he was a school psychologist and special education director. In 1986, he began teaching in family medicine and currently continues in that capacity. Dr. Gunn was the director of behavioral science at the Fort Collins Family Medicine Residency Program in Fort Collins, Colorado. He was codirector of behavioral medicine at Duke University in Durham, North Carolina. For the past 10 years, he has been a faculty member at the New Hampshire/Dartmouth Family Practice Residency in Concord.

He is coauthor of *Models of Collaboration*, a book designed for mental health professionals working in medical settings, and has published articles on the topic of integrating behavioral health into primary care. In addition to his residency work, Dr. Gunn has worked for 20 years as an organizational consultant and serves in that capacity in the local health care system.